Managing
Government Operations

The Scott, Foresman Public Policy Analysis and Management Series
Arnold Meltsner and Mark Moore, Editors

Designing Public Policy: A Casebook on the Role of Policy Analysis
Laurence Lynn, Harvard University

Getting the Facts: A Fieldwork Guide for Evaluators and Policy Analysts
Jerome T. Murphy, Harvard University

Discovering Whether Programs Work: A Guide to Statistical Methods
for Program Evaluation
Laura Irwin Langbein, American University

Managing Government Operations

Stephen R. Rosenthal
Boston University

Scott, Foresman and Company   Glenview, Illinois
Dallas, Tex.   Oakland, N.J.   Palo Alto, Cal.   Tucker, Ga.   London, England

To my parents

Library of Congress Cataloging in Publication Data

Rosenthal, Stephen R.
   Managing government operations.

   (The public policy analysis and management series)
   Includes bibliographies and index.
   1. Public administration.   2. Operations research.
I. Title.   II. Series.
JF1525.06R67   350   81-23323
ISBN 0-673-16462-4   AACR2

Preface

The management of government operations is a subject that tends to generate more heat than light. Citizens complain about the poor quality of municipal services; the media challenge state and federal agencies to be more responsive to public needs; political aspirants decry the weak performance of existing administrations and promise to eliminate waste from bloated bureaucracies. At the root of all such criticism is an increasingly common claim that government isn't worth its cost, that there is much room for improved management. Specific analysis of the underlying reasons for disappointing performance is rare. Even rarer are substantive initiatives to help public managers see how to design and implement better service delivery, given existing economic, bureaucratic, and political conditions.

The field of public management is just beginning to receive the attention it requires. Especially neglected has been the role of the operations managers, those who are responsible for accomplishing government's day-to-day functions. *Managing Government Operations* attempts to fill a key gap in the literature by exploring how the responsibilities and opportunities of operations managers are shaped in predictable ways by the organizational system within which they work. In particular, this book reveals how design decisions at all levels of a public agency combine to determine the agency's productive characteristics. Staff, supervision, equipment, facilities, information, and procedures can all be assessed to determine their collective impact on an agency's objectives. The operational impacts of current or projected external constraints—economic, social, and political—can also be analyzed, as can the operational implications of alternative public policies. These kinds of skills and insights are necessary initial steps toward the widespread improvement of public management practice.

To cast the objective of this book in a familiar modern mold, consider the following two approaches to reducing the cost of government. The first is a simple cost-cutting strategy: slash the operating budget by a fixed percentage and then monitor expenditures to make sure they stay within established budgetary limits. The second approach goes beyond simple fiscal restraint to the notion of improved productivity: get more results for the dollar while stemming runaway expenditures. The first approach has become familiar to most politicians in recent years. At all levels of government, officials promise reduced costs without specifying how such reductions will be accomplished and what the impacts are likely to be. Unfortunately, smaller is not always better. Even during eras of retrenchment, officials and public managers should pay attention to productivity. Accordingly, an increased emphasis on operations management is particularly important during times of fiscal cutback, if government is to achieve even the most basic of its traditional public service functions.

Managing Government Operations emphasizes both analytic skills and managerial thinking. It can be used as either a primary or secondary classroom text in a variety of academic programs in public policy, administration, or management. It is also designed to be useful for practicing public managers and their staff or to anyone interested in the performance of government. For any such potential readers, no prior exposure to the subject is required.

Since this is, to my knowledge, the first book to address the emerging field of public sector operations management, I had to make decisions on what topics to include. Many of the traditional topics developed over the past quarter-century under the label of "production management" are covered here in the context of government operations. I have also included much material not covered in other existing texts. On the other hand, I have chosen to pay little attention to inventory control and queuing theory, two topics that are standard in most operations management texts but are not as central to the themes of this book. Bibliographic references are provided to help the reader gain access to related literature. Frequent comparisons between operational situations in the private and public sectors are intended to help the reader appreciate ways in which existing operations management literature, aimed almost exclusively at manufacturing enterprises, may or may not be relevant to the public manager. Four chapter-length case studies illustrate the various managerial issues and responsibilities described throughout the book. Discussion questions at the end of each chapter give readers the opportunity to apply the concepts and approaches in realistic situations.

I have also written this book with an eye toward certain human realities. Many hardworking public officials and administrators at all levels grow frustrated after unsuccessful attempts to accomplish their goals. Readers of this book will learn how complex sets of operational constraints combine to limit the options available to public managers. As readers become familiar with some rigorous approaches to the design, implementation, and control of government operations, they will understand why the failures of government programs cannot always be traced to the abilities or efforts of civil servants. Armed with a knowledge of the dynamics of operating systems, readers can bring to the study of government operations management a more realistic sense of what is possible and how individuals can work together to achieve a common end.

Almost fifteen years ago, I made a career change that led, gradually and unintentionally, to the writing of this book. Before then, I had been trained in the highly quantitative field of operations research and had been serving for several years on a technical internal management consulting group at Exxon. I left the world of corporate planning, product distribution systems, refinery optimization, and investment analysis to join what was then thought to be the "urban revolution." I had no idea what it might mean to be the first management scientist to work for the City of New York—perhaps the first to work for any state or local government. It wasn't long, however, before I was busily practicing the then-undefined field of public sector operations analysis in areas as disparate as welfare processing, hospital scheduling, housing inspection, and snow removal. Doing analysis to improve government operations was very different from the work I had done in a similar capacity on projects for a major corporation. While projects for the city tended to be much less sophisticated from a technical viewpoint, they required much more attention to such concerns as the definition of feasible alternatives, the existence of multiple objectives, and, perhaps most important, the structure of managerial decision making.

Since that time I have continued to work (in various capacities) on improving the operational performance of agencies at all levels of government. Since 1975 I have been developing and teaching courses in public sector operations management, a variant on the production operations management courses normally offered in business schools. Gradually, my experience as a practitioner in this field has evolved to the point where I feel comfortable talking about the management of government operations as a general set of activities similar in scope to, though different in emphasis from, counterpart positions in the private sector.

Managing Government Operations is drawn from my teaching, research, and consulting experiences in this field. It presents and illustrates the concepts, approaches, and techniques that I have found to be most helpful to managers with operational responsibilities in government. Aimed at both students and practitioners, the book points the way to systematic decision making on critical operational issues. I do not believe that management at the highest levels of government should be (or, in a democracy, ever will be) truly scientific. In every operating agency that I have ever known, however, there is considerable opportunity to improve the allocation and management of resources without sacrificing the essential elements of our political system.

Most of the material in this book was developed for use in the Public Management Program at Boston University, where I have been on the faculty since 1975. Without the leadership of its director, Robert Weinberg, this unique program would not have existed, nor is it likely that I would have written this book. Bob's commitment to creating a management-based graduate degree for government practitioners allowed me to develop a course that drew on my formal education in business-oriented operations research and on my professional experience in public sector operations management. By challenging me in the classroom, my students at the Boston University School of Management helped me to shape my thinking during the years that these materials were being conceptualized and tested. I owe thanks to them and also to students at the Woodrow Wilson School of Public and International Affairs at Princeton University and the Florence Heller Graduate School for Advanced Studies in Social Welfare at Brandeis University, where I recently held part-time faculty appointments.

More specific thanks are due to Arnold J. Meltsner and Mark H. Moore for identifying operations management as a subject important enough to be included in their series of books on public policy analysis and management. The sponsors of the Public Policy Curriculum Development Project, administered jointly by Duke University and the Rand Graduate Institute, provided financial support to prepare the in-depth case studies included in this book. The facilities and support services of Boston University's Center for Applied Social Science helped me to meet my publication deadline. Ann-Charlotte Endahl, in particular, helped me to produce a readable manuscript by cheerfully responding to all requests for detailed review of chapter drafts. Andrew L. Meyers turned out to be more of a partner than either of us had originally envisioned, as he became my indispensable sounding board, friendly critic, and writer of several chapter drafts and many discussion questions. Without Andy, the book and I would have suffered. Finally, I am grateful to Arnold J. Meltsner and Richard E. Neustadt for their helpful suggestions while reading my complete manuscript.

Stephen R. Rosenthal
Newton, Mass.

Contents

Part 1
The nature and relevance of operations management in government

Chapter 1
Why study operations management?

Occasionally local newspapers remind us of the importance of operations management to government. On March 31, 1981, the Boston *Globe* ran a lead article with the bold headline, "Welfare Women Face Sex-Life Quiz."[1] The article described a practice of the state welfare department's Child Support Enforcement Unit. Its subject was the department's new paternity questionnaire concerning the "putative," or presumed, fathers of welfare-dependent children. After the *Globe* published the questionnaire, a public outcry arose in response to certain questions posed to unwed mothers who were applying for welfare assistance for their children. The controversial questionnaire included such items as "Where and when did you have sexual intercourse with the putative father?" and "What are the names and addresses of anyone else you had sexual intercourse with during this period?"

In the days that followed the appearance of this article, press investigations and public hearings revealed the background situation of the small Child Support Enforcement Unit operating in the middle of a vast state bureaucracy. The manager of this unit had been responding to an existing federal requirement when he approved the specific wording and use of the controversial questionnaire. Years earlier, federal officials had determined that for states to be eligible for AFDC (Aid to Families with Dependent Children) funds, they must attempt to recoup certain income maintenance costs that are the basic responsibility of private citizens. Across the country, Child Support Enforcement units were formed to help establish the paternity of AFDC children and to encourage the fathers to pay for child support. Individuals associated with these units have stressed the relative efficiency of their enterprise, especially in the emerging era of fiscal cutback. The Child Support Enforcement program more than pays for itself, since the reduction of AFDC payments made possible by newly negotiated direct child support from the fathers easily exceeds the program's operating costs.

The Massachusetts program manager must have been shocked and surprised by a local newspaper's criticism of his attempt to improve his unit's performance. Readers must have wondered how a responsible public manager could have made such a mistake. Would the manager recover from this negative publicity, or would he lose his job? Clearly, the manager's professional credibility was at stake. The governor already had been embarrassed. Employees of the unit must have been discouraged at the thought that the public did not applaud their sincere efforts to do their jobs efficiently. What had appeared to be a technical decision of internal program operations had turned into a major public debate.

The damage to this manager and to his program already had occurred when, a week later, a *Globe* editorial attempted to restore a reasonable perspective:

> *Intrusive as it seems, the questionnaire, and the process of obtaining child support payments of which it is a part, are necessary ends to a desirable social goal. Bureaucratic snafus are being blamed for the misuse of the questionnaire. Welfare has now given assurances that it will not be used in the welfare intake process nor will any child be deprived of any assistance to which he is legally entitled. Welfare advocates have suggested that the questions not be posed until it is clear that the matter is going to court; lawyers for the Welfare Department argue that they need the information earlier in order to decide whether they have a case worth pursuing. The most intrusive questions . . . are necessary to prove a paternity case. (Boston Globe, April 6, 1981)*

It may be years before the full impact of this "minor" operational incident is known. Although the initial public outcry seemed to center on the policy of establishing paternity, the real criticism focused on the details of program implementation. We may never know the answer to some basic questions such as: Why didn't this manager anticipate potential problems before the public dramatized them? Were the apparent indiscretions in the questionnaire simply oversights, or were they the result of deliberate attempts to strengthen program efficiency? Who actually approved the wording of specific questions that were asked of AFDC mothers, and how much effort went into formulating the scope and content of the questionnaire?

Few government programs receive as much public scrutiny as occurred in this illustration. Most citizens, and the press as well, are generally uninterested in the inner workings of government operations. Nevertheless, external demands for improved performance are likely to remain strong. Public officials therefore must appreciate the importance of program implementation. Furthermore, public managers must learn to emphasize both the productivity and propriety of day-to-day operations.

"Taxpayer revolts," limiting the revenues of state and local jurisdictions, and broad cutbacks at the federal level are recent phenomena that signal changes in public attitudes toward government. It seems that many U.S. citizens now perceive government as wasteful, slothful enterprises that taxpayers are forced to support. During such a period, pressure to understand, measure, and modify organizational performance in the operational activities of government is particularly intense. *Managing Government Operations* provides an opportunity for public managers and others to learn some basic operations concepts, principles, and techniques that can be applied to meet this need.

The growth in government operations is difficult to document with statistics. Trends in budgetary appropriations are not very useful, partly due to inflation, but also because large fractions of government budgets are used for transfer payments (either between levels of government or directly to citizens); these often have minor operational requirements. Despite the growing use of technology in recent decades, government operations are still largely labor-intensive. Therefore, studying public sector operations requires studying its employees. Exhibit 1.1 presents a brief historical perspective on aggregate trends in public sector employment since 1950. While the federal government has a wide variety of

Exhibit 1.1
Civilian government employment in the United States: 1950–1979
federal, state, local

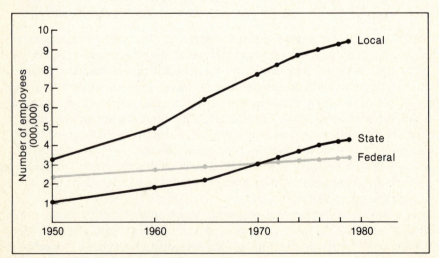

Source: U.S. Dept. of Labor, *Handbook of Labor Statistics,* 1979.

needs for operations management, as is indicated by ongoing shifts in organization and programs, the greatest growth in employment, and therefore operations, has been in state and local government. *Managing Government Operations* is concerned with the business of agencies at all three levels.

Operational responsibilities and trade-off decisions

What do we mean by the "operational responsibilities" of government? Although this subject is discussed in detail throughout the book, for the present an illustrative response should suffice. Exhibit 1.2 lists some government agencies at the federal, state, and local levels, and identifies some of their operational responsibilities. These responsibilities are discharged through "operating systems" of resources, procedures, policies, and management. In a general sense, the "operating system" can be defined as the means through which government conducts its many different forms of business.

Of course the specific activities of government vary from one level to another (although some of the general functions, such as law enforcement, are carried out at each level). Furthermore, the organization of any particular public service varies as does its delivery whether it is among the different states or among the many municipalities within a state. Many choices are usually available in the allocation of resources at a particular level to achieve any specific governmental objective. One must study the general subject of government operations to become sensitized to the broad range of existing options.

By now some of you may be thinking, "But government isn't business. It's politics. So why worry about the management of public sector operations, when so much of government activity is politically motivated?" The broad policy positions taken by a government agency, and the process through which available revenues are allocated to specific programs, of course, often are influenced by politics. This book was written in explicit recognition of that phenomenon. In the chapters that follow, political realities frequently are acknowledged; then possible effects on the practice of public sector operations management are explored. Such realities include, but are not limited to: the legislative process, general economic trends, elections, style and tenure of public officials, the civil service system, special interest groups, trends in the perceived role of government, and available public sector revenues. However, no attempt is made to provide general background on aspects of the American political system, political economy, or bureaucratic politics. Rather, such factors are considered only as they may influence and constrain the management of public sector operations.

Exhibit 1.2
Examples of operational responsibilities in government

Level of Government	Types of Agencies	Operational Responsibilities[a]
Federal	Army Corps of Engineers	Flood control
	Health and Human Services	Funds and monitors Medicare health benefits
	Federal Bureau of Investigation (FBI)	Investigates "federal" crimes
	General Accounting Office	Evaluates many government programs
	Federal Aviation Administration (FAA)	Trains and certifies air traffic controllers
	National Parks Service	Maintains and monitors national parks system
State	Department of Health	Licenses nursing homes
	Rehabilitation Commission	Trains and cares for the disabled
	Turnpike Authority	Maintains and constructs State Turnpike
	Bureau of Taxation	Distributes and reviews income tax forms
	Department of Motor Vehicles	Conducts driving tests and issues licenses
	State Police	Investigates crimes committed outside local jurisdictions
Local	School System	Provides public education
	Fire Department	Responds to calls for fire protection
	City Hospital	Provides health care to city residents
	County Assessor	Assesses property for tax purposes
	City Police	Investigates crimes committed within city limits
	Parks and Recreation	Conducts summer youth sports program

[a] Although many of the agencies listed have multiple operational responsibilities, only one is listed as an example.

The essence of operations management is trade-off. As an introduction to the range of subjects covered in this book, Exhibit 1.3 lists some common operational trade-off decisions in the public sector. Broader questions of organization and management often are beyond the control of any particular operations manager. Choices made in the domains of organizational structure, information systems, orientation to change, and the

Exhibit 1.3
Some common operational trade-off decisions in the public sector

Decision Areas	Typical Trade-Off Decisions	Typical Trade-Off Options
Organization and Management	Type of organizational structure	Organized by function, division, or geographic area
	Information management emphasis	Operational, evaluative, or planning focus (reflected by extent, frequency, and level of detail of data collection and analysis)
	Orientation to change	Maintenance of status quo or commitment to innovation
	Role of top management	Direct involvement in operational matters or complete delegation to subordinates
Design of the Operating System	Level of service	Comprehensive, special, or single-purpose service using a relatively large or small work force
	Degree of service integration	Planning and design for independent services or for "integrated" (multi-service) delivery systems
	Type of production process	General-purpose (line operation) or special-purpose (job shop or single project)
	"Make or buy"	Direct agency "production" or purchase of services from outside contractors
	Number and location of facilities	Centralized (few, large facilities) or decentralized (many small facilities)
	Cost to "customers"	Total subsidy from tax revenues or (full or partial) fee-for-service
	Degree of stability in service delivery scheduling	Fixed or adjustable schedule
	Relative emphasis on reliability	Strict quality-control system or informal monitoring
	Allocation of responsibility for quality control	Centralized (at supervisory level) or decentralized (at level of individual worker)
	Extent of job specialization	Single tasks (specialized jobs) or autonomous groups (general-purpose jobs)
Operational Planning and Control	Primary location of budgetary control	Centralized or decentralized fiscal planning and monitoring
	Use of budget	For fiscal accountability only or also for performance evaluation
	Type(s) of program evaluation	External overview, internal management, or both
	Timing of program evaluation	Included in periodic planning and budgetary cycle or independent, idiosyncratic process
	Allocation of resources	Emphasis on meeting peak demands or on smoothing service delivery patterns
	Quality assurance mechanisms	Emphasis on consistency or flexibility (discretion)
	Type of maintenance	Regular preventive maintenance schedule or emergency repair
	Inventory levels	High inventories with infrequent replenishment or low inventories with frequent replenishment

role of top management directly affect the options for more specific operational decisions. The category labeled Design of the Operating System involves a wide range of trade-off decisions. Not all of these decisions will be made by the same person, nor is it likely that they will be made at the same time. However, taken together, this set of decisions will determine the major operating characteristics of any government program. Not every decision element will apply to every situation, but generally all the decisions must be made. The trade-off decisions labeled Operational Planning and Control also are generally applicable, although some items, such as maintenance or inventories, may not apply in a given situation. *Managing Government Operations* attempts to introduce aspects of almost all the trade-off decisions listed in this exhibit. The book intentionally omits discussions of topics such as the techniques used for facility location and inventory control (the direct applications of which are relatively infrequent in government) which already are covered in depth in existing operations management literature.

Managerial challenges

Despite this catalog of trade-off decisions, observers of and participants in this country's government often proclaim that "public management" is impossible, that the two words are a contradiction in terms. Not surprisingly, *Managing Government Operations* takes issue with this line of "conventional wisdom." It takes the counterposition: that program operations, public or private, always are being managed. The questions are, "How well?" and "Compared to what?" This book argues (and attempts to demonstrate) that one can (and should) study government operations to gain skills in the improvement of public sector performance, whether this sector is growing, stable, or declining. In any situation, the management of government operations requires a commitment to try to answer these important managerial questions:

☐ What is being accomplished with available resources? Who is being served? In what way? With what degree of success? At what cost?

☐ How well are current public policies being implemented through the programs and processes of government? Can program managers identify the policies which guide their daily operational decisions? Are these the same policies that public officials and the public at large assume to be in effect? Are the accomplishments of the programs, and the mechanisms through which they are delivered, consistent with stated policies?

☐ How should existing government operations be changed to reflect new objectives, service delivery options, or resource constraints?

These guiding questions encourage the manager to define issues that are worth analyzing, rather than to seek solutions to a predetermined, limited set of well-structured problems. A book which attempts to address the subject of public sector operations management with these questions in mind is, admittedly, ambitious. At the outset, therefore, it is important to identify the range of managerial challenges that necessarily are addressed. An appreciation for these challenges motivates the particular strategy for studying government operations that has been adopted in this book.

Formulate feasible public policy

Can government deliver what its officials promise? The challenge to public officials is to consider operational realities before establishing new policies. They must learn to recognize the implications of unavoidable external constraints on government performance and to assess what can be accomplished.

Design appropriate operating systems

Can steps be taken in advance to create productive systems for service delivery and other public sector operations? The challenge to public managers is to select operational approaches through which public policy is implemented. They must learn to view day-to-day operations in the context of underlying organizational structures and processes.

Adopt a production orientation in government

Can a government agency be run to achieve a stated level of performance? The challenge to managers at all levels is to make responsible resource allocation decisions in government. They must learn to plan for required levels of resources within existing budgetary constraints. They must avoid the traditional, mindless process of increasing the operating budget, regardless of how that budget is to be spent. Rather, they must become proficient at assessing the use of resources and at measuring outcomes. Furthermore, they must learn to monitor system performance in ways that reveal needed changes in resource allocation and operating procedures.

Accept complexity and uncertainty

Can a note of informed humility be introduced in the management of government operations? This challenge applies to those who critically observe the workings of government, such as members of the media, as well as those who hold policymaking or administrative responsibilities. All these people must learn to appreciate the complexity of government operations and the uniqueness of many government enterprises. They must learn that in government programs "improvement" is an ambiguous term, since people with different values will assess the same public program. Public managers must learn to live in a world in which perhaps the one constant is that the "rules of the game" are in flux; shifts in public expectations, legislative mandates, the type and amount of available resources and technologies, and the orientations of government employees cannot be anticipated completely. Increasingly, these managers will need the support of technical advisors and analysts. They must learn to manage these "experts," not merely to rely upon them to the point of ignoring political judgments on technical grounds.

A strategy for studying government operations

These challenges indicate how the subject of public sector operations management ought to be studied. The following guidelines served as a basis for the preparation of this book.

Follow a systems approach

Public managers need to understand the typical performance patterns in the organizations that they run. Operating systems have familiar structures that can be learned. Such knowledge, based on a systems approach, can be transferred from one application area to another. A good public sector operations manager must have this skill, since government engages in many different kinds of business. As a public manager rises in professional responsibility, he or she also will benefit from the ability to understand hierarchies of operating systems. In our increasingly "intergovernmental system" (federal programs passed through state agencies for local implementation), this ability becomes particularly important.

Require rigorous analysis

Public managers must avoid the temptation to make unfounded generalizations about government operations. For example, familiar claims that "there are never enough resources," "government employees can't be managed," or "politics makes management impossible in government" are based more on willingness to sidestep the issues at hand than on responsible analysis and reflection. Public managers must learn to be explicit in their statements of problems and to be aware of internal operational relationships and interactions between specific policies and their operational implications. Furthermore, they must learn how to collect valuable data on the performance of government operations, and to use such information to stimulate debates on even the most value-laden operational issues.

Acknowledge complexity

Since the world of the public manager is complex, those who study government operations should acknowledge such factors as the inconsistency among different public policies existing in the same field, conflicting expectations among prospective beneficiaries of the same government program, and the subtle influences of bureaucratic cultures on operational performance. Students of public management should retain a practical "world view" which incorporates these kinds of complexities, while they seek out important issues and concrete solutions. A public manager normally is concerned with finding feasible solutions to complicated operational questions. Rarely does optimality become a meaningful criterion of success.

Focus on decisions

The study of operations management, or any subject which purports to be "scientific," can lead the student too far along the path of "rational decision making." It is essential to keep in mind the context within which such learning is to be applied. For example, while additional information often will improve the quality of operational decisions in government, it is costly and time-consuming to acquire the full set of "required" data. Furthermore, time deadlines for analysis and decision making in the public sector can be short and the need to respond to public pressures can be sudden. A good public manager will respect such constraints and, when studying an operational issue, will make a decision before a *de facto* resolution has been made. On the other hand, the study of government operations should help a manager to avoid naive, "quick-fix" responses which at best postpone the problem and at worst aggravate it. In addition, students should be encouraged to approach operational design with an eye to program implementation, evaluation, and improvement.

In summary, the practice of operations management in government needs development. The lack of literature on this subject is not surprising, as it has not yet attracted much systematic research. It also has been ignored in the traditional training of public administrators (although in recent years there have been some notable exceptions). The better operations managers in government have learned through years of experience, not from reading a conceptual treatise on the nature of their jobs. *Managing Government Operations* is not an attempt to replace experiential learning. Rather, it is designed to supplement and structure the experience of practitioners. For those interested in public management careers, the book should serve as a useful point of reference. In proceeding through the chapters which follow, any reader may wish to regain an overview by referring to the challenges and perspectives outlined above.

Structure and contents of this book

Managing Government Operations attempts to bridge the gap between theory and practice. While presenting the central concepts of traditional operations management, the book also emphasizes ways in which operational problems arise in the world of government. The study of concepts encourages orderly cumulative learning about an empirical phenomenon, and yet these concepts may appear artificial and useless when presented apart from specific operational programs and processes of government. Therefore, illustrations from a wide range of government programs are provided in all chapters; in addition, discussion questions at the end of each chapter provide a focus for applying new concepts and for appreciating their relevance and limitations.

Although short illustrations help to bring life to the conceptual dimensions of operations management, they do not stand alone. Accordingly, chapter-length descriptions of program operations in four different kinds of government agencies have been included in this book to fulfill the important "bridging" function. These "problem chapters" offer a counterpoint to the linear presentations of standard topics in operations management. Each such chapter presents a particular organization in need of operational analysis and improvement. Each is placed immediately after chapters that introduce related issues and concepts or methods. The problem chapters present a range of issues and data and encourage the reader to appreciate the full range of activities and responsibilities of the operating manager in government. Discovering the most important issues embedded in these illustrative situations can be as challenging as developing solutions to them. The questions listed at the end of each of these problem chapters may guide student assignments and discussions. These chapters are intended to provide a sense of what it feels like to be an operations manager in government. Some of the skills emphasized are: obtaining accurate and relevant data, being sensitive to the political environment of government operations, knowing what facts to emphasize and how to interpret them, and planning for and achieving change in public sector operational settings.

The book goes beyond the narrow definition of operations management to touch upon related issues in areas of legislation, budgeting, personnel, and program evaluation. Such topics, however, are covered only as they impinge on (and are affected by) the role and function of the operations manager. This is not a comprehensive text on public management, but it is designed to be part of the basic education of everyone with managerial responsibilities in government.

The book is organized into four parts. Part 1, which contains this chapter and chapter 2, addresses the nature and relevance of public sector operations management. Chapter 2 describes the functions of operations management and presents the concept of an operating life cycle. It outlines the stages from the conception of a public program until its termination. It identifies how managerial attention naturally shifts to different issues as a program proceeds through this cycle. Part 1 provides fundamental perspective for those who would attempt to manage or improve the operational performance of government.

Part 2 contains chapters 3–10. It is the core of the book and deals with the analysis of public sector operating systems. It includes a series of technical approaches to understanding government operations. Chapter 3, "Process Analysis," explains how flow charting and the measurement and cost of existing operations can lead to a rigorous assessment of an operating system. It also defines the three basic types of production processes. Chapter 4, "Capacity Management," identifies the central importance of productive capacity. It presents techniques for measuring capacity and related program attributes, such as service quality and equity. Chapter 6, "Personnel Planning and Work Measurement," looks at the labor input to government operating systems. It presents criteria, methods, and organizational approaches for planning personnel levels from a production point of view. It also discusses implications for work measurement and the setting of performance standards. Chapter 7 discusses how public managers can affect the demand for, as well as the supply of, services. It explains the growing policy significance of the strategy of "demand management." Chapter 9 focuses on information as a major resource of the operating manager in government. It identifies different types of information systems and presents approaches for assessing the costs and benefits of each system. This section also includes three examples—chapters 5, 8, and 10—which provide ample opportunity to conduct the types of analysis covered in the other chapters. Part 2, then, presents analytic approaches to the various problems that an operating manager faces in planning, designing, and controlling government operations. It contains references to more in-depth coverage of specific quantitative techniques that are beyond the scope and direct purpose of this book.

Part 3 describes a major species of public sector operating systems, dealing with the processing of "cases." Chapter 11 presents a conceptual framework for understanding the relationships between public policy and operations in case processing systems. Chapter 12 discusses the role of information in supporting case management. Both chapters draw directly on the concepts presented in Part 1 and on the approaches included in Part 2. Chapter 13 is an example in which all of the typical "case management" issues are present.

Part 4 contains the concluding chapter, " 'Managing' in Government." This chapter summarizes the political and structural climate within which public sector operations currently are "managed." It proposes how the public sector operations manager, grounded in the material covered in this book, can improve the performance of government, despite the existence of a variety of familiar institutional barriers.

Managing Government Operations offers both analytic skills and practical perspectives to those who wish to improve public sector performance. Since the topics covered are highly interrelated and the conceptual foundation develops sequentially throughout the text, readers are urged to approach the material in its entirety and in the order presented. Part 1 provides an introductory set of managerial perspectives; Part 2 presents a series of techniques and approaches that build upon each other; Part 3 describes a common though complex application area which requires the synthesis of prior topics; Part 4 provides realistic and hopeful conclusions.

Summary

Every government office has a core set of tasks to perform if its services are to be delivered or its regulations enforced. Operations management deals with these "systems of production," from their initial design, through the day-to-day control of their activities, to their possible revision. *Managing Government Operations* is designed to promote competence in this field. It explains how to analyze and design the processes through which human resources, facilities, equipment, and information combine to form a productive organizational entity.

Productive systems of all types attract the attention of public managers and policymakers. A citywide network of police patrols, a state highway system, and an entire municipal hospital are traditional public sector examples of complex, interrelated systems of production. Like their counterparts in the private sector, such systems often involve large groups of people, sophisticated machinery, expensive facilities, and complicated communication networks, all of which must be designed, developed, and organized into a productive unit. The successful performance of such public systems is of direct concern to the policymaker and program manager alike. The importance of this field for such practitioners and their staff can be seen as a two-way link between policy and operations combining:

☐ The extent to which an operating agency can deliver the services which legislative or administrative policy promises; and

☐ The manner in which policies occasionally must be reformulated in response to inherent limitations of existing service delivery systems.

Notes

[1] The *Boston Globe* article "Welfare women face sex-life quiz" by Walter Robinson, March 31, 1981, and the excerpt from "Welfare's Questionnaire," a *Boston Globe* editorial which appeared April 6, 1981, are reprinted courtesy of the *Boston Globe*.

Chapter 2
Public management through the operations life cycle

Every government program has at least one operations manager and usually more. Their titles vary. They may be called program director, area chief, office supervisor, project manager, or branch head. From agency to agency, and across the various levels of government, the responsibilities of specific operations managers are also structured, as well as labeled, in different ways. The student of public management, accordingly, would do well to become acquainted at a more general level with the functions of operating managers, and with the range of issues which they must address at various points in the development of government programs.

The functions of operations management

Operations management is the selection, design, operation, control, and updating of production systems. Each of these activities is briefly defined below.[1]

Selecting involves choosing a particular approach to implementing a public policy. This choice may lead to direct or indirect delivery of service by government. Alternatively, the application of traditional government tools, such as regulation, taxation, or administrative reform, may provide "nonservice" strategies in which government collaborates with others in the pursuit of social policy objectives. For example, needed social services may be delivered to clients directly by a government agency, they may be purchased by government from a "third party" (independent contractor), or they may be delivered by local volunteers who provide "self-help" with government encouragement. An enforcement agency, to give another example, must decide whether it will respond to complaints received directly from the public, or whether it will send out investigators to identify potential compliance problems. Policymakers often underestimate the importance of selecting an appropriate and feasible productive system. This strategic choice is often made in the absence of anyone with a formal responsibility for the management of the associated operations. Instead, the selection of a productive system may emerge from the interaction of political forces in the legislative process, or it may occur behind closed doors as policymakers negotiate with constituents who represent special interest groups.

Designing consists of a series of tactical decisions to make operational the production mode which has been selected. Such decisions include specifying the particular jobs to be performed by clerks, technicians, and supervisors working together to deliver a particular public service. The design function also includes identifying criteria for making operational choices, such as setting priorities for the day-to-day handling of a wide range of agency matters. The formulation of standard operating procedures is another important aspect of public sector operations design.

Operating involves making decisions on subjects that range from short-term questions of how to handle the current program work load to long-term choices of future levels of service delivery or enforcement. Acquiring and training staff to meet forecasted levels of demand are examples of the general operating responsibilities of a public manager. Resolving an ambiguity in proper program procedure is another. Most familiar, perhaps, is the ongoing supervision and direction of those who put out the fires, collect the garbage, or otherwise protect the public safety and health.

Controlling is an information-processing function aimed at improving all operational aspects of program performance. Control activities may affect ongoing operations or longer term plans. In either case, they require looking for signals that something is wrong and then suggesting operational corrections through shifts of organizational resources. Social workers perform a control activity when they review clients' treatment plans, such as the kind or duration of service being offered, after they have observed the impacts of treatment received. Law enforcement officials regularly examine their crime prevention procedures in light of actual crime patterns. Sanitation department inspectors routinely spot-check to see if garbage is being collected in a timely and thorough fashion. These kinds of control activities are generally called "program monitoring." Public sector programs that involve the collection of revenues through taxes or fees need to review some of these returns to ensure against misuse. Auditing, therefore, is also a traditional form of operational control in government. Increasingly common is another class of control activities—special studies to examine how well an agency is accomplishing its goals. These efforts, called "program evaluations," often explore operational issues and may serve as a form of periodic control. The success of any operational control function in government is partially determined by the quality of existing information systems. This relationship is discussed in chapter 9.

Updating is the revision of a public service delivery system in light of changes in policy, demand, resources, technology, or managerial capacity. Sometimes the need for updating will be triggered by internal control activities that signal particular failures of existing operations to meet stated objectives. Perhaps more commonly, external forces—emanating from the executive office, legislature, judiciary, media, or a special interest group—provide the catalyst for major program change. A new administration, committed to imposing broad budget cuts, may force many government programs simultaneously to update their operations. Each program will have to modify its production system to function with a reduced complement of resources. A less extensive example is the changing of medical procedures in a public hospital to incorporate the use of a new type of diagnostic equipment. The housing inspection activity of a municipal agency might require significant overhaul (work priorities, job skills, information systems) in response to major revisions in the housing maintenance code.

One conclusion to this brief view of the functions of public sector operations management should be clear: rarely does a single person serve all of these roles in a program of any complexity. In practice, a number of individuals will be involved. Furthermore, each of them will engage in combinations of these activities, rather than work in a structure where each distinct function is neatly assigned to a different manager. Indeed, one of the major challenges for those who study public sector operations is to identify the actual role and responsibility of the key actors and to determine whether some of these important managerial functions are going unattended while others are unnecessarily duplicated. A top manager of a complex government program will also need to know this. However, the balance of managerial responsibilities for government operations will change through time. Analysts and managers will improve their understanding of the dynamics of operations management if they begin to think in terms of an operations life cycle.

The operations life cycle

To implement public policy, production processes are initiated, stabilized, modified, and (finally) eliminated. Broad expressions of public policy are not converted into government operations through a single, fixed pattern of events. There is, however, a standard operations life cycle which includes all of the necessary implementation activities. This cycle contains seven stages: birth, service definition and process selection, operational design, start-up, steady-state, revision, and termination. These stages logically relate to each other in the sequence shown in Exhibit 2.1. In practice, however, some of them—particularly the first four—may occur almost simultaneously. In this chapter, examples are provided with the presentation of the life cycle concepts to illustrate some of the typical patterns.

Birth

The birth stage begins with conceptions for a new public service and ends with the delivery of policy and financial commitments necessary to its development. The manner in which ideas are conceived will vary, as will the actors involved. Some of the underlying determinants will be: the level of government initiating the service, the type of service, the degree of urgency, and the constituents who participate in service decisions. The central action in the birth stage is often the passage of enabling legislation; President Johnson's "War on Poverty" was initiated with considerable new legislation. If the general role of government has been established in a field and an agency is already in business to serve that role, an administrative initiative may be sufficient to give birth to a new program. For example, lead paint detection programs arose in cities and states throughout the country in response to health administrators' decisions.

Exhibit 2.1
Stages of the operations life cycle

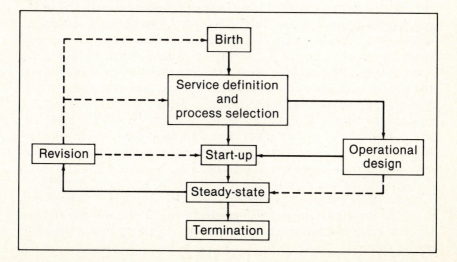

In the private sector, the birth stage would be the appropriate time for an organization to determine whether the service (or product) under consideration is consistent with its existing goals and distinctive competencies. When IBM decides to introduce a new computer, or AT&T a new communications service, the birth stage is a very deliberate top management activity, resulting in clear specification of the desired goals. In reaching this consensus, top corporate management is likely to consider the existing strengths of its organization and the likelihood that the new product or service will be a successful venture. Government does not behave this way. To begin, public sector goals are often expressed vaguely, in terms of launching a new service (a tautology which isn't helpful), or of promoting the public welfare (too general to be of much use to operations managers). In either situation there is likely to be little advance attention paid to operational issues inherent in the new venture. In particular, the existing capabilities of government are often the last factor to be considered in deciding whether to launch a new public program. Government tends to take on new responsibilities when officials decide that a service (that the private sector won't supply) must be provided or when they see the need to impose a new regulation on the private sector. Capabilities of various governmental organizations may be stressed, however, when it is clear that a new program is needed and when rival managers battle for the right to implement it.

The process by which a new government program emerges in the birth stage varies from situation to situation. In complex cases (for example, a national welfare program) a combination of social, political, and economic factors will be introduced. In simple cases, political factors may prevail: "The Sierra Club would be furious if we proceeded any further with our idea to dam that wilderness river, but we must take action to stop the annual flooding." Increasingly common is the use of the economic argument: "We wanted to build four municipal tennis courts this year, but the budget is tight so we can only build two." Some students of government may argue that all economic decisions of this type are basically political in origin. Others may take the opposite position that economic forces generate political arguments. For our purposes this type of disagreement does not have to be resolved. Let us agree that a new public service is conceived when the intention to deliver it is expressed by the responsible public official, and born when it first becomes a legal, administrative, and budgetary entity. The birth stage thus includes the formulation of a service concept and the necessary commitment to implement the service. However, it does not always include the operations management activity of selecting the production approach. Exhibit 2.2 illustrates the birth stage by summarizing how the United States Environmental Protection Agency (EPA) got started. It is not uncommon for the birth stage of a major new government initiative to last a period of several years.

Exhibit 2.2
The birth of the Environmental Protection Agency (EPA)

The late 1960s witnessed a growing public awareness and concern for environmental issues. Constituent pressures led both President Richard Nixon, a Republican, and Senator Edmund Muskie, a leader in the Democrat-controlled Senate, to express a desire to establish an expanded federal program to deal with the environment. Both legislative and executive policy analysts stressed the need for a unified approach to managing the environment. In 1969, Congress established the Council on Environmental Quality to examine issues that required attention by the Nixon administration. In February 1970, President Nixon outlined over thirty goals to be achieved. At the same time, Senator Muskie sponsored several pieces of legislation to deal with specific environmental issues. Public concern was solidified on "Earth Day," April 22, 1970. Finally, as one of Nixon's Presidential Reorganization Plans, the Environmental Protection Agency (EPA) was created in late 1970. This new agency brought together all existing entities throughout the federal government that had responsibility for particular environmental and pollution concerns. The EPA was initially composed of many unintegrated units, and was funded by the original budgets of these units.

Service definition and process selection

Before the new production system gets underway, decisions are required on several basic questions. What are the characteristics of the needed service? Are there to be a range of services offered or just one? Who will deliver the service and through what process is this to be accomplished? To whom will the service be made available? The formulation of broad, initial answers to these questions comprises the second life cycle stage: service definition and process selection.

In the private sector, a separate department may specialize in this stage. There may be a well-defined review process through which the new idea is formally advanced as a "preliminary design" subject to a subsequent business analysis. Sometimes this kind of review will occur in the public sector. Initial plans for a new highway, for example, are produced in response to a general policy agreement that a particular expansion of the transportation network might be advisable and that the funds for such a construction project could be forthcoming.

Often, however, public service systems are defined and production processes are selected in a fragmented manner. Some of these decisions follow from prescriptions made during the birth stage, particularly those expressed in enabling legislation. The Civil Rights Act of 1964, for example, established the Equal Employment Opportunity Commission (EEOC) and charged it to respond to individual complaints of job discrimination. Based on this mandate, the newly formed EEOC had to promulgate a set of regulations. The regulations, in effect, defined the type of service that the agency would offer the public. At the same time, the EEOC selected the primary production process that it would employ—a complaint response system (a kind of "job shop" as described in chapter 3).

Sometimes, service definition and process selection is more independent of the birth stage. A program manager may have to decide what a new service will be: what type of "technical assistance" should a State Office of Economic Development provide to small businesses? A related issue is what type of production process to adopt. Should the agency simply respond to inquiries as they arise, should it actively seek potential clients through a selective "outreach program" or should it start with a mass production approach, such as the preparation and dissemination of written materials answering all major questions on the subject? Process selection is a strategic matter which (as described in chapters 3 and 4) has important implications. The raising of standard marketing issues and the conduct of market research (for example, the identification of market segments) may occur in the course of the service definition and process selection stage, but to date this practice has been rare in government.

In theory, a variety of government employees might usefully participate in these "predesign" decisions, depending on whether the item under consideration is a matter of policy or of administration. In practice, the service definition and process selection activity varies widely in terms of participation, level of effort, and exploration of alternative options. No standard rules are followed either in terms of who participates or what specific decisions are actually made during this stage of the operations life cycle. Exhibit 2.3 returns to the EPA example and illustrates the activities in this stage. The major challenge in this stage is to address the important strategic design questions without getting buried in the details of operational design.

Operational design

Before the public service delivery system can begin, a more refined set of decisions must be made. The definition of the service and its production strategy must be supplemented by the selection of equipment, the design of jobs, the definition of work methods and procedures, and the identification of performance measures. Systems for achieving quality control, cost control, and accurate demand forecasting must also be designed. Decisions regarding these items may be considered "preliminary" designs but sometimes get bureaucratized to the point that they are hard to change, while "final" designs have a way of becoming obsolete and requiring revision (as described below). Designing may be explicit or implicit, depending on the formality of operating management. Staff skills and managerial styles will largely determine the extent to which such designs are

---

Exhibit 2.3
Service definition and process selection at the EPA

In December 1970, President Nixon appointed William Ruckelshaus as administrator of the EPA. Ruckelshaus needed to establish policies to permit the new
agency to cope with a wide range of environmental concerns, including water
pollution, air pollution, and solid waste disposal. The specific areas in which the
EPA had expertise were determined by the functional units which the newly-
formed EPA had inherited from other federal agencies. However, before they
made any operational decisions, Ruckelshaus and his initial staff had to refine the
focus of the agency and set up agency-wide guidelines and policies. An overall
approach to improving the environment needed to be established. What combination of activities, such as supporting research, providing incentives to eliminate
pollution, and demanding compliance with rigorous guidelines, would result in the
most effective outcome? How could the EPA draw on centralized control for rapid
enforcement of existing regulations, while it established the strong decentralized
(regional) authority required by the Nixon administration's "New Federalism" policy? In his search for answers, Ruckelshaus drew on the expertise of employees
from the individual departments that had been combined to create the EPA, while
he also kept in mind the general direction that had been advanced by President
Nixon.

This initial planning activity was quite short and left many basic questions unresolved, since only slightly more than a month elapsed between Ruckelshaus'
appointment and the official starting date of the new agency. As a result the service
definition and process selection stage overlapped in time with the operational
design and start-up stages.

"intuitive" or "analytic." In the public sector, a manager must develop
the intuitive insights about operating systems to the point where he or she
can wisely decide when to employ analytic skills and specialized design
techniques.

Regardless of how such design decisions are made, a traditional planning sequence would require that they be resolved (at least in a preliminary way) before the new program begins operations. In practice, this
rarely occurs in the public sector. Instead it is quite typical for the birth of
a new service system to be accompanied by a public statement—often in
the enabling legislation—declaring when the service will be available. As
in the case of the formulation of the EPA, programs that reach this formal
stage of approval have been selected as top priority, with the result that
there is likely to be great pressure to start them as soon as possible.
Policymakers who set the start-up date for a new program often underestimate the range of detailed design decisions yet to be made. Start-up
usually begins, therefore, long before operational design is really completed. This occurred at the EPA, as indicated in Exhibit 2.4. In the face
of such realities, one should probably consider operational design as starting after service definition and process selection but continuing through-

---

Exhibit 2.4
Operational design at the EPA

At the EPA Ruckelshaus was locked into many operational constraints already functioning in the independent departments. Although each unit that was inherited had clear programmatic responsibilities, there were considerable functional overlaps within these agencies. Each had a regulatory branch, an enforcement branch, a research branch, etc. Ruckelshaus was uncertain if maintaining a programmatic structure was preferable to instituting a functional structure. Furthermore, the geographic allocation of staff resources required his attention. However, even more pressing was the need for Ruckelshaus to bring together the resources to meet the January 31, 1971, deadline, set by law, to promulgate air quality standards. Ruckelshaus was aware that making many operational changes would be further constrained by budgeting limitations during the current fiscal year. With these issues in mind, Ruckelshaus set up an early operational design that (1) would demonstrate that EPA was serious about the pollution problem by taking several specific immediate actions against polluters, and (2) would allow EPA the time to resolve the other operational problems after the formal start-up of the agency.

---

out the life cycle of a public service delivery system, rather than being completed prior to start-up. Operational design may be viewed as a life cycle of its own, as illustrated in Exhibit 2.5.

Start-up

Installing a new operating system requires several types of actions. A budget must be allocated. A manager must be designated. Staff must be assembled and trained according to specified procedures. Facilities and equipment must be acquired. And prospective clients must be notified that the service is available and informed about how they might obtain it.

In a manufacturing organization, the start-up period has a simple transitional function: to test the production system and to reach an acceptable level of efficiency. In such settings the start-up period offers an opportunity for management to minimize the time needed to reach full-scale production. It represents a period when technical personnel spend considerable time checking the feasibility of their production designs and making necessary adjustments. Then, when production is satisfying the desired standards, the start-up period is declared to be over and normal production commences.

In the public sector, in contrast, the start-up period is more than a transition period, a necessary buffer between the birth of a new idea and the efficient delivery of the desired service. Most new public services need further definition, policies must be sharpened, procedures must be refined, capacity requirements must be defined, roles and responsibilities must be worked out, and initial client contacts must be established. All of

Exhibit 2.5
The operational design cycle

Stage	Contents	Product
1. Preliminary Design	Specification of organizational structure, basic staff complement, and outline of operational responsibilities	Written draft for review
2. Executive Review	Preliminary design reviewed for consistency with existing policy and resources (personnel budget)	List of changes to preliminary design
3. Detailed Design	Specification of jobs, operating procedures, decision rules, information systems, and performance criteria	Written draft for review
4. Operational Review	Detailed design is examined by the different levels of operating personnel to assess feasibility	List of changes to detailed design
5. Complete Design	Full specification of "who does what when"	Final report

Note: There may be a repetition of stages 1 and 2 preceding executive approval. Similarly, stages 3 and 4 may require recycling to achieve operational approval.

this takes time and is hard to predict fully. For public management, the start-up period is a crucial time of learning about the new operation and its associated problems of control.

Sometimes the start-up stage of a public program serves a market-testing function. A subset of the client population (e.g., a single county in the state or a particular age group or an income category) is selected to receive the service for a specified period, before any attempt is made to provide it to all who are eligible. Special transportation services for the elderly and the handicapped, for example, have followed this approach. In such cases, the start-up stage has both a beginning and an end. Start-up, in short, presents an opportunity to reevaluate the viability of the services before proceeding to full-scale operations.

Sometimes, however, government cannot initially limit the scope of the production system. A new housing code enforcement program to provide fuel and emergency repairs to city residents must be launched "full-scale" at start-up, since limiting the service at first to a single neighborhood or type of resident could be legally and ethically unjustifiable. Gradually the service will be brought under control through the direction of its management. In such cases, it is difficult to say when the start-up stage is complete. Exhibit 2.6 outlines the start-up stage at EPA.

Exhibit 2.6
Start-up at the EPA

As in many governmental agencies, the EPA was forced into the start-up stage with several issues from earlier stages unresolved. Ruckelshaus had only a month to make organizational sense of the geographically dispersed units that made up the EPA. He needed to assess the capabilities of his staff and appoint some new managers. He had to decide whether to phase the EPA into pollution control gradually or try to start with a full-scale program.

Ruckelshaus chose the latter strategy. Shortly after the official start-up, the EPA filed suits against several major polluters. The agency also took steps aimed at establishing clean air standards by January 31, 1971. These two actions committed EPA resources in ways that were consistent with the major policies of this new agency.

Throughout the start-up stage, Ruckelshaus had to deal with the past practices and budgets of the inherited units. Since many of the staff of the EPA were transferred directly from existing agencies, many traditional start-up activities were absent. Instead, Ruckelshaus had to break the inertia that existed and to commit agency staff to support the new directions. Ruckelshaus also spent considerable time planning the budget and staffing for the next fiscal year. Throughout the start-up stage, organizational changes and operational adjustments were also common as Ruckelshaus attempted to make the EPA a well-run agency. In summary, there was considerable overlap at the EPA between the start-up and the operational design stages.

Steady-state

Regardless of how the start-up stage is conducted, the service eventually reaches ''steady-state.'' This stage occurs when the program's budget has stabilized (at least to the point of being on a predictable trend), its policies and procedures are well established, and changes are either relatively insignificant or infrequent. At this point, program staff will have acquired a reasonable level of expertise. Operations managers will understand the nature of the production system (as described in chapters 3 and 4) and will have identified those aspects of service demand and supply that need to be watched most closely. The monitoring and control of day-to-day operations can become highly refined during the steady-state stage—if it lasts long enough.

Private sector manufacturers often allow the operations of their more established product lines to remain in steady-state for years or even decades. Naturally, there will be product improvements, technological innovations, turnover of management and employees, and shifts in market emphasis. But the product itself may remain viable and the company may wish to stay in the business, while it grows more and more competent in supplying its particular markets. With some luck, the industry may even be relatively stable during this time and customer requirements may not shift very much.

In service organizations, this type of scenario is more unusual, especially in the public sector. The operations manager's job in steady-state is to maintain satisfactory performance of the production system and to identify opportunities and methods for its improvement. A new government program or service, however, is often faced with a particularly unstable set of conditions. Administrative turnover is frequent and broad-based. Priorities tend to shift dramatically. Fiscal outlook is highly uncertain. To make matters worse, the need for many public services is highest when the economy is depressed. In such situations, one of the most fruitful strategies for improving the long-run performance of government operations may be for operations managers to assume that the steady-state will be transitory—if it is perceptible at all. Managers would also do well to consider options for revision during this stage. The one thing that can be safely claimed about the steady-state period for most government operations is that it can be counted on to collapse at some point.

Revision

Minor adjustments in resources, practices, and procedures are likely to be underway at most points throughout the life of an established governmental program. If such adjustments can be accommodated without significant structural changes—that is, within existing constraints of budget, manpower, management, and organization—the program remains in steady-state. If, however, adjustments become more substantial, program operations will be subject to the revision stage. The need for program revision may arise in different ways. A recent trend at all levels of government has been for the onset of a fiscal crisis to force a considerable cutback in the scope of existing programs or services. (The management of demand, a primary strategy in such situations, is the subject of chapter 7.) Alternatively, sharp increases in public expectations may lead to broad criticism of an existing service, thereby triggering significant policy and program reform. Sometimes a public official may take the initiative by selecting a particular governmental area as a target for improvement in performance or efficiency.

Regardless of the origin of the revision stage, it is at this stage that the weaknesses of the program will become articulated. Analysis, reformulation, and redesign are then needed to save the program, unless the objective is simply to terminate the program as soon as possible. Much of systems analysis, program planning, and management science falls into this category. If properly anticipated, program revisions may proceed without interrupting service delivery until steady-state is again reached. If revisions are extensive, the service might have to undergo a new start-up stage. When the revision involves changes to enabling legislation or major

Exhibit 2.7
Illustration of the revision stage: the department of social services

In the late 1970s there was growing concern in Massachusetts that the social services provided to welfare clients had become fragmented and ineffective. This was particularly critical in programs aimed at children who were indirect welfare recipients. The current Welfare Department was highly centralized and the organizational and fiscal structure was set up to emphasize assistance payments. Pressure from constituencies arose for a change in the approach used to provide social services. Social service staff members had become frustrated with their inability to modify services to meet the specific needs of their clients and requested greater local autonomy. Advocacy groups voiced the same concern and, in a report to the state legislature, outlined problems that existed. They stressed existing gaps in the social service system and overlaps among agencies that created redundant services. A blue-ribbon panel, commissioned to study these changes, surveyed existing social service programs and concurred that a major revision was needed. The panel recommended new legislation to create a Department of Social Services (DSS), which was to be responsible for all social service programs currently handled by the Department of Public Welfare and to have oversight responsibility for other statewide service programs for children.

The law was passed in 1979. The newly formed Department of Social Services attempted to correct many of the perceived problems by moving quickly toward a regional organization. Local autonomy was provided by allowing regional offices across the state to tailor their programs to their own clients' needs. Funding was changed from a centralized, programmatic base to a regional base so that regional managers could decide how much of their total budget to allocate to each type of social service being delivered. New staff were hired to provide the right mix of support for providing these services. The new DSS began to resolve many of the issues that had instigated earlier revisions of the welfare system in Massachusetts, particularly the separation of welfare payments (income maintenance) from social services.

In this case, an agency in a mature stage of the operations life cycle suddenly entered the revision stage, through legislative mandate. After the agency was split into two organizational entities, each part had its own independent operational life cycle—DSS started at birth, while the department that provided welfare payments returned to steady-state.

policy reformulations, the service may even be subject to another birth stage. Unfortunately, some of these more dramatic instances of revision are unexpected, since public officials often view policy and program changes as incremental, when, in fact, substantial operational upheaval is required. This was the case in the formation of the Massachusetts Department of Social Services, which took over existing programs from the Department of Public Welfare, as outlined in Exhibit 2.7.

Termination

Occasionally, a government program will fall into such a severe state of crisis or be faced with such an obvious lack of market, that revision is no longer an option. At this point termination is a distinct possibility, and the strategic issue is how to salvage the remaining resources. Program termination is probably an appropriate decision much more frequently than actual practice would indicate. (Some factors currently inhibiting termination in public sector ventures are outlined in chapter 14.) Whenever termination is not a viable option, it becomes even more important to design and manage government so that a process of rejuvenation, through a timely reversion to an earlier stage of the operations life cycle, will occur.

Managerial priorities during the operations life cycle

The major value of thinking in terms of the operations life cycle is that it signals important patterns in managerial priorities. In the birth stage, policymakers must concentrate on taking actions that avoid severe unintended consequences. In particular, they must try to anticipate fundamental operational problems that are likely to arise. The birth stage, on the other hand, is not the time to try to resolve all operational ambiguities. This can be done in the service definition and process selection stage, but only if the birth stage provides adequate time for program design and implementation. The birth stage must, however, provide budgetary resources commensurate with an acceptable type and level of program activity. In short, the basic managerial priority during the birth stage is to avoid creating a guaranteed disaster. Though this requirement may seem easy to satisfy, it generally demands that those who draft or approve legislation and administrative mandates become sensitive to operational realities which they might normally tend to overlook.

In the service definition and process selection stage, the priorities become more precise. Public managers must then focus on articulating their goals and objectives in ways that indicate what services will be provided to specific population groups. They must recognize that production systems involve people and equipment acting together to achieve particular outputs. Managers must be able to envision how the new program will function and the type of demand it will satisfy. From these initial specifications, the type of production process (for example, line or job shop or project, as defined in chapter 3) will emerge. Such specifications become more precise and require more technical skills as the operational design stage is entered. The top managerial priority is then to ensure that the design cycle is sensibly matched to the program implementation sequence.

The skills needed at start-up are different from those required for maintaining a program in steady-state. In start-up, a diffuse set of resources must be brought together to form a productive entity. Managers must aggressively seek to identify operating difficulties and draw on analytic support to remove the underlying problems. The assembly of a good team and the scheduling of major start-up efforts, project management approaches such as those outlined in chapter 4, may be appropriate.

In steady-state, program maintenance skills are most critical. Managers need to be able to monitor existing operations and to motivate staff to achieve the targeted level of performance. They need to emphasize the solution of exceptional situations while relying on a sensible set of responses, policies, and procedures to handle standard situations. When the flow of exceptions grows out of bounds, public managers must be able to identify alternative operational systems. They must then be skilled in assessing such alternatives and in making informed judgments on the best revisions to attempt.

In the revision stage, managers must demonstrate skill in dealing with organizational change. Planning a revision may be easier than implementing it. Managers must be sensitive enough to the difficulties of change to anticipate problems that may arise in setting new goals and objectives. If a program is to be terminated, a major managerial priority is the transfer of existing resources to other operations.

Prerequisites for successful life cycle management

It is hard to generalize about successful life cycle management of public system operations. Each program or service tends to have its own context and requirements. Perhaps the most important prerequisite is that all operations managers begin with an awareness of the existence of a life cycle and that they understand the different tasks and priorities of each stage.

Each stage of the life cycle draws in different ways on the five basic functions of operations management, described at the beginning of this chapter. Taken together, these functions call for a wide range of skills. In practice, for any sizable government operation, these functions are likely to be shared among several individuals. All operations managers in a government agency must realize that individual efforts at any point in the life of a program will affect other managers who have related but distinct responsibilities for that program.

The importance of the design stage deserves special mention. Government programs must be designed to operate in a chaotic environment. Crises are the rule, rather than the exception, in many parts of government. It would be naive to assume that major disruptions would vanish if operations management were strengthened. Program designs, accordingly, must be flexible enough to ensure that basic service delivery continues even at times of particular crisis.

Finally, uniform concepts of and standard analytic approaches to operations management are required for successful life cycle management. Operating systems are usually sufficiently complicated that intuitive attempts at program designs or evaluation will not work. Standard reliable information must be collected, analyzed, and retained for future comparative purposes. Some degree of stability in program management and operating personnel is also required. Finally, someone must take a long-term view of the operating system, even while others are preoccupied with the immediate situation.

Summary

The general functions of operations management are to select, design, operate, control, and update productive systems. Government programs normally have several operations managers who share these responsibilities. As a public program proceeds through the operations life cycle, these managers shift their emphasis. At first it is important to select an appropriate production process and to determine its functional design. Later the execution of day-to-day operations and related control activities demand the most attention. As time passes and conditions change, the need for maintaining steady-state operations will yield to requirements for program change. Then the managerial abilities to redesign and adapt the productive system become crucial. Finally, programs will need to be terminated, at which time skills in phasing out existing operations are required. At any stage in the operations life cycle, public managers must be able to identify the existing production process and to measure its capacity and performance. Approaches for doing so are presented in succeeding chapters of this book.

Discussion questions

1. Pressures from external constituencies change during the life of public sector service organization. For example, a public interest group might lobby against the elimination of services in the revision or termination stage. What forces must public managers be prepared to face in *each* stage of the life cycle? Looking at each stage individually, consider the possible effect of such external pressures on the kinds of operational decisions that must be made in that phase of the life cycle. Give specific examples.
2. A newly formed government agency may lack clear demarcations between the stages of its operations life cycle. Identify some of the kinds of overlap in stages that might be observed in such situations. Should a manager be concerned if all service definition and process selection tasks are not completed by start-up? Finally, a newly hired public

manager may suspect that the different programs in his or her agency are in different stages of the life cycle: some in start-up, some in steady-state, some in revision, etc. What characteristics should the manager look for to determine the current life cycle stage of each program?

3. One of the functions of an operations manager is controlling. In which life cycle stages would a manager most likely perform control activities? What specific control activities would be required of a manager in these stages?

4. The major functions of an operations manager—selecting, designing, operating, controlling, and updating—were discussed. If you were the chief of police, what activities would be associated with each of these functions? What specific managerial actions might you take to accomplish these activities? By what criteria would you expect the mayor to assess your performance of these functions? What information would be necessary as background for such assessments?

Notes
[1] Much of the basic terminology of the functions of operations management and the life cycle stages were adopted from Chase and Aquilano (1981). However, the author knows of no development of these terms along the lines of this chapter.

Bibliography
Chase, Richard B., and Nicholas J. Aquilano. *Production and Operations Management.* Homewood, Ill.: Irwin, 1981.

Part 2
Analysis of operating systems

Chapter 3
Process analysis of public sector operating systems

In order to set and achieve reasonable objectives, a public sector operations manager must understand the basic structure and process of public sector operating systems. The ability to allocate wisely available productive resources, while taking into account the constraints imposed by the agency's external environment, is also essential. So, too, is the skill needed to conduct a periodic process analysis of existing operating systems. This chapter and chapter 4 discuss the perspectives necessary for building such skills. These two chapters introduce basic concepts which a public manager should understand before he or she addresses the practical issues of how to improve government performance.

An operating system is a productive transformation process through which a set of inputs is converted to desired outputs; in other words, it is a production process through which resources are combined to produce goods or services. Those who have been exposed to other views of organizations as systems (for example, as discussed in Churchman, 1968, or Katz & Kahn, 1966) will see direct analogues to the concepts presented here, but none of these other models or vocabularies (jargon) is necessary to our discussion.

Definition of an operating system

A simple operating system may serve one of a number of functions: manufacture, supply, transportation, or service. Standard texts in operations management usually compare and contrast these functions, while they stress the manufacturing function. A public manager, however, is not likely to be responsible for manufacturing. Service delivery is the most prevalent public sector operation, although transportation and supply operations are also common. Illustrations of many types of government operations are presented throughout this book. Any operating system can be defined in terms of its inputs, its outputs, and the nature of the production process.

Identification of inputs

Inputs are the resources that are consumed, used, or converted by an operating system in the production of a good or service. Such inputs include labor, energy, equipment, and raw materials. Labor and energy are consumed in the operation of the system; vehicles, tools, or other equipment are used; raw materials are converted to other forms as a product is made.

In manufacturing or construction systems, identification of the resources that are direct production inputs is usually quite straightforward. At each stage of a production process some labor inputs may be required: a certain number of person-hours for making each ton of steel, a certain number for forging or installing each beam. Capital input requirements include facilities and equipment necessary for executing the production process. Energy, of course, heats or cools the facilities or fuels the equipment.

In the production of goods, raw materials are particularly important. The particular stage of the production process determines the raw materials required: iron ore is needed to make steel, steel to make beams, and beams to support buildings. Labor and equipment, as well as raw materials, are required. The mix of requirements for these different kinds of inputs varies from industry to industry. It also varies from firm to firm, depending on the extent to which the product is mass-produced.

In contrast, service delivery systems are usually labor intensive (i.e., labor inputs are more extensively required), although other inputs, especially equipment, are frequently needed. Some public sector operating systems may also accommodate different sets of inputs. Iron ore is always needed for steel production, but no one input is *always* required to put a law enforcement system into motion. A concerned citizen may call the police station, a burglar alarm may go off, or the police may observe a suspicious act. In each case, the law officers investigate the situation and attempt to make an arrest if such action is warranted. Thus, the same output (arrest) may be accomplished through a variety of inputs (citizens' calls for help, police observations, etc.). Similarly, a request for special medical treatment may lead to the same health care response for a hospital patient regardless of whether the request was initiated by a nurse, an aide, or a doctor. A public manager must be alert to the spectrum of inputs that may be used by a service production system.

Simply identifying the inputs is an insufficient basis for planning desired production targets and estimating production costs. A manager must be able to determine the required level of inputs. Input levels are measured initially in units unique to the kind of input (tons of iron ore, person-hours, or kilowatt-hours). Translating the physical input levels into their monetary values allows a manager to compare the cumulative cost of all inputs to the value of the output. Clearly, this process is necessary in the private sector: without the conversion to common units it is impossible to know if producing thirty tons of steel from a combination of fifty tons of iron ore, twenty tons of coal, and twenty tons of limestone is worth the effort. In the public sector, input cost information is essential for a manager to assess whether the worth ascribed to the output warrants the continuation of the service. Similarly, without first establishing specific costs for all inputs, a manager cannot assess alternative production designs; only when the cost of all inputs has been determined can the net costs of changing the mix of inputs to produce the same outputs be assessed.

Identification of outputs

A production (or operating) system yields specific goods, such as steel, or specific services, such as an arrest, as "output." Identifying the precise nature of such outputs is a fundamental step in describing any production system. The simple fact that a good is produced, or a service delivered, does not describe adequately the output of an operating system. Manufactured products must physically meet certain specifications which define an acceptable level of quality. Likewise, the output of a service delivery system has a built-in quality dimension. For example, if a police department makes many arrests, but each case is dismissed by the court because of a consistent error in arrest procedures, the output is unacceptable and the operating system should be examined closely for areas that need improvement; there might be problems with the quality or nature of the input or with the process that converts the input to output. It is inappropriate to assess the output of an operating system unless the dimension of quality is explicitly addressed.

A value must be assigned to production outputs, as well as to inputs. For most goods and services, the value of production outputs is established in the market. Consumers who desire the good or service are willing to pay a price which reflects its economic worth. Measuring the value of outputs in terms of price permits direct comparisons with the aggregate cost of the inputs. Although this method works well for purchased goods or services, it is inappropriate for the many public services provided at no direct cost. Many studies have attempted to answer such questions as "How much is an arrest worth?" or "How much is rapid transit worth?" to establish the value of government's operational outputs. (In the area of fire protection, for example, see Walker, Chaiken, & Ignall, 1979.) Although citizens do not pay a police officer for each arrest, each arrest is "worth" something to society as a whole. However, progress in measuring the value of government outputs has been mixed. A competent analyst may be able to determine the total costs of inputs in a law enforcement system, yet the question, "Does the output (number of arrests) justify this cost?" might be difficult to answer.

A public transit system provides a slightly more complex example. A charge of fifty cents a ride represents the direct cost to the user, but the total cost of public mass transit is typically greater than the fares paid by riders. Most communities are willing to use tax revenues to subsidize a portion of the service provided by a transit system. Deciding on an acceptable level of subsidy, in effect, determines the value of the transit system "output." While some quantitative analysis may be valuable, public managers must determine appropriate output levels by drawing cues from similar situations elsewhere, from a sense of prevailing societal norms and values, and from an understanding of the characteristics of the output and the use to which it will be put. Often, however, these decisions are political and are made by voters and elected officials, rather than by operating managers.

The production process

Those who manage government operations are responsible for some aspect of a production process through which inputs are transformed into outputs. Each task in a production process needs to be managed, as do the interdependent elements of the entire production system. The production process typically is represented by a flow chart, such as that in Exhibit 3.1. This exhibit depicts a firm which assembles a particular product from three purchased parts. The firm maintains an inventory of each part, assembles the parts in two steps, and maintains an inventory of the final product. In this process flow chart, the solid arrows represent the physical movement of the product as it is produced.

Any process flow chart must display the three significant characteristics of a production process: operations, movement, and storage. By

Exhibit 3.1
Process flow chart of a simple assembly operation

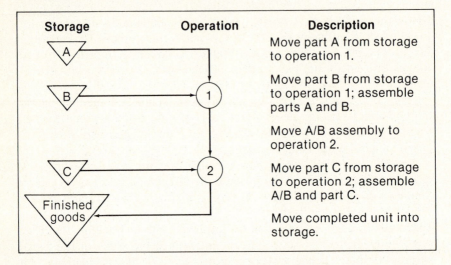

Storage	Operation	Description
A		Move part A from storage to operation 1.
B	1	Move part B from storage to operation 1; assemble parts A and B.
		Move A/B assembly to operation 2.
C	2	Move part C from storage to operation 2; assemble A/B and part C.
Finished goods		Move completed unit into storage.

convention, the symbols used are O = operation, → = movement, and ▽ = storage. Operations are defined as the set of productive activities through which inputs are transformed to interim or final products. Movement is the transfer of inputs, information, or partially completed products from one operation to another, or to a storage area. Storage occurs between operations or movements. Parts may be stored before they are used, information may be stored for later analysis, and outputs may be accumulated and stored to meet subsequent demand.

The flow of information, as well as of goods, is essential to the successful operation of a production process. In the production process shown in Exhibit 3.1, the records office needs to know when a part is removed from inventory, where any particular batch of partially assembled products is located, and when a batch has been completed and delivered to the finished goods inventory. Such flows of information can be represented graphically, as shown in Exhibit 3.2. The use of broken lines is a standard convention to indicate the movement of information. While no return information is indicated in this exhibit, that might not be the case in an actual operating setting, and the flow chart easily could be expanded to include information feedback. A well-designed flow chart tracks each input as it is transformed by the production process into the desired output. The flow chart of an existing operating system must describe the actual process performed, not what is desired.

Exhibit 3.2
Process flow chart of a simple assembly operation including flow of information

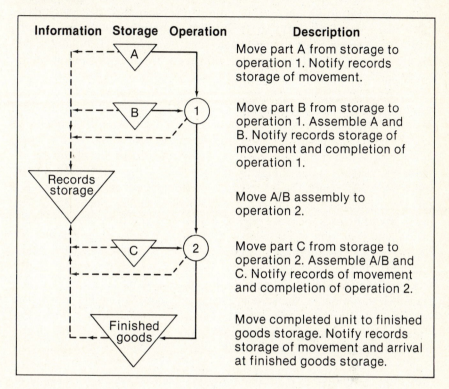

Information Storage Operation	Description
A	Move part A from storage to operation 1. Notify records storage of movement.
B 1	Move part B from storage to operation 1. Assemble A and B. Notify records storage of movement and completion of operation 1.
Records storage	Move A/B assembly to operation 2.
C 2	Move part C from storage to operation 2. Assemble A/B and C. Notify records of movement and completion of operation 2.
Finished goods	Move completed unit to finished goods storage. Notify records storage of movement and arrival at finished goods storage.

Process flow charts for service production can follow a similar format. However, such charts may become complex, as processing in service systems often requires discretion, and the resulting decisions may lead to one of several paths. Also, the production of many public services largely consists of processing and analyzing information. Accordingly, the inclusion of information tracking on a flow diagram is crucial. Flow charts of service delivery systems, however, often lack storage steps, since (as discussed later) services cannot be inventoried for subsequent use. Developing a flow chart similar to Exhibit 3.2 will clarify how each component is indicated on a process diagram. The preparation of a flow diagram is the necessary first step to understanding a production process. This is followed by the analysis of the production process, specifically the measurement of capacity and performance.

Basic types of production processes

Operating systems traditionally are categorized into three types: line (or flow) operations, job shops, and projects. In practice, a government agency is likely to be engaged in production processes that encompass more than one of these types. Nevertheless, parts of processes, corresponding to these ideal types, usually can be isolated. Ultimately, the management of each type may be enhanced by an appreciation of its particular features.

Line (or flow) operation A line operation is a continuous processing system. The desired service (or product) is produced according to a fixed sequence of activities. Operations flow from one task to the next without deviations. While there may be a delay before the processing of any one of these tasks begins, no task may be skipped. Nor is there any discretion in the sequence in which the given tasks are completed. In the private sector, a familiar line operation is the automobile assembly plant. An example in government is the placement of new clients into the welfare (income maintenance) system. A line shop with six tasks is represented graphically in Exhibit 3.3. By definition, a line operation is highly specialized and inflexible. It produces what can be termed a standard service. If the nature of the service is changed, the line operation may have to be redesigned. If variations of the standard service are needed, either more than one line operation will be necessary to accommodate the range of new "products," or a composite operation which does not correspond to the line format will have to be designed.

Job shop A job shop is an operating system that produces a range of services or products, each of which follows a different set or sequence of tasks. The full range of operating activities must be available whenever any particular job is handled. Some of the tasks are likely to be required almost all of the time, while others are reserved for special processing circumstances. Consequently, the flow pattern through a job shop varies from job to job. A company that makes custom-ordered, hand-built furniture is likely to structure its production system as a job shop. In government the response of a fire department to a call for assistance, from the receipt of the call until the completion of all response activities, follows the job shop structure, since the response depends in part on the nature of the call. A simplified diagram of a job shop of a fire department handling three different types of situations is shown in Exhibit 3.4.

Project A project is a one-time production process. A unique service or product requires the design and implementation of a temporary operating system. This system must include all of the resources needed for satisfactory completion of the project, and these resources must be available to

Exhibit 3.3
Sample flow chart for a line operation (welfare processing)

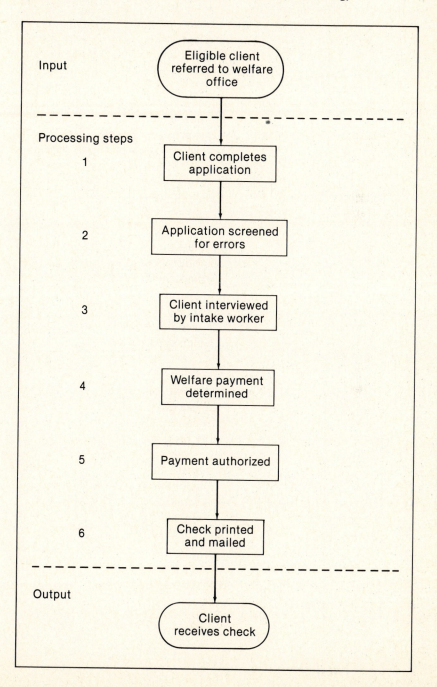

Exhibit 3.4
Sample flow chart for a job shop operation (fire department)

1. Alarm received	2. Alarm screened	3. Initial response made based on apparent severity of fire	4. On-site evaluation	5. Subsequent on-site action	6. Total response level
Alarm sounds at dispatch	Is alarm from firebox or phone? — Firebox / Phone — Caller questioned by dispatch — Is initial response needed? — Yes / No — Process complete	First alarm sounded; 2 pumpers 1 ladder truck 15 fire fighters dispatched	First unit arrives on scene and determines severity of condition — Is additional alarm needed?	False alarm — Return to station. Minor fire — Initial response sufficient, extinguish fire and return to station. Major fire — Request next alarm. Yes — Extinguish fire and return to station. No	First alarm response average time for false alarm: 20 minutes. First alarm response average time for 1 alarm fire: 2 hours. Up to 8 alarms and 16 units can be dispatched average time for multialarm fire: 4 hours.

the project as needed. Often, these resources never before will have been assembled into a productive entity. The central operating problem for a project, usually called project management, is to schedule the use of the required resources to achieve the objectives of the particular project. Major construction efforts typically are managed as projects. The most familiar and glamorous public projects are perhaps those in the aerospace field, notably the Apollo missions to put a man on the moon. An emergency domestic initiative such as a (threatened but not yet implemented) gasoline rationing system also would be managed as a project. Projects traditionally are displayed in graphic form as a network of interrelated, time-sequenced production activities. An example of such a network and further discussion of project management in government is included in chapter 5.

Exhibit 3.5 lists some familiar examples of operating systems in government to illustrate each of the three basic types of production processes. The selection of any one of these production processes will affect the operational work environment, the skills required by operating personnel, the cost of delivering a public service, and techniques for assuring quality and reliability. Public managers involved in the selection of the production system—the second stage of the operations life cycle—should attempt to assess such impacts before they make their decisions.

Exhibit 3.5
Examples of production processes in government

Type of Service Delivery	Type of Process	Example
Public Works	Project	Sewer system construction
	Job shop	Pothole repair
	Line	Highway paving
Criminal Justice	Project	Crime prevention task force
	Job shop	Court operations
	Line	Arrest processing
Health and Human Services	Project	Swine flu vaccination program
	Job shop	Social services
	Line	Welfare payment processing
Public University	Project	Presidential search committee
	Job shop	Career counseling
	Line	Course registration and payment

Elements of a Process Analysis

A public sector operations manager usually will want to know several
things about a production process. How much can it produce during the
next planning period? How well used are the available resources? Is the
level of production satisfactory? What are the actual costs of production?
What are the most significant external constraints on the operating system? To answer these questions, an operations manager must develop
skills in identifying a system's capacity, efficiency, effectiveness, costs,
and environment. Taken together, these are the key elements of a process
analysis.

Capacity

The capacity of an operating system is the amount of output produced in a
particular period of time. Public managers need to determine whether the
existing capacity is appropriate. They must be able to answer questions
such as: Is capacity sufficient to meet service delivery requirements?
Should there be enough capacity to handle the average demand level or
should capacity meet peak demands? When should capacity be expanded
or contracted? How should this be done? These and other issues regarding the management of capacity are discussed more fully in chapter 4.

For now it is sufficient to point out that a process analysis must distinguish between theoretical capacity and effective capacity. Theoretical
capacity is the maximum rate at which output can be produced over a
short time. A machine running at full speed in a perfect environment
theoretically could produce a fixed and finite number of units of output.
Unfortunately, it rarely is possible to attain this maximum capacity over
an extended period, since the occurrence of any unexpected events would
preclude maintenance of this rate. A power shutoff, a jammed part, or the
brief departure of an operator from a machine would reduce the output
below the theoretical maximum capacity. Therefore, determination of
effective capacity clearly is more valuable. Effective capacity is the actual
output of the production process over a longer time period. An operating
manager uses effective capacity to determine the total output of goods and
services that can be achieved over any particular planning horizon and,
therefore, to assess the likelihood that a production system will meet
demand. In assessing effective capacity, public managers are faced with
many uncertainties. The difficulties grow with increases in the number of
operations, the number of people involved in the process, the level of
employee discretion in the process, and the variability of demand on the
production system.

Efficiency

Efficiency is a concept that relates the output of a process to the required inputs. It is common to try to measure the inputs in the same units as the outputs. In production systems, costs of input and price of output are convenient measures. In the private sector, with its emphasis on profits, setting aside opportunity costs, an output price in excess of the input costs would reflect a process efficient enough to justify continued production. If an analyst discovers that input costs per unit exceed the output price, a decision on the feasibility of continued production is warranted. (In practice, many other factors must be considered in such a decision, including the means used to establish cost of inputs, the objectives of the process, the long-term prospects for improvement, and the overall goals of the organization.)

In government, however, the traditional bottom line is not easily established and the measurement of efficiency can be more complicated. Often the input costs of public services significantly exceed the price paid for the output. Welfare services, for example, are "free" to the recipient. Frequently efficiency must be measured in terms of units of output per dollar spent, or output per unit of input. As mentioned earlier, the dollar equivalent of input usually can be determined in the public sector, but it is difficult, and often impossible, to accurately and totally compute the value of output. Measures such as passengers carried per dollars spent or claims processed per employee must be used.

Efficiency measures are useful only to the extent that they quantify measures that have managerial significance. Many traditional efficiency measures, such as arrests per police officer, cases closed per social worker, or complaints resolved per investigator, are difficult to interpret as a basis for action. Is the police officer who prevents crime and has few arrests a less efficient officer simply because his or her total output of arrests is low? Is the social worker who handles a large number of straightforward cases and closes them rapidly more efficient than one who deals conscientiously with fewer, more complex cases, which inevitably remain open for a longer time? A public manager must wrestle with these kinds of questions before settling on any particular measure of efficiency. Another common pitfall is selecting a single measure to be used throughout an organization. If the measure chosen contains a "work load bias," inequities in evaluating independent components of the system may arise. "Arrests per police officer" raises this kind of problem since a police officer in a high crime area *should* have more arrests than an officer in a low crime area. Accordingly, it may not be reasonable to compare the performance of individuals throughout an agency with this type of biased efficiency measure. Finally, it is improper to make operational decisions based solely on efficiency measures, since there are often trade-offs between achieving efficiency and effectiveness in a government program.

Effectiveness

Effectiveness is a measure of comparison between the actual output from a process and a standard or target output. Since standards may have more than one dimension, identifying an appropriate unit of measurement becomes an important managerial decision. For example, standards could reflect either the quantity or quality of output or the time needed for its production. Note that cost standards, which commonly are developed for accounting purposes, are not used for effectiveness measurement, since production costs refer to the inputs rather than the outputs of an operating system.

The setting of standards is common in government operations: 250 unemployment claims should be processed this week; all complaints should be investigated within 3 days; 95 percent of all bus runs should leave on time. If a service delivery system fails to meet production standards, its manager should examine the process to find the source of the performance gap. Often the source is simply that the standard itself is unrealistic. Standards should be feasible targets, not ideal dreams.

Output standards must reflect the nature of the production process, taking into account characteristics such as complexity of operations, variability in service requirements, and the need for employee discretion at many points in the system. Attempting to reach an unattainable goal has managerial implications beyond the mere report of low effectiveness. Employee morale may suffer, thereby hindering future performance. The agency might become subject to more frequent external review in response to apparent lack of effectiveness. Operations managers therefore must carefully establish meaningful standards to be used as a basis for improving program effectiveness. Furthermore, they must be willing to adjust the standards whenever those initially selected are proven faulty. Finally, if the standards seem reasonable but the production system yields a low measure of effectiveness, improvements should be sought. The necessary alterations might involve changes in the mix of program inputs or a revision of the production process itself.

A public manager naturally seeks to develop a production process that is both efficient and effective. Unfortunately, however, these two types of performance indicators often are in conflict. In the quest for improved effectiveness, an operations manager might alter the mix of production inputs such that the resulting process is less efficient than before. Suppose, for example, that a municipal sanitation department uses 4 trucks and has established a refuse collection target of 250 tons per day, but has been able to achieve only 230 tons per day, on average. If the commissioner of sanitation were to purchase another collection truck, the department might be able to meet the target on a regular basis and program effectiveness would be improved. At the same time, however, the addition of a new truck might force a rerouting of the fleet of trucks so that all trucks are used for less work (tons collected per truck) each day than before. The overall efficiency of the department's refuse collection activities will have dropped from 57.5 (230/4) to 50.0 (250/5) tons per day per truck. At a later date, the commissioner might act in the opposite direction to improve program efficiency. If the oldest truck is retired and only the four best trucks are used, efficiency might be raised to 55 tons per day per truck. Effectiveness, meanwhile, would decline because the resulting output of 240 (4 × 55) tons per day is less than the 250 tons per day target. Operating managers must be alert to the trade-offs between program efficiency and effectiveness and should strive to reach a balanced level of both.

Costs

Operating managers or program planners who conduct process analyses must know how to establish the costs of a production system. Adequate cost information is important whether the program is growing, declining, or in steady-state. When a program is growing, a public manager needs to account for the costs of existing operations to justify additional expenditures to produce the desired levels of output. When operating funds are being reduced, a manager must be able to assess the costs of all elements of the system to help determine where desired savings can be achieved without unduly affecting overall program performance. If a system is in steady-state, operations managers routinely monitor the costs of operations as part of their ongoing control function.

Annual budgets for public organizations specify the costs that will be allowed for service production. Typically, operating managers are legally required to provide services within the authorized budget ceiling. Unfortunately, budgets for individual programs are sometimes arbitrarily established, or they are restricted artificially by legislative mandate. Understanding all the costs of the production process permits a public manager to adjust the process to remain within the program's budget.

Since it depends on comparisons between program costs and revenues, the breakeven calculation, a traditional tool of financial management, has had little application in most public sector settings. However, the importance of this technique in government process analysis has been growing in light of the recent public sector trend to replace free and highly subsidized programs with fee-for-service programs. As more public programs are forced to "stand on their own feet," use of the following technique will become more widespread.

A breakeven analysis determines the level of service production needed to cover all operating costs when a given output price is in effect. This kind of analysis requires information on three cost components: fixed costs, variable costs, and price (the cost of the output to the consumer). Fixed costs, such as those associated with purchased machinery and buildings, are incurred as long as production levels remain within a predetermined range. In the long run, an organization could sell its machinery or buildings, but in the short term, the costs associated with these assets are incurred whether the operating system is occasionally idle or whether it is working to capacity. In contrast, variable costs, such as those associated with raw materials and energy, change with the level of production. A breakeven analysis determines the surplus often called "contribution margin" between price and variable costs for each unit of output and calculates how many units must be sold for the sum of the contribution margins to equal the fixed costs:

$$\text{Breakeven quantity} = \frac{\text{total fixed costs}}{\text{price} - \text{variable costs}}$$

Production that meets or exceeds this breakeven quantity produces a profit. Lower production levels incur a net loss.

Public service delivery programs are increasingly charging user fees as taxpayers become more reluctant to subsidize these programs. This trend has increased the relevance of revenue production as a strategic variable in the design, operation, and evaluation of government operating systems. A modified breakeven analysis can be performed for revenue-generating public programs to determine the split between costs covered by user charges and those covered by taxpayers. For example, the manager of a municipal transit system, faced with a service demand less than the breakeven quantity, needs to determine required public subsidy. Suppose that the passenger fare on this transit system is 50 cents per ride and the total cost of operating the system is about $1 million per day. Assume further, that 500,000 rides are taken daily for a total daily revenue of $250,000. If the $1 million daily cost represents fixed costs of $800,000 and variable costs of 40 cents per trip, then a traditional breakeven analysis would reveal that for the system not to lose money, 8 million rides are needed.

$$\text{Breakeven quantity} = \frac{800,000}{.50 - .40} = 8,000,000 \text{ rides/day}$$

This level of ridership may be highly unrealistic considering the size of the metropolitan area and past transit demand levels. However, if the analysis is carried a step further, the manager could compute the subsidy needed to make 500,000 rides the breakeven point. The same breakeven formula can be used to solve for x, the sum of price per ride plus subsidy per ride.

$$500,000 = \frac{800,000}{x - .40}, \text{ or } x = \$2.00 \text{ per ride}$$

Therefore, the subsidy needed for each ride is $1.50, the difference between x and the $.50 fare. Once this information is known, a decision can be made to provide the needed subsidy, to provide a lower subsidy with proportionately reduced service, or to raise the fare so that with the subsidy a breakeven balance is achieved. (Some combination of these options also might be used.) This type of analysis can be applied to any service production system funded partially through user charges and partially through public funds.

In today's economy, inflation has a growing impact on many operational cost analyses. A service that is delivered successfully at this year's cost may not be adequate when constrained by next year's inflated cost. A sophisticated understanding of costs is necessary to answer the question: "Can the same service be provided next year without raising total operating costs to account for inflation?" In response to inflation, public managers will have to decide whether to cut service or to reduce expenses selectively while they attempt to maintain service levels. It is not always easy to identify those cost reductions that will have the least impact on service. In resolving this problem, managers must be wary of a common trap which can be illustrated by a public transit system example. As inflationary pressures began to affect a particular transit system during the mid-1970s, initial cost-cutting actions were aimed at operational activities which apparently would not reduce service levels. Such actions included drastic cutbacks of vehicle maintenance programs. The system continued to provide satisfactory service in the short run, but the equipment began to deteriorate. A few years later, the entire fleet of rail cars needed to be replaced. A shortsighted cost reduction decision had unanticipated, costly ramifications. If both the short- and long-term costs of the operating system had been combined in the same analysis, a wiser decision could have been made.

"Life cycle costing" is another concept which affects the decisions of an operations manager. A life cycle cost is the total expense (using an appropriate discount rate over the life of the asset)[1] of maintaining a particular operating capability from a program's inception to its termination. Such cost elements include start-up cost, capital purchase cost, maintenance cost, operation costs, and eventual termination costs.

Traditionally, the development and operation of a government program requires two independent cost decisions: capital cost and operational cost. Government decisions to purchase major items are based on the availability of capital funds and the actual cost of the item. Often, public organizations are mandated by regulations to purchase the lowest cost item sufficient for adequate operations. Such purchasing restrictions were established to eliminate possible conflict of interest among public employees, to prevent collusion between suppliers and purchasers, and to remove subjective and discretionary decisions from the public manager. As a result, when they decide on a purchase, public managers traditionally pay little attention to subsequent operating costs. Recent inflationary trends and energy shortages have created pressures in the opposite direction. No longer is it enough to know the cost of purchasing a police car; the chief of police also must know the costs of fuel and service over the entire useful life of a patrol car. When life-cycle costing techniques are used, all such costs are considered.[2] It is necessary to select the option which provides service at the lowest total cost, in order to encourage the long-term efficiency of an operating system. As operating costs consume more and more of each available service delivery dollar, the importance of life cycle costing will continue to grow.

Environment

As you will recall, an operating system is defined as a specific production process through which a set of inputs is transformed into outputs. At this point, you should have a general understanding of the inner structure of an operating system and the various meanings of performance. A final and important consideration in conducting a process analysis is the impact of external constraints on the system. These constraints collectively are called the environment of an operating system. An understanding of the operating environment helps public managers to forecast the extent and variety of demand that will be placed on an operating system. Appreciation of environmental forces also allows managers to make successful operational decisions despite prevailing external constraints. Toward these ends, environmental analysis is appropriate at any stage in the system's life cycle—during design, steady-state, or revision.

A service manager designing an operating system must assess the environment with specific attention to the likely variability of demand. If demand for a manufactured product declines in one area, unsold output can be shipped to an area with excess demand. This flexibility does not exist in service production systems, since it is impossible to store or transport services. A service, by definition, is consumed by a customer or client in the act of being produced: barbers cut the hair of those who can come to the shop; waiters take orders from current patrons; airlines provide transportation to those who arrive at the point of departure at the scheduled time. Accordingly, a manager should explore the likelihood that either the demand for the service or the nature of the service demanded will change. An obvious example in the field of public health is that the need for organized efforts to combat a particular disease (such as polio) will decrease rapidly when the disease itself is controlled. The manager who monitors the environment and is fully aware of the implications of demand on the structure and scale of the operating system will be able to respond most effectively to these changes.

Many operating systems are called upon to continue to produce the same output even when there are drastic changes in inputs. Electric utility companies may switch their production technology to use coal rather than oil in response to increased shortages or higher costs of petroleum products. When a scarcity of doctors leads to the training of physician's assistants, hospitals must reorganize staff responsibilities to use these new paraprofessionals without changing the quality of medical care. A production process must be designed with flexibility to adjust to these alterations. While it is often difficult to measure the responsiveness of a system to such environmental changes, a complete process analysis should include an assessment of the ability to adapt to an uncertain, or turbulent, environment.

The existence of new technological options for possible use in a production system is another environmental factor to be considered. Whenever different methods of producing the same output are available, the operations manager must be prepared to evaluate each of the options and to make a sound choice. This assessment may not be easy, since changes in production technologies often have a major impact on costs, input needed, and exact specifications of output. In the long run, failure to consider the possibility of technological change when designing a new operating system can have severe unanticipated consequences. Henry Ford's innovative use of the assembly line significantly modified automobile production techniques and resulted in a standardized product. Recent increases in the use of robots, and other highly automated assembly systems, have had an impact on various manufacturing processes, while changing the required mix of worker skills. The office of the future brings the latest document preparation and transmission capabilities to business and government alike, as it revolutionizes traditional clerical roles and activities. Furthermore, technological advances often breed technological dependency: for example, increased need for integration among an organization's various computerized information systems can cripple an organization which lacks such a capability. Managers must remember that while the selection of a state-of-the-art technology initially may seem attractive, direct analysis of the costs and benefits of competing approaches may produce a different decision.

Finally, one must understand environmental constraints other than input availability and technological options. External regulation is particularly prevalent and must be understood. Legislatively or judicially imposed restrictions have an immediate and often dramatic effect on operating systems in both business and government. The imposition of air pollution guidelines forced many industries to revise their production processes to comply with new regulations. The courts may take over municipal services during periods of performance crisis, thereby adding to the environmental constraints that some public managers face. If voters place limits on spending, availability of funding is likely to become an environmental constraint at all levels of government. The impact of the environment is a growing concern of all managers who must design or adapt systems to function in our rapidly changing world.

Summary

Sometimes a public manager needs to design a new operating system to meet a unique or novel situation. At other times, the manager must evaluate an existing system to assess its current performance. In either event, a rigorous process analysis allows the manager to define the components of the system and their interactions.

There are no shortcuts in analyzing an operating system. The analysis begins with the specification of inputs and outputs and the description of the production process. Flow charting is a standard device for displaying program operations. Once it is clear whether an operating system fits the model of a line, job shop, or project, specific analytic approaches can be applied. In any event, a public manager must be able to measure the capacity of an operating system and to assess its effectiveness. Cost analysis also is becoming increasingly important, as government tries to run itself in a more businesslike manner. Finally, government operations always will be constrained by social, political, economic, and technological forces which managers who are trying to improve operating systems must learn to assess.

Discussion questions

1. The trade-off between efficiency and effectiveness constantly must be monitored by a public manager. Clearly understanding each measure is critical to balancing their interactions. If, as a town manager, you were told by the board of selectmen that meter maids were inefficient because they were not ticketing enough illegally parked cars, how would you respond? What information would you need to defend adequately the program as it is or to make adjustments in response to the selectmen's complaints?
2. Several examples of line operations and job shop processes were dis-

cussed in this chapter. Select one of the following service production systems with which you are familiar, and develop a process flow chart that reflects the steps and sequence of individual operations.

a. University course registration
b. Hospital admissions
c. Military induction processing
d. Hospital in-patient services
e. Welfare fraud investigations

3. The uncertainty and variety of funding sources for public service programs are major environmental constraints facing managers. Further, certain funding sources restrict the kinds of costs for which they can be used. How could these constraints affect the decisions on expenditures during the various life cycle stages of a production system? During what stages of the life cycle are the capital costs likely to be greatest? The operation costs? At what point in the life cycle should a manager be able to predict accurately the operating costs of the system?

4. Defining the appropriate inputs and outputs of a service production system is integral to determining the efficiency of that production process. Normally, outputs can be defined in terms of the service provided, such as arrests, ambulance runs, welfare claims processed, driving road tests conducted, or miles of road paved. Develop a list of inputs that would be needed to produce each of the above outputs. Be sure to consider all possible input categories: labor, energy, materials, equipment, and capital. In each case, how would you determine the total worth of the inputs? The total worth of the outputs? List any assumptions you make.

5. Any discussion of a production process must consider the effect of pressures from the external environment on the system. In the public sector, changes in the political environment can have a major impact on production systems in steady-state, leading to revision or termination of those programs. What specific external changes, generally beyond the control of the operating manager, must the public manager be alert to when the political climate changes? Can such changes be anticipated prior to their occurrence?

Notes

[1] A detailed examination of discounting and other analytic approaches to capital purchase decisions is found in Chase and Aquilano (1981) or any standard finance text.

[2] Practical applications of life cycle costing technique can have immediate and direct impact on operational decision making. For example, the effects of life cycle costing on the decision by a medium-sized police department to purchase a patrol car are discussed in a recent issue of *Municipal Police* (Edgerton, 1980).

Bibliography

Chase, Richard B., and Nicholas J. Aquilano. *Production and Operations Management.* Homewood, Ill.: Irwin, 1981.

Churchman, C. West. *The Systems Approach.* New York: Dell, 1968.

Edgerton, William B. "Cost Effective Vehicle Purchasing." *Municipal Police*. Hudson, Mass.: The Municipal Police Institute, November 1980, pp. 12–15.

Hatry, Harry P.; Louis H. Blair; Donald M. Fisk; John M. Greiner; John R. Hall, Jr.; and Philip S. Schaenman. *How Effective Are Your Community Services?* Washington, D.C.: The Urban Institute, 1977.

Hatry, Harry P., and Richard E. Winnie. *Measuring the Effectiveness of Local Government Services*. Washington, D.C.: The Urban Institute, 1973.

Hatry, Harry P.; Richard E. Winnie; and Donald M. Fisk. *Practical Program Evaluation for State and Local Government Officials*. Washington, D.C.: The Urban Institute, 1978.

Katz, Daniel, and Robert Kahn. *The Social Psychology of Organizations*. New York: John Wiley and Sons, 1966.

Levitt, Theodore. "Production-line Approach to Service." *Harvard Business Review*, September-October 1972, pp. 41–52.

Walker, Warren E.; Jan M. Chaiken; and Edward J. Ignall, eds. *Fire Department Deployment Analysis*. New York: North Holland, 1979.

Chapter 4
Capacity management

Throughout the life of a production system managers are continually faced with capacity questions. Those who plan operations must both determine the overall level of required capacity and decide how it is to be managed. Once a productive system is operational, managers need to be aware of how capacity decisions affect trade-offs among the objectives of effectiveness, efficiency, and equity. As operating problems are identified, managers must decide what capacity changes are appropriate. Determining both the amount and the location of such changes is an important step in the management of capacity. Finally, managers must be able to implement changes in productive capacity as the need arises.

Capacity measurement and related concepts

The proper measurement of capacity is an essential prerequisite for informed capacity management. Recall from chapter 3 that the capacity of a system is the output that can be produced in a given period of time. In manufacturing processes, output for any particular period (and therefore capacity) usually is determined easily by counting the number of units produced during that period. In service delivery, such measures often are less obvious. Exhibit 4.1 lists examples of capacity measures.

Note that any capacity measure contains certain assumptions. Are "passenger-miles" the most appropriate measure of the output of a transit authority? Is one measure of capacity adequate or are multiple measures

Exhibit 4.1
Examples of capacity measures

Production System	Capacity Measure
Automobile Manufacturer	Cars assembled/week
Public Transit Authority	Passenger-miles provided/day
Movie Theater	Seats available/performance
Highway Department	Miles of roadway maintained/year
Hospital	Beds available/day or inpatients handled/year
Airport	Airplane landings/hour or passengers carried/month

required? Answering such questions requires considerable appreciation of the production process and of its objectives.

Effective versus theoretical capacity

Every system has a "theoretical capacity" which represents its maximum rate of production. Suppose one clerk at the Division of Employment Security working at peak performance for a full eight-hour day could handle 10 unemployment claims. If ten such clerks staffed this office, its theoretical capacity would be 700 claims per week. In reality, however, this capacity would not be achieved. First, since the office is closed on Saturday and Sunday, there is no productive capacity over the weekend; similarly, no real output occurs on legal holidays. Sickness, distractions, breaks from work, and interruptions by other job demands are some factors that might reduce actual output below its theoretical maximum. Perhaps during one or two weeks in a year 500 claims will be processed. However, in other weeks fewer claims will be handled. An average weekly capacity over a full year might be 400 or even as low as 350 claims. The output that is actually produced by the system in an average time period is called the "effective capacity." A manager who asks, "How much is my operating system likely to produce in a fixed period of time, given existing resource constraints and productivity?" wants to know the system's effective capacity.

Multiple measures of capacity

Operating managers in government must be sensitive to the needs of the various constituencies being served by government programs and to the dimensions of productive capacity important to these groups. As indicated in Exhibit 4.1, the capacity of an airport can be measured in terms of either airplane landings or passengers carried. Both are indicators of the level of service provided, but each is of particular importance to a certain constituency. Pilots, air traffic controllers, and the Federal Aviation Administration tend to focus on the number of landings that can be safely handled. In contrast, passengers are most immediately aware of the extent to which airport services meet their travel needs (which is not to say that passengers ignore obvious safety concerns). If capacity measures are based on the number of passengers carried per month, approximate estimates may be made for parking, baggage handling, restaurants, and ticketing. Such capacity requirements are largely independent of the capacity to land aircraft; adding a new terminal with parking space for 1500 cars and gates for 10 planes will not increase the number of planes allowed to land. It is perfectly reasonable to expect airport management to deal with both aspects of capacity—planes landed and passengers carried. It must be understood that ensuring adequate capacity for one set of constituents will not necessarily guarantee that the capacity needs of the others will be met. This is a somewhat unusual, but very important, issue in capacity measurement. Failure to grasp and apply this concept can lead to confused planning and operations, with potentially disastrous practical and political results.

Multiple measures of capacity also are required when a production system is divided into a set of subsystems. Exhibit 4.2 provides some familiar illustrations. In such situations, it is important to acknowledge that each subsystem has its own type of production capacity. Since capacity of the various subsystems is directed at meeting different kinds of demand, each manager is likely to be guided by a different measure of capacity. Although organizations usually have separate operations managers in charge of the various subsystems, the subsystems must be managed consistently. This requires top management coordination of capacity measures for the independent subsystems.

Spatial distribution of capacity

In many organizations, it is important not only that sufficient capacity exists to meet total demand, but also that the capacity is located near the sources of demand. This requirement is not as necessary for a manufacturing organization, since products can be shipped from one area to another to adjust for spatial mismatches between supply and demand. However, shipping is not an available option in service production systems since, as already mentioned, a service is available only at the time and place of its delivery.

The problem of spatial distribution of public service capacity became

Exhibit 4.2
Multiple capacity measures for illustrative organizations

Type of Organization	Productive Subsystem	Capacity Measure
Hospital	Inpatient Facilities	Total beds/day
	Operating Room	Operations performed/day
	Outpatient Clinic	Outpatient appointments/day
Internal Revenue Service	Accounting	Returns processed/day
	Auditing	Audits conducted/day
	Information Service	Telephone inquiries answered/day
University	Course Registration	Students/semester
	Student Housing	Dormitory beds/semester
	Food Service	Cafeteria meals/semester

particularly apparent during the 1950s and 1960s, in the face of large population shifts from the cities to the suburbs. During the early stages of this shift, before government operations were adjusted in response, an excess of municipal services tended to exist in the cities while service capacity in the suburbs was inadequate. Public school systems were especially affected; schoolrooms in the city had many empty chairs, but crowded schools in the suburbs often were forced to run double sessions to accommodate pupils.

Therefore, to say that the government provides adequate educational capacity "on average" is to avoid the critical question of whether children in different neighborhoods receive comparable resources. Qualitative dimensions of these resources may turn out to be as important as quantitative ones. Examples of qualitative elements are: the layout of a school building, as well as its size; the training and orientation of the school's teachers, as well as their number; and the currency of texts and teaching aids, as well as their availability. Similarly, to say that a city provides sufficient trash collection "on average" is no consolation to citizens who find the service in their neighborhood considerably below average. In general, a public manager must understand that merely providing adequate overall capacity is not enough. The equity of service delivery depends on how aggregate capacity is assigned to the various groups who demand service.

Capacity and equity

Equity considerations begin during the initial development of a service delivery system and continue through subsequent modifications of that system. Equity is not always measured only in terms of the amount of allocated capacity. It also includes the timing of available capacity and the quality associated with the production output. To understand the issue of timing, consider garbage collection services in two neighborhoods. In one neighborhood, the weekly collection took place at midday, while the same service was provided at 6:00 A.M. in the other neighborhood. Citizens in the latter locale justifiably might complain that being awakened so early by noisy trucks on collection day constituted inequitable treatment by the local government.

Inequities also may arise in the distribution of support services as well as in the extent of equipment and facilities provided. For example, city management could claim that by locating a public park in every neighborhood an equitable recreation system has been offered to the citizens. However, if program personnel were provided at only some parks, the level of the service would not be equitable, since parks that had such staff could be said to represent higher quality services than those that did not. If the city decided to close some of the recreational facilities but provided staff at all the remaining parks, the distribution of capacity would no longer be equitable even though the quality of existing capacity would be consistent.

Similar questions of equity can be raised in almost all public service delivery systems. Responsible public managers must be sensitive to the effects of capacity availability on program equity. Many forces can alter an apparently rational and equitable allocation of public sector resources and, as a result, can affect the production capacity available to different population groups. An elected official, responding to the interests of vocal constituents, might interfere with the internal allocation decisions of agency managers. For example, pressure on the mayor from a local community group might generate a city hall request that the police chief allocate more police officers to patrol that community, even if the actual crime rate there did not indicate the need for increased coverage.

The public often is unaware of the equity criteria upon which capacity decisions have been made. Furthermore, government agencies do not always explicitly formulate equity-based criteria for capacity decisions. Even when such criteria have been formulated, public officials may hesitate to make them available for fear of alienating some constituencies. Finally, if the criteria are made public, only a small percentage of the population is likely to become informed. The subject of equity is particularly complex because it is possible to apply any of several different principles of service allocation. Such principles include equal output of service per client, equal inputs per region (regardless of population), equal inputs per capita (regardless of region size), and equal service for equal payment. (See Savas, 1978, for a discussion of these options.) During periods of service reduction, similar equity considerations exist. For example, which school should be closed or which fire station should be phased out? Public managers must make such decisions carefully, considering the social, economic, and political dimensions of reduced service capacity. The bases for these decisions are often subtle and it is not uncommon for managers to overlook matters of equity when they make service delivery decisions.

Despite the care given to equity considerations, there always will be some individuals or groups who feel that any existing allocation system is inequitable. Public criticism must be expected by operating managers in government. Such criticism should not force a manager to change an operating system, but valid complaints may indicate that straightforward improvements are needed in public service delivery. On other occasions, such criticism may become a catalyst for major program revisions. Issues of equity often shape the course of new programs, as public reactions are felt in the start-up stage. Occasionally, similar forces will drive a program out of steady-state. In fact, the importance of equity considerations in public sector operating management is one reason why, as mentioned in chapter 2, steady-state is such a tenuous period.

Capacity and type of production process

The nature of an operating system can affect its productive capacity. Two traditional production processes (described in chapter 3) are the job shop and the line operation. Each has unique, capacity-related characteristics.

Capacity in a job shop is determined by the complexity of the sequence of operations required to process orders. If the process is one in which several independent jobs follow various paths through the production system, capacity depends on the difficulty and length of these jobs. Altering the workload to include a greater number of less complex jobs will increase capacity without changing the level of resources.

To illustrate this point, consider the operation of a municipal criminal justice system. Exhibit 4.3 outlines some of the various processing paths that may follow an arrest. Many of the basic tasks are required in all cases, but the amount of effort needed for activities such as investigation or witness presentation will vary from case to case. For example, the nature of the crime will determine whether a jury is needed or can be waived. Since most judicial systems have a scarcity of available court rooms and judges, and a judge can hear only one trial at a time, the capacity of the diagrammed system is likely to be limited by the trial portion of the process. Some types of cases (for example, shoplifting)

Exhibit 4.3
Criminal justice system job shop (simplified version)

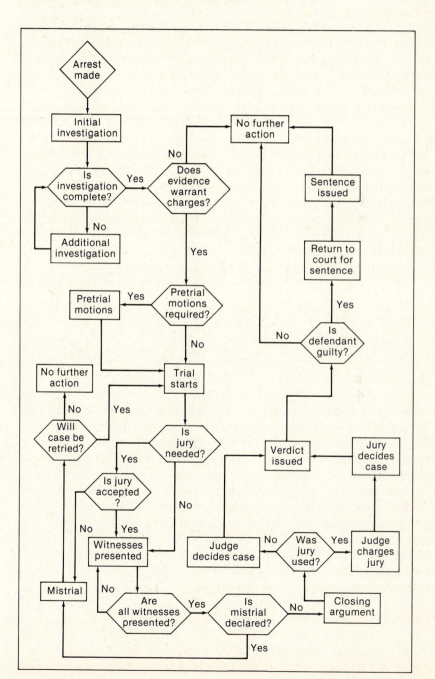

require less time before a judge than others (for example, armed robbery). If armed robbery arrests are increasing at the same time that shoplifting arrests are decreasing, the overall capacity of this criminal justice system will decrease.

Therefore, the number of cases that can be processed in this job shop is directly related to the complexity of the case and to the amount of production time needed for each work activity. Since a job shop, by definition, handles different types of demands, the actual distribution of production time for each work activity cannot be determined in advance. Given this uncertainty, a production planner cannot completely eliminate bottlenecks. For these reasons, the capacity of a job shop will vary from one time period to another.

In contrast, a line operation—in which standardized orders follow a fixed path through all sequential stages of a production process—offers the potential for more direct measurement of capacity. The *cycle time* of a line operation is the time needed for each unit of production to be output from the system. A simple numerical example will show the relationship between cycle time and capacity in a line operation.

Consider a three-step line process with processing times as indicated to produce one unit of output:

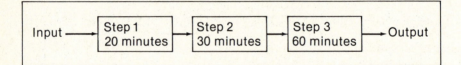

Every twenty minutes one unit is completed at Step 1 and moves to Step 2, where processing takes thirty minutes. From Step 2 the unit moves to Step 3, where processing requires sixty minutes. After Step 3 the unit is completed and becomes output from the system. Since the longest step in this production system requires sixty minutes, it is impossible for more than one unit to be completed each hour. The rate at which resources arrive for processing at Steps 1 and 2 has no effect on the rate at which final output is generated (that is, the cycle time). In this example, the cycle time is one hour per unit and the capacity of the system is clearly one unit per hour. By definition, the capacity of a line operation is always the inverse of the cycle time: capacity = 1/(cycle time).

Waiting time and throughput time

The capacity of a system and its related cycle time are not affected by the amount of internal waiting time. Consider the simple illustrative line oper-

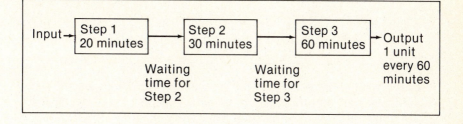

ation after it has been in continuous operation. As shown above, all facilities will be fully utilized, but backlogs will develop at Steps 2 and 3. It should be clear that the output will be one unit every sixty minutes regardless of the backlog awaiting processing at Step 2 or Step 3. The waiting time for any single order will depend on the backlogs that develop at Steps 2 and 3.

Waiting time, whether in a job shop or in a line operation, will affect "throughput time," even though it has no effect on capacity. Throughput time is the total time it takes a unit of output (i.e., client, case, order) to travel through the production system. Throughput time includes both the actual processing time and the waiting time before each work activity. Consider again the same simple three-step example illustrated in the previous section.

With the production line functioning in this sequence, waiting time will develop at both Step 2 and Step 3 for all but the first unit of production. Exhibit 4.4, which traces the throughput time of the first six units produced, shows how throughput time can increase as each unit of production must wait to be processed at Step 2 and Step 3. In this system, as long as the rate of input continues unchanged at Step 1, the throughput time will increase infinitely. Obviously, this arrangement quickly becomes unwieldy.

The development of bottlenecks or waiting lines is likely to have a more direct impact on the customer in service production systems than it does in traditional manufacturing systems. If Exhibit 4.4 represented a manufacturing process, space would be needed to store partially completed products between Steps 1 and 2 and between Steps 2 and 3, but the quality of the ultimate output would not be harmed by such in-process waiting lines. In contrast, when a customer or client is forced to wait at various intermediary stages in a service production system, the quality of the output, as measured by timely, convenient service, is directly affected. Regardless of the specific characteristics of the output, the cost associated with ever increasing throughput times (see Exhibit 4.4) eventually will result in loss of customers.

As an alternative, consider a production system with the following process:

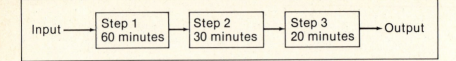

The cycle time of this process is still sixty minutes and the capacity is still one unit per hour, but for each unit of output the resources at Step 2 are idle for thirty minutes and at Step 3 for forty minutes. From the consumer's perspective this process ensures a constant throughput time. However, from a management perspective the arrangement is less attractive than the prior illustrative process because resources are not fully utilized: workers at Steps 2 and 3 must wait for the completion of Step 1 tasks.

Many of the same costs are incurred whether a production system is running at maximum capacity or sitting idle: equipment and facilities have fixed cost components. Most government operations also increase fixed costs associated with salaried employees in civil service positions. Cost considerations motivate an operating manager to run the system at full capacity, thereby spreading fixed costs across the highest feasible volume of output. As mentioned above, however, this approach may not be in the consumer's best interest, since the quality or timeliness of the resulting service might not be optimal.

Therefore, a manager must balance waiting time (and increasing throughput time) and the cost of inefficient use of resources, carefully weighing the trade-offs. Often making slight changes in the production process can improve efficiency without decreasing the quality of service. Consider these alternatives to our original example.

☐ A second Step 3 operation could be added so that the units output from Step 2 could be processed at either Step 3.

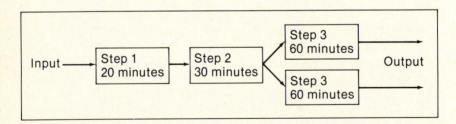

Now, two units of output can be produced every sixty minutes. This would result in a cycle time of thirty minutes and a capacity of two units per hour. Waiting time, in turn, occurs only before Step 2.

☐ The process at each step could be revised so that the time required for each step was more nearly equal. This is the concept of line balancing. If part of the Step 3 processing could be completed in

Exhibit 4.4
An illustration of throughput time

Unit Produced	Processing Time (Minutes)			Waiting Time (Minutes)			Throughput Time (Minutes)
	Step 1	Step 2	Step 3	Step 1	Step 2	Step 3	
1	20	30	60	0	0	0	110
2	20	30	60	0	10	30	150
3	20	30	60	0	20	60	190
4	20	30	60	0	30	90	230
5	20	30	60	0	40	120	270
6	20	30	60	0	50	150	310

Step 1 and part in Step 2, the new production process could appear as:

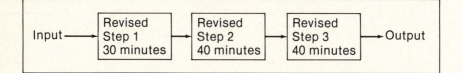

In this system, output is produced at the rate of one unit every forty minutes (cycle time) and the capacity is one and a half units per hour. In this new process, waiting time only occurs before Step 2.

These kinds of relationships among waiting time, throughput time, and capacity utilization force managers to design their productive systems carefully. A line operation that is perfectly balanced has the potential for achieving the highest utilization. In practice, achieving the balance can become quite complex since both demand patterns and production times are random variables rather than constant rates as assumed in this simple illustration.

Capacity utilization

For efficiency or cost reduction reasons, managers of any production system are concerned with the utilization of existing capacity. *Capacity utilization* is a measure of the amount of effective capacity actually used in some particular production period. It is usually expressed as follows:

$$\text{Capacity utilization} = \frac{\text{actual production output per period}}{\text{available effective capacity}} \times 100$$

In applying this formula, one must be careful to use the same length of time to compare production with capacity. Since both of these elements are measured in units of output/time, and by definition, the available effective capacity cannot be exceeded in practice, capacity utilization is measured as a percent and must fall between 0 and 100. For a single step in a production operation, the calculation of capacity utilization is straightforward and is based only on the output from that step. In a multistep operation, such as the example used in this chapter, the overall capacity utilization is determined by adding the actual output at all steps and dividing by the sum of the capacities at each step. Line balancing is an attempt to achieve maximum capacity utilization (through minimum cycle times).

Waiting line decisions and queuing theory

Operations managers of service systems must be aware of the issues associated with the attempt to match productive resources and processes to external demand patterns. In particular, a manager of a service delivery system should understand how waiting lines develop and should appreciate the costs of such delays to the agency and to its clients. This chapter is not intended to provide either theoretical grounding on waiting lines—technically known as *queuing theory*—or computer simulation approaches for studying such systems; standard texts, such as Chase and Aquilano (1981) or Buffa (1979), cover the basic formulas and models. Instead, the following discussion is meant to provide an intuitive feel for some of the questions that should be asked and some of the problems that may be encountered.

As previously discussed, a production system with an extensive waiting time is likely to be achieving a high utilization of capacity, while it is perceived by the client or customer to be offering poor quality service. It is a managerial challenge to develop a production system that has both high utilization and a reasonable waiting time. Some of the fundamental dimensions of this problem are outlined below.

Arrival patterns   The length of waiting lines will depend in part on the arrival pattern of customers. To the extent that arrivals occur in a regular and completely deterministic pattern—as in an assembly line operation—no waiting need occur. Random arrival patterns, in contrast, may lead to delays in receiving service. Actual data on rates of arrival can be fit to statistical distributions, allowing a probabilistic analysis of waiting line behavior. At a municipal airport, plane arrivals follow a general schedule, but random variations in arrivals lead to "stacking" as planes are forced to circle the airport while they await clearance to land. Effective management of airport landing capacity requires that a manager periodically assess changes in arrival patterns.

Nature of the service production process   Four traditional patterns of service delivery account for the great majority of service production facilities.

☐ In single-channel, single-phase service, the entire production system contains one line of users being processed at one work activity (for example, paying a parking ticket at the police station).
☐ In single-channel, multiphase service, one line of users, upon reaching the front of the line, receive a sequence of related services (for example, receiving comprehensive diagnostic screening in an outpatient clinic).

☐ In multichannel, single-phase service, more than one waiting line is available, but only one production task is performed (for example, the traditional alignment of toll booths on an interstate highway).

☐ In multichannel, multiphase service, many lines are available and multiple production services are performed sequentially (for example, large neighborhood multiservice centers that provide assistance for problems of health and social welfare).

One goal of any service delivery system is to achieve a successful balance between resource utilization and customer waiting time. Exhibit 4.5 shows the nature of this fundamental trade-off. At some point, an increase in productive capacity will not decrease waiting time enough to justify the additional operating expense (not shown in the exhibit). The optimal solution depends on the costs (inefficiency) associated with excess capacity and the benefits (effectiveness, equity, timeliness) of marginal reductions in waiting time.

Often some form of priority system for service delivery must be instituted to ensure that waiting times are consistent with service delivery

Exhibit 4.5
Waiting time and capacity utilization

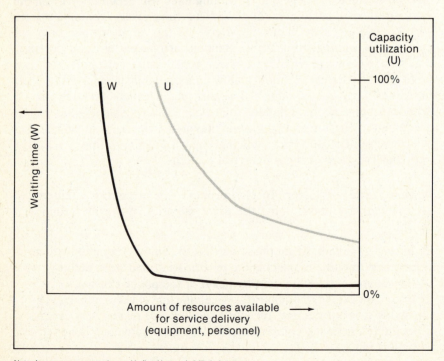

Note: Assumes aggregate demand is fixed but probabilistic in nature.

objectives. Several common priority rules are "first-come, first-served," "previous clients only," "reservations," or "emergencies first, others as possible." The decision rule chosen to determine service priorities depends on the service being provided. Hospital managers would be unlikely to adopt a first-come, first-served system, while the Department of Motor Vehicles might find this decision rule to be appropriate. These options essentially are directed at managing the demand on public service delivery systems, which is the general subject of chapter 7.

Quality/quantity trade-off

As discussed in the section on throughput time, one measure of quality is the total time taken in the production system. Obviously, another is the physical quality of the output. If a system is operating at capacity, pressure to increase the quantity of output can have a deleterious effect on quality even if the throughput time has not increased. Consider the example of processing welfare claims. To process additional claims, welfare workers simply can perform less work on each application. However, if interviews are shortened, investigatory work is decreased, or review for errors is eliminated, the potential for a drastic reduction in quality is evident. A municipal department of sanitation, forced to dismiss employees because of budget restrictions may have to reduce the frequency of trash collection. Again, the quality of service would be decreased to allow a lesser capacity to meet a fixed demand. The issues of capacity utilization and quality of service are complex. Public managers must carefully consider such issues when they plan new programs or when they make changes in existing programs.

Capacity planning

Operating managers are not simply passive observers of government programs. They must be active in developing a program's initial capacity and in implementing needed changes. Managers must be able to forecast requirements and act to ensure a satisfactory match between available capacity and the demand for the product or service. In this section we will discuss capacity planning, which assumes that demand is an uncontrollable external factor. The strategy of demand management, which assumes that policymakers and operations managers can affect the demand for government services, is the subject of chapter 7.

The amount of capacity needed in a production system is related directly to the demand for its output. The difficulty of determining the necessary amount of capacity similarly is correlated with the degree of uncertainty associated with the predicted level of demand. If demand were fixed, a constant capacity could be provided. If demand fluctuated in a completely predictable way, the level of capacity could be adjusted to meet varying demand. Demand may be cyclical, with predictable peaks and valleys, as illustrated by the Internal Revenue Service's need for additional staff between January and April. However, demand instead may be totally erratic, as in the need for hospital beds during a medical emergency; in the midst of a flu epidemic, a municipal hospital is likely to be filled. Does this mean that there is insufficient hospital bed capacity? Should more hospitals be built to meet peak demand? Or should some beds be removed (that is, hospitals closed down), if this would result in aggregate capacity which more nearly matched average demand? Determining the most appropriate level of capacity is a challenge faced by many operating managers.

The value of excess capacity

The higher the cost of not meeting demand, the greater the needed capacity, even if it sits idle much of the time. Traditionally, production systems are designed to provide capacity in excess of average current demand. For example, electrical generating plants are designed to produce more electricity (capacity) than is needed during periods of average use (demand).

Excess production capacity allows the production system to meet unplanned contingencies, such as plant shutdowns, or to accommodate future growth. At a large generating station, one turbine could be out of service for repairs while the remaining turbines produce sufficient output to meet demand for electricity. In addition, excess capacity permits demand to grow without the need to expand capacity immediately. Although there will always come a point, as demand grows, when increased capacity will be required, the existence of excess capacity provides a time cushion for new increments of capacity to be developed and implemented. This cushion is often described as the *lead time* needed for incremental capacity increases. Lead time is discussed in detail in the following section.

An example will help to clarify the concept of the value of excess capacity. As demand for electricity grows, the production capacity of existing facilities eventually becomes inadequate. Planning and construction of additional facilities might require as long as twenty years. Therefore, close monitoring of demand for electricity is necessary to ensure that the existing excess capacity (and increments already in development) will meet demand while new facilities are being completed. Ideally, the new facility will be ready to produce electricity just as the original capacity is exceeded by current demand. As additional excess capacity is introduced into the production system, the forecasting and expansion cycle can continue without major production shortages.

The importance of excess capacity also is apparent when one tries to assess the cost of failing to meet demand. In the private sector, such cost is defined as the revenue foregone on *lost transactions*, those that could have been completed had there been sufficient capacity. An auto manufacturer who cannot produce a high enough volume of a specific model (lack of capacity) may lose sales when potential customers decide to buy another model rather than wait. Thus, this manufacturer forfeits the profit that could have been made.

Determining the cost of insufficient capacity in government operations is often less straightforward. Failure to provide sufficient municipal parking places in the business district could reduce profits of local merchants. Failure to provide sufficient welfare workers could produce delays in processing claims for income maintenance. It is an analytic challenge to measure the cost of these kinds of occurrences. If an analyst could produce acceptable cost estimates in these (or other) public service contexts, arguments for incorporating specific amounts of excess capacity in the production system would follow.

The importance of lead time

Lead time in capacity expansion projects is the time required for the implementation of additional capacity. Exhibit 4.6 depicts the importance of lead time in the face of a perceived increase in demand. Lead time is responsible for the delay between the realization that more capacity is needed and its final acquisition. In the illustration in Exhibit 4.6, capacity never falls behind demand, but this is not always the case.

In businesses with long lead times (for example, the generation of electrical power), existing capacity must exceed current requirements if existing capacity is to meet growing demand while new capacity increments are being developed. In contrast, some organizations can expand rapidly as the need arises, thereby avoiding the costs of excess capacity. As the unemployment rate increases, the Division of Employment Security, faced with an increase in unemployment claims, can hire and train additional clerks in a relatively short time.

A number of factors peculiar to the public sector may cause delays in expanding the productive capacity. Perhaps the most familiar example is that of a capital construction project which requires the acquisition of funds, issuances of a request for proposal, review of bids and selection of

Exhibit 4.6
Lead time and capacity change

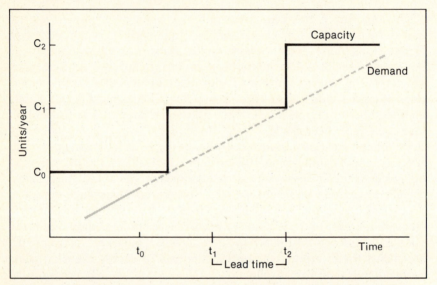

Note: At time t_0, a demand projection indicates growing demand will continue and current capacity (C_0) and capacity increases already in progress (C_1) will be insufficient by time t_2. The lead time needed to incrementally increase capacity from C_1 to C_2 is determined, and the latest time at which the project must begin is computed (t_1).

(———— = historical demand; — — — — — = projected demand)

a contractor, followed by the various stages of construction itself. Such public projects often require site selection and approval, activities which can be very time-consuming if the facilities in question (for example, refuse incinerators) or the programs to be housed in them (for example, welfare, corrections, or mental health programs) are undesirable to local communities. Furthermore, obtaining approval involves legislative debating over the amount of funds to be allocated for capacity expansion; this may include questioning the need for additional capacity and postponing fund allocation (possibly for years) until this need is established to legislators' satisfaction.

Requests for the additional manpower required by most expansion projects may also be delayed by bureaucratic and political problems involving budget approvals. Acquiring the personnel components of capacity can take more time than other capacity expansion efforts. Civil service requirements often affect the options for hiring new personnel and for upgrading and training existing staff.

Critical path methods and project management

A public manager who has not anticipated these sources of delay will end up valiantly trying to "stretch" existing capacity while awaiting the planned increases. Therefore, a public manager, preparing for the implementation of a major capacity expansion project, has a strong incentive to analyze the impact of all possible delays. After assessing how independent delays may combine to affect the total time needed to adjust capacity, a manager will be able to obtain a more realistic understanding of the entire project. Standard project management techniques such as PERT (Program Evaluation and Review Technique) or CPM (Critical Path Method) exist for this purpose. The data needed for such techniques are the sequence of tasks required for the project and the time and cost (perhaps with probability distributions) for its completion. A network, such as that shown in Exhibit 4.7, can be constructed to show the precedence relationships among these tasks. From these data one can calculate the project's *critical path*, which is the longest sequence of connected activities through the network. Managers may choose to accept the time and cost implications of the critical path and monitor the progress of a project to ensure that this schedule is met. Alternatively, they may use the same techniques to evaluate the time and cost implications of completing some of the critical path activities on an expedited (top priority) basis. See Levy, Thompson, and Wiest (1963) or any standard text of operations management techniques (for example, Chase & Aquilano, 1981) for an introduction to the techniques of critical path scheduling.

A PERT chart enables a manager to display the steps, time, and resources needed to carry out a specific project. The chart's major value may be its use as a planning tool employed to convince policymakers of the necessity to begin a project in a timely manner and assure them that a structured management approach will be used to monitor progress. PERT does not provide answers to the questions: What are we trying to accomplish? And how should we do it? Further, the direct impact of PERT can diminish during the project implementation as managers revise timetables to meet changed production schedules, begin to question the original analysis, and find that time and resources to update the PERT data are unavailable. However, the symbolic value of this technique may live on as participants continue to behave as if project management was still being imposed (Sapolsky, 1972).

In the private sector, most projects have clearly defined goals, and it is the manager's responsibility to assemble a team to define and execute the process to achieve the goal (Stewart, 1965). For example, a financial analyst, an architect, an attorney, a construction engineer, and an industrial engineer could develop a comprehensive PERT chart listing how a

Exhibit 4.7
PERT chart for initial activities required to widen two-lane road (simplified)

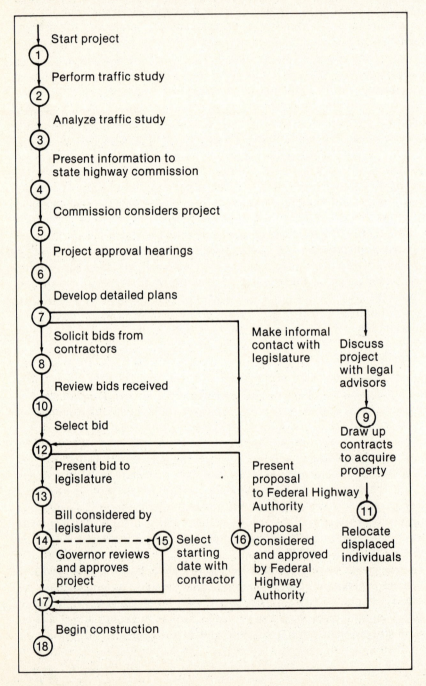

well-defined project ought to be accomplished. This team has the practical experience to specify each participant's responsibilities.

In the public sector, project goals often are less well defined, and prior experience with similar projects often is lacking. Nevertheless, project management may be used. During the development of many large public programs, a project approach is used for the birth, service definition, process selection, and operational design stages. A start-up team may be assembled to translate the policy concerns of the legislature into actual program operations. Initial program goals often are vague, and as the start-up team moves toward implementation, its members must refine the goals and objectives of the program. During this phase of the operational life cycle, analysts must assess the external demand for the program as a basis for initial capacity estimates. For example, if a new benefits program is being developed to provide monetary assistance to the needy for fuel oil purchases, public officials must specify the means of program delivery and eligibility criteria before capacity requirements can be estimated. Once it has been decided to establish community offices to serve those households with incomes below $10,000, analysts can forecast the amount and location of required capacity, including facilities and staffing needs. After a start-up team has resolved all such program design issues, it can begin to implement the program by establishing the capacity to meet demand. Project management, in short, is one approach in government for planning and then acquiring new productive capacity.

Capacity reduction

This discussion of capacity change started with consideration of capacity expansion. However, it is increasingly important for public managers to be skilled in planning and implementing decreases in productive capacity. The development of local tax limitation initiatives at all levels of government is forcing public sector managers to scrutinize existing programs and to develop alternatives which provide adequate service with reduced capacity. Although most constituents favor tax containment, convincing a community group that service reduction inevitably must result is often difficult. Even equitable reductions of service may be resisted by the affected constituencies. Public managers must be prepared to face conflict when they decide what capacity to reduce and by how much.

The impetus to reduce capacity often develops from a desire to control program costs. However, the actual reduction in expenditures often is more illusory than real. Recall that only variable costs can be eliminated, while fixed costs continue whether or not capacity is available. Further, even variable costs cannot be stopped abruptly. Lead time is required for capacity decrease just as it is for capacity increase. Users of services increasingly tend to seek judicial intervention to prevent elimination of services. The resultant delays can significantly affect a manager's ability to reduce capacity expeditiously.

Many public programs are interrelated so that cutting back or eliminating one may put unexpected, increased demand on another. Public managers must be aware of the impact of their activities on other programs. Several examples illustrate this point. A decision to reduce Federal Drug Enforcement Agency capacity in order to save expenditures could lead to an increase in illegal drug use, putting greater demand for service on state drug treatment facilities and local law enforcement agencies. A reduction in public transit service could prevent many social service clients from traveling to the necessary office. As a result, the social service agency might be compelled either to open satellite offices within walking distance of its clients or to provide clients' transportation as part of the service package. Finally, a reduction in a federal work assistance program (such as CETA) would force the unemployed to seek other means of financial support, thereby most probably creating greater demand for unemployment insurance or welfare payments. In each of these examples, the cost savings from the reduction of service capacity in one program might be overshadowed by the additional costs to compensating programs.

As public managers and policymakers attempt to reduce capacity, their ability to understand the impact of their decisions, to communicate to constituents the need for reductions, and to obtain accurate information and documentation on savings will be vital. Without a substantive understanding of the associated operating systems, they will be unable to reduce capacity effectively and equitably. (See Behn, 1980, for a discussion of strategic dimensions of cut-back management).

Improving capacity management

Managers are under pressure to improve the output of government programs often without commensurate additions to available resources. This calls for increases in the effective capacity of a program. In most organizations, effective capacity can be improved by changes in the utilization of either staff or equipment.

Staff utilization

Improved staff utilization usually requires training and incentives, in addition to supervision. Managers must do their best to ensure that staff are trained to perform routine operations more quickly and with fewer errors. They also should train staff for related production jobs so that a competent worker can substitute for an absent employee, thereby reducing some of the capacity loss caused by absenteeism. Finally, any success in reducing staff turnover is likely to improve overall utilization as production is measured through "the learning curve" (Abernathy & Wayne, 1974).

Public managers also should offer meaningful incentives to employees to motivate them to improve capacity. Profit sharing or bonuses for extra production are some incentives commonly used in the private sector. Although the public sector generally is not known for being highly innovative in incentive plans, some jurisdictions are introducing experimental programs of this sort. One pioneering discussion of such programs is available in the Urban Institute's study of monetary incentives and work standards (Greiner, Dahl, Hatry, & Millar, 1977). Admittedly, as outlined in chapter 14, civil service systems and public service unions present several barriers to this type of reform. Nevertheless, there is reason to believe that an increased emphasis on public sector productivity in the future will stimulate such innovations.

Maintenance of equipment

For some public service delivery systems, improving productivity requires better utilization of equipment, as well as of staff. Upgrading the maintenance of machinery, thereby reducing downtime, improves the effective capacity of a production system. It is important to weigh the trade-off between the costs of this increased maintenance and the savings realized by eliminating breakdown costs. Exhibit 4.8 illustrates the preventive maintenance trade-off curve and shows that total cost can be minimized by a judicious maintenance policy. In assessing the expense of increased maintenance, a manager must remember that such costs will be reflected immediately in the operating budget: staff to repair equipment will have to be hired, supervised, and housed. In contrast, purchasing extra production equipment as a backup system, rather than improving maintenance, will place an additional burden on the capital budget. Typically, capital expenditures are budgeted separately from operations costs. For state and local services, capital expenditures often are more readily approved than those that draw on limited operating funds. However, if one can manage the initial fiscal liability of increased emphasis on maintenance, this strategy is attractive since it may enhance the effective capacity more quickly than would the direct purchase of additional productive capacity.

Short-term strategies for using excess capacity

Development of uses for facilities or resources that would otherwise sit idle will improve the capacity of a productive system. Public school sys-

Exhibit 4.8
The preventive maintenance trade-off decision

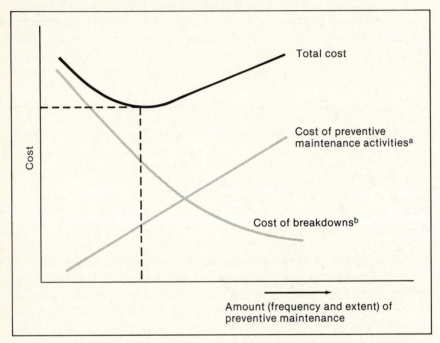

a Includes direct costs of inspection, adjustment, and replacement, as well as lost production time due to
  maintenance disruptions.
[b] Includes direct costs of maintenance and replacement, as well as lost production time due to breakdowns.

tems offer a classic example. School buildings are used intensively for
nine months, yet those buildings traditionally are vacant during the summer. Meanwhile, the community incurs certain costs while no service is
being provided. An emerging trend toward "year-round" schools
(Shepard & Baker, 1977) permits productive use of formerly idle school
capacity. Developing a complementary use for a fixed resource also will
take advantage of a currently unused capacity. For example, a community
that provides ice skating rinks for its residents during the winter months is
simultaneously creating excess capacity in the summer months. A complementary use, like roller skating, for such a facility can provide an
equivalent demand during warmer months when the rink is not being used
for ice skating.

   Similarly, during the winter, snow-covered municipal golf courses can
be used as cross-country ski trails. The inclusion of a complementary use
for an existing facility provides a constant, though differentiated, demand
on a fixed productive capacity and thereby reduces the total amount of

unused capacity. Exhibit 4.9 illustrates this strategy, which has the benefit of providing additional service to the community and the possibility of
generating additional revenues.

Turning from facilities to labor-intensive government services, we can
make a similar argument for handling cyclical demand by seasonal shifts
of public personnel. The housing code enforcement program described in
chapter 8 provides a good illustration of this phenomenon. In the winter
months, the volume of housing complaints will increase in response to
shortages of adequate heat. Since each complaint requires that an inspector assess the problem and recommend a solution, a backlog of unin-
spected, nonemergency complaints arises every winter. Then during
warmer months, when inspectors are not needed to handle heating complaints, they are able to resolve other code enforcement problems that had
been postponed.

This same approach is seen in communities that rely on volunteer fire
protection. These communities have an ongoing capacity to fight fires, but
they do not pay for full-time personnel who are basically idle (that is,
unutilized) until called to fight a fire. Under the volunteer system,
firefighters are employed full time in other jobs, and nearly all excess
manpower capacity is eliminated. An obvious risk in overusing this type
of capacity management strategy is that the development of multiple uses
for the same resources may reduce effective capacity below an acceptable
level. For example, it would make little sense for police officers also to

Exhibit 4.9
Complementary demand for the same productive capacity

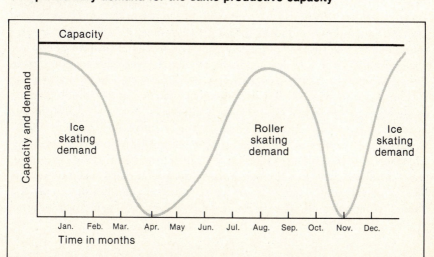

serve as volunteer fire fighters because often both services are needed simultaneously.

These solutions to the cyclical demand phenomenon have been aimed at changing the supply side of a service delivery system. Another approach to excess capacity problems that arise from cyclical demand is to take actions that make the effective demand for services more constant; then a public manager need only provide enough capacity to meet the smoothed demand pattern. Such demand management strategies are discussed in chapter 7.

The above discussion of cyclical demand has focused on annual variations. However, in some service production processes, the cycle time is much shorter. In welfare offices, for example, it is possible that most clients arrive during the first hour in the morning and the first hour in the afternoon. This pattern results in long waiting lines at some times and idle welfare workers at others. If public managers are able to design jobs so that the workers who process applications during peak times have additional responsibilities during other hours, they may improve the overall capacity and utilization of the operating system. By approaching job redesign with this purpose in mind, a manager may be able to handle critical mismatches between the demand for a service and the capacity to deliver it, at no increase in operating cost.

The employment of temporary resources is another short-term strategy for alleviating shortages of production capacity. For example, the Internal Revenue Service traditionally hires part-time workers between January and April. This allows the organization to increase capacity without a major increase in year-round operating costs. As soon as the peak demand subsides, the temporary workers are discharged and their associated costs are eliminated. This approach may result in some quality problems, as the newer workers may be less competent in their jobs and more prone to error. However, the cost of supervising these workers and correcting their errors is likely to be less than the alternative of maintaining a year-round capacity sufficient to meet this abrupt seasonal peak in demand.

Government also handles instances of capacity shortage by purchasing the additional capacity from external producers who have an existing surplus or who can develop the needed capacity more rapidly than a public agency. A transit system often contracts services to private bus lines to augment its regular service. A public university can lease additional space in private buildings instead of constructing new facilities. This public management strategy of "third-party contracting" is not always possible, but when the appropriate situation arises, this method can offer a cost effective means to increase capacity. Contracting out always should be considered when demand is cyclical, the need for additional productive capacity is only short-term, and the production activity is familiar to existing private (or nonprofit) enterprises.

Long-term strategies when demand exceeds capacity

Constant increases in demand for services may require revisions of an agency's internal productive capacity. The most basic change would be an expansion of the entire production system. A city may establish a new refuse disposal site or expand its resource recovery plant. A state consumer protection office may be enlarged, after an initial trial period, to handle the projected public inquiries and complaints for the coming decade.

Long-term capacity expansion also requires the location of new facilities to meet shifts in the spatial distribution of demand and to maintain program equity. Generalized mathematical models may be used to help weigh the cost trade-offs in deciding where to locate facilities, whether they be fire stations, power plants, or neighborhood health centers. These models, which are introduced in standard Operations Management texts (and are discussed more fully in specialized texts such as Francis & White, 1974), identify optimal locations which minimize travel time, cost, or some other measure of service delivery. Ultimately, however, many decisions regarding the location of public facilities require compromises based on political realities.

It is often economically or politically unreasonable for public managers to try to maintain service quality while expanding program capacity and, therefore, cost. Another strategy, in the face of increased demand, is to reassess the nature of the system's output. More specifically, it may be necessary to reduce the quality of the service, effectively increasing capacity without expanding the resource base. Thus, it may be appropriate to provide slightly less individual service to all clients, if such a strategy will enable a larger segment of the population to be served.

Public officials facing fiscal crises are beginning to ask whether it is necessary for the government to provide a particular direct service. Often a "nonservice" approach will be more cost-effective. In such a situation, incentives would be available for the private or voluntary sector to provide the needed service, and the public sector production system would be dismantled (or would never be developed in the first place). Tax incentives might encourage private employers to hire the unemployed, thereby reducing the need for public service work programs. In some communities, human services are provided by "self-help" groups of private citizens, rather than by government programs established to meet these needs. For some surveys of existing nonservice approaches to public programs, see Waldhorn, Gollub, Henton, Hentzell, Gardner, and King (1980).

Summary

This chapter has presented a series of capacity-related issues that must be considered by a manager in the public sector. A major managerial responsibility is to ensure that the capacity of an operating system is sufficient to meet the demand for its services. To accomplish this, managers must be skilled in selecting the measures of the capacity in a productive system. Managers also must know how to measure throughput time (including waiting time) and the utilization of the production process. The extent of waiting time must be considered when the adequacy of capacity in a service production system is assessed. Managing capacity to maintain both high utilization and high quality of output is particularly critical in the public sector. This requires an in-depth understanding of the structure of the operating system.

Managers must also be able to anticipate likely changes in demand that will require changes in existing capacity. The lead time needed to increase the capacity of a production system must be evaluated in any capacity planning exercise. To perform these tasks, the public manager requires a considerable amount of data including the current capacity, the availability of additional resources or financial constraints on the system, and trends in demand for the service (for example, growth rates, geographical shifts in population, or changes in the clients' demographic characteristics).

Finally, managers must develop techniques to resolve both short- and long-term mismatches between demand and capacity. Short-term strategies for improving the overall utilization of staff and equipment include the employment of temporary resources to cover periods of peak demand. Long-term strategies, such as expansion of facilities and other program resources raise certain managerial issues of scale, timing, and location. When government capacity must be reduced, other strategies—such as selective reduction in the quality of direct service delivery or increasing emphasis on nonservice approaches to governance—need to be explored. The examples discussed in this chapter illustrate various responses to problems of insufficient capacity. As managers gain insight into capacity management, they also will be able to develop creative responses to new environmental pressures. Public managers, in particular, are likely to feel pressures not to increase operating costs. Accordingly, they face the challenge of trying to maintain services without raising productive capacity.

Discussion questions

1. Exhibit 4.3 displays a simplified version of the criminal justice system as a job shop.
    a. What actions might a district attorney take to improve the throughput time for defendants who are processed in this sytem? What public policy and management issues are associated with these alternatives?
    b. What actions might a judiciary task force recommend to improve the capacity of this sytem? How would these alternatives and the associated policy and management issues differ from those discussed in (a)?
2. Public managers continually face capacity shortages in service systems. Sometimes this is the result of poor planning, but more often, it is the result of the many constraints facing a public manager. Discuss some of these problems and suggest actions a public manager might take to overcome them. In systems requiring long lead times to increase capacity, a manager often has great difficulty in getting the process started in time to match future capacity and future demand. Discuss why this issue is particularly perplexing in the public sector. What options are open to the public manager?
3. A university is a set of service production systems designed to provide academic training and the ancillary services to support this education. Develop a list of services and the appropriate capacity measure(s) for each. What actions must the university administration take to ensure that the available capacity for each system is adequate for student demand? Should each system be responsible for planning its own capacity or are there interrelationships that must be considered? If there are, include a list of these relationships.
4. At the town meeting, a selectman states unequivocally, "Equity must be maintained at all costs." Do you agree with this statement? If you do not, what arguments and illustrations would you use to persuade the selectman to your point of view? As the selectman begins to accept your perspective, he says "How do you think we should measure equity in public services?" What is your answer?
5. Wilderness County is a large geographic area containing many fine sites for hunting and fishing. Currently, one office processed all hunting license applications and no license is required for fishing. The

office is staffed year round, although the greatest demand is limited to a few months each year. At this time, the operation requires the completion of the five tasks listed below. Each task must be completed in the order shown. Assume that the processing times are all constant (not random variables).

Station Number	Task Description	Processing Time
1	Clerk assists applicant in completing application form and hands the applicant a test on hunting regulations.	2.5 minutes
2	Applicant moves to testing area and completes the self-administered test.	10 minutes
3	Applicant waits while clerk grades test.	5 minutes
4	Clerk photographs applicant and attaches photo to license. Applicant takes license to cashier.	5 minutes
5	Applicant pays fee to clerk and receives completed license.	2.5 minutes

The costs of this operation are offset by the current license fee of $25.00 for those who pass the test and $10.00 for those who do not pass the test.

Office rental	$9100/year
Clerks' salaries (total)	$38,400/year
Application forms	$ .50/applicant
Photos	$ .75/applicant

In answering the following questions, make these assumptions:

Applicants are processed between 8:30 A.M. and 4:30 P.M. Monday through Friday;

The passing rate for the test is 75 percent;

A different clerk handles the processing at each station that requires assistance; a supervisor fills in for the clerks as each goes to lunch;

Each clerk is able to perform each task if need be;

The time taken by the applicant in moving from station to station is included in the processing time;

All clerks receive the same salary;

No clerk is needed to monitor testing;

Space exists for as many as ten applicants to be taking the test at the same time;

The clerk at Station 1 is responsible for ensuring that no long lines develop inside the office during the day and for closing the processing so that all daily applicants are processed within the eight hours.

Now answer these questions concerning the operations of the hunting license processing office of Wilderness County.

a. What is the cycle time of this operating system?

b. Assuming that a line forms before the office opens at 8:30 A.M., how long, on average, will an applicant who passes the test spend in the office (not counting any waiting time)?

c. Where is a waiting line likely to form in this process? How can waiting time between Steps 1 and 5 be kept to a minimum without adding staff or changing the work activities?

d. What is the daily capacity of this operating system?

e. What is the utilization of clerical capacity from 2 P.M. until 4 P.M.?

f. The county commissioner expected the office to process up to 115 applications on any given day. What is the current effectiveness? Is the commissioner's standard realistic?

g. Can this system be made more efficient without changing the operating steps or the processing times? If so, how? What are the monthly savings?

h. With the current fee structure, how many licenses must be processed for the office to break even?

i. Last year the office processed 2500 applications, and 75 percent of the applicants passed the test. What was the average cost of processing each license?

j. There has been talk of requiring a fishing license in Wilderness County, but the county commissioners would authorize a fee of no more than $4.00. The fishing season does not coincide with the hunting season. Given the economics of the situation, should the current office begin to process fishing licenses in addition to its present responsibilities? (The processing requirements would be essentially the same as for a hunting license.)

Bibliography

Abernathy, William J., and Kenneth Wayne. "Limits of the Learning Curve." *Harvard Business Review*, September–October 1974, pp. 109–19.

Behn, Robert D. "Leadership for Cut-Back Management: The Use of Corporate Strategy." *Public Administration Review* 40 (November/December 1980): 613–20.

Buffa, Elwood S. *Modern Production Management*. 5th ed. Los Angeles: Wiley/Hamilton, 1977.

Chase, Richard B., and Nicholas J. Aquilano. *Production and Operations Management*. Homewood, Ill.: Irwin, 1981.

Francis, Richard L., and John A. White. *Facility Layout and Location, An Analytical Approach*. Englewood Cliffs, N.J.: Prentice-Hall, 1974.

Greiner, John M; Roger E. Dahl; Harry P. Hatry; and Annie P. Millar. *Monetary Incentives and Work Standards in Five Cities*. Washington, D.C.: The Urban Institute, 1977.

Levy, F. K.; G. L. Thompson; and J. D. Wiest. "The ABCs of the Critical Path Method." *Harvard Business Review*, September–October 1963, pp. 98–108.

Sapolsky, Harvey M. *The Polaris System Development*. Cambridge, Mass.: Harvard University Press, 1972.

Savas, E. S. "On Equity in Providing Public Service." *Management Science* 28, 8 (April 1978): 800–808.

Shepard, Morris A., and Keith Baker. *Year-Round Schools*. Lexington, Mass.: D. C. Heath and Co., 1977.

Stewart, John M. "Making Project Management Work." *Business Horizons* 8, 3 (Fall 1965): 120–38.

Waldhorn, Steven A.; James O. Gollub; Douglas C. Henton; Shirley Hentzell; Sidney L. Gardner; and James R. King. *Rediscovering Governance*. Santa Monica, Calif.: SRI International (unpublished report), July 1980.

Chapter 5
"Snow removal"

On Sunday, February 9, 1969, New York City was the victim of a major fifteen-inch snowstorm. The storm caught the U.S. Weather Bureau, and therefore the rest of the city, by surprise. When the city officials responsible for snow removal activities became aware of the severity of the situation, additional personnel were called in to supplement the minimal Sunday work force. Many workers could not get to their work stations due to rapid snow accumulation on major traffic arteries and breakdowns in the public transit system. Efforts of those who managed to report to work were thwarted by equipment failure, abandoned cars, and high winds that created deep snowdrifts. The snow fighters could not catch up with the storm.

During the next few days, this storm became a highly politicized event as the snow had not yet been cleaned away and the city was still crippled. Many residents of the outer boroughs of Queens, Brooklyn, the Bronx, and Staten Island were particularly voluble. These citizens felt that they had not received their fair share of snow removal activity compared with residents of Manhattan. Mayor John Lindsay, who was facing a reelection challenge later that year, was highly criticized for mismanagement of the city's snow removal resources and thereby, for exhibiting favoritism toward Manhattan at the expense of the rest of the city.

Meanwhile, remedies for future events of this type were offered by special interest groups. One suggestion was that the Department of Sanitation (which is responsible for snow removal, in addition to its major year-round work on refuse collection and disposal and street cleaning) should keep more sanitation workers on duty around the clock during the winter. Others pushed for the hiring of more mechanics to maintain the existing equipment. Still others wanted the city to buy more snow-removal equipment. Allowing sanitation workers to report for snow removal duty wherever they found it most convenient was another idea that was expressed. And owners of large bulldozers claimed that the city should hire privately owned equipment (at premium rates) when such snow emergencies arose in the future. Finally, it was not uncommon to hear within the ranks of Sanitation Department employees the whispered slogan: "God puts the snow here and he also takes it away."

In the midst of this confusion, the systems analysis group in the mayor's office of administration initiated a thorough study of the city's snow-fighting capability. The study team gathered a considerable amount of data and descriptive information, with the intention of presenting an analysis for the mayor's review and action. The analysts felt the time was ripe to try to identify and eliminate the major shortcomings in the snow removal program. Their basic approach was to see whether the supply of snow removal services made sense given the nature of the demand.

Snowfall statistics and climatic conditions

An historical analysis of U.S. Weather Bureau records disclosed that:

☐ Snowfall in New York City averages thirty-three inches annually.
☐ An average season has two storms with snowfall greater than four inches.
☐ During the period from 1910 to 1967, there were only five snowstorms in New York City which had a snowfall of at least fifteen inches.

Exhibits 5.1 and 5.2 present further data on snowfall patterns in New York City. Coping with a snowstorm in New York City involves using a variety of equipment to accomplish up to three sequential activities: spreading salt, plowing, and hauling away snow. Salt spreaders, crosswalk plows, and snow loaders are used only for snow removal activities. Other equipment, such as the trucks used for plowing, serve different functions when they are not being used for snow removal. Spreading salt is the usual first line of defense and is done perhaps twelve times a year; that is, salt is spread for the six or seven snowfalls which turn out to be greater than one inch, for others which appear threatening but ultimately deposit less than an inch, and also for freezing rain. The backbone

Exhibit 5.1
Frequency distribution of snowstorms, by depth, 1948–1967

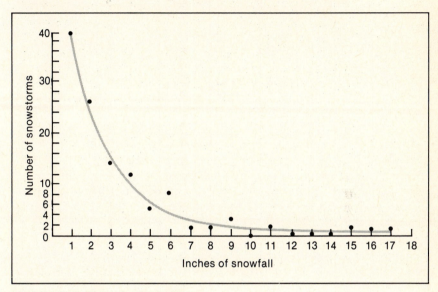

Source: U.S. Weather Bureau, New York City Office.
Note: Only includes snowfalls of at least one inch.

Exhibit 5.2
Frequency distribution of snow seasons by number of snowstorms
1948–1967

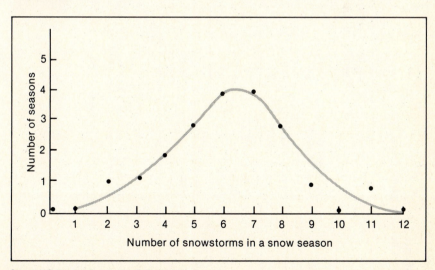

Source: U.S. Weather Bureau, New York City Office.
Note: Only includes snowfalls of at least one inch.

Exhibit 5.3
Snow accumulation rates

		Final Depth	Number of Storms	Accumulation Rates (in Inches)									
				1 hr	2 hr	3 hr	4 hr	5 hr	6 hr	7 hr	8 hr	9 hr	10 hr
Peak Accumulation Rates[a]	Average during Peak Period[b]	4-9	14	1.0	1.7	2.4	2.9	3.3	3.6	4.0	4.3		
		9+	9	1.7	2.9	3.9	4.8	5.6	6.3	6.9	7.4		
	Maximum during Peak Period[c]	4-9	1	1.4	2.6	3.3	4.2	4.7	5.2	5.5	5.6		
		9+	1	2.5	4.1	5.4	6.7	7.6	8.6	9.5	10.4		
Initial Accumulation Rates	Average for Initial Period	4-9	9	.1	.4	.8	1.1	1.4	1.9	2.4	2.9		
		9+	4	—	.1	.5	.8	1.2	1.8	2.5	3.2		
	Maximum for Initial Period	4-9	1	.5	1.2	2.1	3.3	4.4	4.9	5.4	5.7	5.8	6.0
		9+	1	.4	.6	1.1	2.0	2.9	4.1	5.7	7.7	10.0	11.5

Source: U.S. Weather Bureau, New York City Office.

[a] Based on the twenty-three storms equal to or greater than four inches during the period from 1958 to 1967.
[b] For example, if one looks at the three-hour period of heaviest snowfall for each of the fourteen storms whose final depth was 4-9 inches, the average accumulation during those three-hour periods was 2.4 inches.
[c] For example, the greatest five-hour accumulation for any storm was 7.6 inches; this occurred for a storm whose final depth was greater than 9 inches.

of the Department of Sanitation's snow removal fleet is the refuse collection truck which can have a plow mounted on the front end when it is needed for snow removal rather than refuse collection. Plowing is done three or four times in an average year, whenever snow depths are expected to approach four inches or so. (Specific decisions about plowing will depend on such factors as current ground temperature, predicted air temperature, wind, and traffic conditions—because salt is more effective in melting snow when traffic is relatively heavy.) Removal of snow by hauling is relatively rare, being reserved generally for snowfalls greater than six inches when the temperature is expected to remain below freezing for an appreciable period of time.

Salt spreading alone is usually sufficient for removal of snow up to six inches in depth, if temperatures rise above freezing. Continuing low temperatures, however, impede snow removal and limit lower-cost dissipation techniques by retarding natural snow shrinkage and inhibiting salt's melting action. (Salt becomes virtually ineffective at temperatures below 10° F.) Low temperatures also freeze the moving parts of all mechanical equipment, thereby reducing overall productivity. Flushing, scattering, and "sewering" (all low-cost operations) are effective only at temperatures above freezing. Hydrants cannot be used at temperatures below 34° F.; in very cold conditions, snow scattered in traffic blocks the cars rather than being crushed and melted by them; under such conditions snow deposited in sewers would clog rather than melt away. Also, snow dumped at waterfront bulkheads can pile up and prevent further dumping, rather than being washed away.

One of the important variables in responding to a snowstorm is the rate of snowfall. A heavy initial rate of fall could make streets impassable before sufficient snow-fighting equipment could get out into the streets. Statistics on snow accumulation rates are presented in Exhibit 5.3.

Successive storms that occur within a one-week period prolong snow removal operations, test the endurance of workers and machines, and strain the budget to a greater extent than storms spaced over a longer period of time. Conditions worsen materially when the successive storms are large, although this is a relatively rare event. (Between 1910 and 1968 there were no more than eight instances when snowstorms of four inches or more occurred in New York within one week of each other.)

Street priorities, mileages, and snow removal routes

The Department of Sanitation subdivides the city into a set of ten boroughs, each of which includes a number of districts (and within districts there are sections). See the sample map shown in Exhibit 5.4. The department periodically realigns its districts to accommodate population

Exhibit 5.4
Sample map of portion of Manhattan
Showing Department of Sanitation districts (large-type numbers)
and the sections (small-type numbers) within them

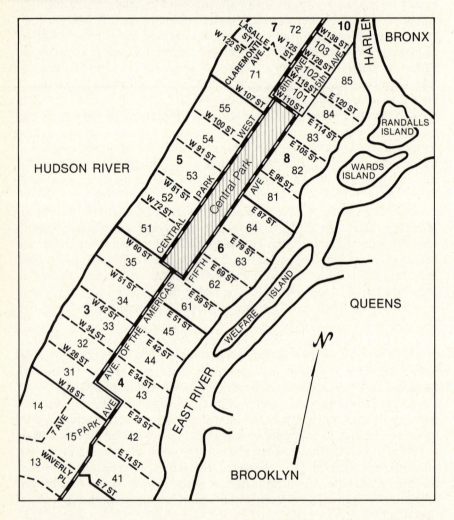

shifts; although the total population of the city has remained relatively constant for decades, there has been an extensive redistribution of residents within the city. (Especially notable is the growth of the outer boroughs of Queens and Richmond.) Each district operates a garage where all the district's equipment is housed and where routine maintenance is performed.

All city streets are classified in terms of their priority for snow removal. The three priority levels, called primary, secondary and tertiary, are de-

Exhibit 5.5
Definitions of snow removal street categories

Primary
Streets considered main traffic arteries, thoroughfares, or lifeline streets such as highways, parkways, expressways, drives, or bridges;
Feeder approaches to, and exits from, bridges, tunnels, ferries, highways, and airports;
All bus routes, private and city-owned;
All streets within concentrated food-produce, industrial, financial, theatrical-amusement, shopping, hospital, or maritime (passenger and freight) areas;
Streets on which are located vital facilities, such as firehouses, police stations, hospitals, newspaper plants, fuel distribution depots, and transportation terminals.

Secondary
Streets with reasonably heavy traffic, other than primary streets (includes all non-primary streets south of 59th Street in Manhattan);
Alternate routes for primary streets;
Short lengths of residential area streets that feed into primary streets;
Main local shopping streets;
Main access streets in limited industrial or commercial areas (unless a primary street).

Tertiary
All other streets.

Source: Department of Sanitation, *Snow Removal Manual.*

fined in Exhibit 5.5. The grid of all primary and secondary streets was designed to permit police, fire, and hospital vehicles to advance within one or two blocks of an emergency on a tertiary street. As shown in Exhibit 5.6, primary streets comprise 43 percent of the linear street mileage, but 45 percent of the spreader miles, and 55 percent of the plow miles in the city. (Depending on the width of the street, a vehicle may have to traverse it more than once in order to salt it or plow it, while spreaders and plows have different effective widths.)

The Department of Sanitation reviews its snow removal route network annually, noting changes in bus routes, street directions, and other area characteristics; snow clearance and disposal procedures; and specialized problems. For each sanitation district, separate schedules and routes are prepared for spreading salt, plowing, and hauling snow. A small fraction of the primary streets (a total of 619 miles in 1969) are designated and marked with signs by the Department of Traffic as Snow Emergency Streets, on which travel during a snow alert is restricted to cars with skid chains or snow tires and vehicle standing or parking is prohibited.

Snow removal is less cumbersome during weekends than during weekdays. Generally, Saturday traffic is light enough for snow vehicles to get

Exhibit 5.6
Street mileage: existing street network

Class of Street	Linear Miles		Spreader Miles[a]		Plow Miles[b]	
	Number	Percent	Number	Percent	Number	Percent
Primary	2530	43	2733	45	7330	55
Secondary	1978	34	1978	33	3493	26
Tertiary	1331	23	1331	22	2444	19
Total	5839	100	6042	100	13,267	100

[a] Spreader miles are assumed to be linear miles for all types of streets, except parkways and expressways, for which it is assumed that there are two spreader miles per linear mile.
[b] Plow miles are determined by multiplying linear miles by number of traffic lanes, less lanes utilized by parked vehicles or used by snow ridges or piles. (On primary streets this amounts to approximately 2.9 times linear miles; on secondary and tertiary streets, approximately 1.8, since on highways, expressways, and parkways, there is no parking.)

through easily and heavy enough to wear down the snow significantly. On Sunday, although there is less interference from traffic, the lighter traffic does not help enough to clear the roads. Parked cars are the greatest impediment to plowing, affecting nearly all streets except highways—where abandoned cars may present a problem. Plows are not very maneuverable, and although they can swing around illegally parked cars on major streets, operators are instructed to skip side streets where parked cars may make passage difficult. Snow removal routes are generally confined to the sanitation district boundaries which govern all operations of the department. Snow removal routes, however, differ considerably from routes followed for refuse collection. Sanitation Department officials claim that the snow removal routes are so designed that each one can usually be covered at least once every two hours as a plow completes its round trip. Successive plow trips are made continuously until the storm has ended, at which time the route should be entirely cleared of snow.

Normally, during a snowstorm, the Department of Sanitation works two shifts per twenty-four-hour day. Each shift is eleven hours long, with one hour in between. In any one shift, however, only about two thirds of the time is spent on productive work (plowing or spreading salt). The remainder of the time is required for refueling or loading, meals, and rest breaks. For each shift, about one hour and twenty minutes is required for various start-up activities and travelling to the beginning of a route. To aid in rapid mobilization of snow removal forces, plow blades and chains are attached to operable refuse collection trucks and street flusher trucks every Saturday night and on evenings before holidays during the snow season. Plow blades and chains are removed if they are not needed before normal (nonsnow) usage begins. From one to two man-hours are required to mount a plow on a truck.

The salt-spreading activity

Salt spreaders are ordered out (1) when there is freezing rain or sleet and the air temperature is less than 32° F., or (2) when any snowfall is equal to or greater than one inch. Spreaders remain in use for the duration of a storm to prevent icy road conditions, to reduce the accumulation of ice and snow, and to spread salt on streets that have already been plowed. Spreaders lose their effectiveness once snow accumulation exceeds about four inches.

A light snow of up to five inches, or even more, may require only salting and traffic, if the Sanitation Department gets a prompt start. Traffic assists by mixing the salt with the snow and breaking up ice layers that have been weakened by salt. However, if no salt or other chemicals of the proper mix have been applied at the beginning of a snowfall and traffic has had an opportunity to pack the snow, larger quantities of chemicals and a longer period of time are required to penetrate and remove the ice or very hard snow that results.

The salt spreaders are fully loaded at the start of a snowstorm. Some spreaders hold nine cubic yards of salt while others have a fourteen-cubic-yard capacity. Spreader speeds vary from four miles per hour on some streets in some boroughs to ten miles per hour on highways, with an average of seven miles per hour. Salt-loading spots are located throughout the city. In Manhattan the distance is not a significant problem; but in Queens loading may take over an hour, depending on the location of the nearest loading point. Equipment allocation and associated spreader workloads for the ten Department of Sanitation boroughs are presented in Exhibit 5.7.

The snowplowing activity

The Department of Sanitation has a total of 1760 collection and flusher trucks to which plow blades can be attached to clear snow from the path of moving traffic, from bus stops, at intersections, and around fire hydrant areas. Streets are plowed according to their priority level, except that emergency calls for police, fire, or ambulance service take precedence. If the department is alerted that an ambulance is going to a house on a side street, the nearest plow is dispatched immediately, even though this may

Exhibit 5.7
Spreader unit allocation and spreader-miles
of streets by sanitation borough and type of street

| | | Spreader Miles[b] | | |
Sanitation Boroughs	Number of Spreader Units[a]	Bus Routes, Parkways, and Expressways	Primary Streets Only	All Streets
Manhattan West	23	112	214	285
Manhattan East	26	104	179	275
Bronx West	14	133	165	314
Bronx East	15	158	244	503
Brooklyn West	25	167	261	547
Brooklyn North	19	138	202	386
Brooklyn East	12	128	171	592
Queens West	36	201	414	938
Queens East	38	318	611	1336
Staten Island	15	102	272	866
Total	223	1561	2733	6042

[a] One spreader unit has the capacity of a nine-cubic yard spreader. Therefore, a fourteen-cubic-yard spreader equals one and a half spreader units. The department has 160 nine-cubic-yard spreaders and 42 fourteen-cubic-yard spreaders.
[b] As defined in Exhibit 5.6.

mean clearing a secondary or tertiary street and delaying main artery clearance. The allocation of equipment for plowing and associated work-load indicators for each borough are shown in Exhibit 5.8. Plows generally function effectively in snow up to about eight inches deep. However, if the snow is particularly dense, plows may become immobilized following lesser accumulations.

Traffic affects plow speeds at different times of the normal weekday. A plow can be run at fifteen miles per hour if it is not interrupted by traffic. In the morning and evening rush hours the average speed is five miles per hour. Between these rush hours, during the late morning and early afternoon a plow speed of eight miles per hour is possible. Average speeds in Manhattan are lower than those in the outer boroughs.

Equipment breakdown

The Department of Sanitation's Snow Removal Manual specifies how the equipment is to be readied for snow removal use: inspecting equipment

Exhibit 5.8
Plow equipment allocation and plow miles
of streets by sanitation borough and type of street

Sanitation Boroughs	Number of Plow-Bearing Trucks[a]	Plow Miles[b]		
		Primary Streets	Primary and Secondary Streets	All Streets
Manhattan West	162	626	739	746
Manhattan East	189	473	583	584
Bronx West	157	485	680	820
Bronx East	148	726	919	1240
Brooklyn West	194	699	922	1154
Brooklyn North	203	548	778	942
Brooklyn East	173	495	740	1387
Queens West	226	1079	1787	2034
Queens East	238	1523	2215	2745
Staten Island	70	676	1460	1615
Total	1760	7330	10,823	13,267

[a] A combination of collection trucks and street flusher trucks.
[b] As defined in Exhibit 5.6.

early in September to determine required repairs; performing repair work later in the month; field testing in early November, and checking the functioning of snow removal equipment operation at frequent intervals. In general, vehicle breakdowns are felt to be related to vehicular age and storm duration, rather than to the level of equipment maintenance. Some spreaders, the smaller nine-cubic-yard units, are more than thirty years old and their downtime is 40 percent. The newer fourteen-cubic-yard units have a lower breakdown rate of 25 percent. A spreader usually lasts from ten to fifteen years. Most spreader breakdowns are minor and can usually be repaired within one shift.

On average, 40 percent of the plow units are not functioning during the course of snow removal activity. Sanitation collection trucks and street flusher trucks to which plow blades are attached have an expected productive life of six years (but regular day *and* night utilization for nonsnow duties accelerates aging). In practice, most of this equipment is from eight to ten years old, and the older units have a higher breakdown rate. The disabled rate increases during a storm, when plow parts—rather than the trucks themselves—fail. In such an event, the plow trucks are returned to the garage, the plow parts are repaired, and the trucks are restored to service within one shift.

Manpower planning and availability

There are more than 9000 uniformed workers in the Department of Sanitation who can be assigned to operate the department's 2800 pieces of snow removal equipment. The Department of Sanitation provides citywide residential service throughout the year. Frequency of refuse collection varies among districts but remains constant for any one district unless there are major budgeting cutbacks. The complement of workers and equipment assigned to a district is geared to meeting the weekly workload as determined primarily by refuse collection and street-sweeping schedules.

In planning and scheduling operations during the snow season, the department takes several steps to ensure that a sufficient number of workers will be available and prepared for snow-fighting duties. Among these steps are:

☐ The hiring of mechanics on a snow season basis, on or about September 15, who, with the over 900 sanitation workers assigned to garage duties, maintain equipment in a high state of readiness. These mechanics are assigned to garages throughout the city in order to ensure equal maintenance capability citywide.

☐ The switch of personnel and equipment from day to day-and-night refuse collection, on or about November 15, when shift times are changed and personnel are reassigned within each district. When there is no snow, the night workers collect refuse and carry out other assignments. Collection operations during the day shift alone are resumed in the spring.

☐ A review by sanitation borough superintendents with each respective district superintendent by November 15. The review covers district personnel assignments to the day and night plow organization and to the day and night snow removal organization. It is meant to assure that a sufficient number of workers are assigned to each shift.

☐ The request to other city departments to furnish workers to perform various snow removal activities, mainly hauling snow. Such assistance provides only minor additions to the Sanitation Department's own capacity. During an emergency the commissioner may also order the hiring of private laborers and truck drivers to remove snow. (All personnel from outside the department are prohibited from operating the existing Sanitation Department vehicles.)

☐ The instruction, at the Sanitation Training Center, of department employees, personnel from other city departments, and persons from Civil Service eligibility lists, in the duties of their assignments.

The wintertime aggregate assignment of manpower by shift is charted in Exhibit 5.9. From Monday through Saturday there are three levels of

Exhibit 5.9
Planned winter shift levels for manpower in field

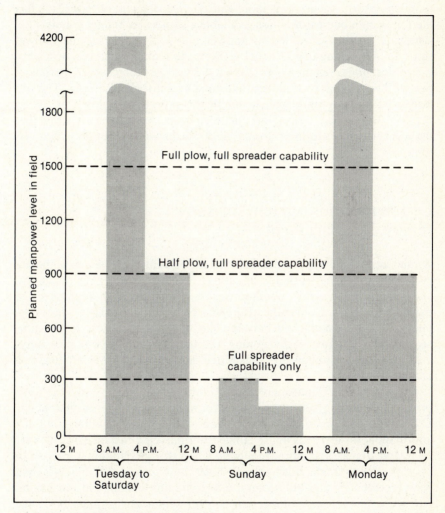

Note: Exclusive of Administrative and Garage Personnel.

response capability: from 8 A.M. to 4 P.M. a total force of more than 1500 workers—capable of operating all spreaders and plows—is on duty; from 4 P.M. to midnight, there are 900 workers, enough to operate all the spreaders and half of the plows; from 12 midnight to 8 A.M. approximately 300 workers are on hand, enough to operate all spreaders. On Sundays, there are approximately 300 workers from midnight to 4 P.M.—full spreader capability only—while from 12 midnight Sunday night to 8 A.M. Monday, no field forces are assigned. On Mondays at 8 A.M. the full complement returns to duty.

When a storm occurs or is imminent, the Department of Sanitation has the following courses of action available—subject to budget constraints: (1)relying on the scheduled manpower only; (2) extending the current shift; and (3) calling in additional workers. In making such resource allocation decisions, reliance is placed on the weather forecasts, experience, general operational procedures, and long established priorities. The objective is to make manpower levels fit the severity of the storm. When personnel are called in on a nonscheduled basis, work rules prescribe that the workers report to their normal field offices within their assigned districts.

Communication system for snow removal management

As shown in Exhibit 5.10 the Department of Sanitation has an elaborate communications network for updating forecasts, mobilizing resources, and reporting on snow conditions. The Department maintains close liaison with the U.S. Weather Bureau's New York forecaster on a telephone hot line established between the two agencies during the snow season. This line is used for getting weather information at regular intervals, and storm warnings are transmitted on it as soon as they are foreseen and/or develop.

The Sanitation Department also contracts, via public bidding, for a private forecasting service whose information supplements that of the U.S. Weather Bureau. The private contractor relays weather condition information three times daily, under normal circumstances at 6 A.M., 2 P.M. and 10 P.M., and more frequently when storm conditions threaten or develop. For example, during the 1968–69 snow season, 520 messages had been received by mid-March on the teletype unit installed in the Sanitation Department's communication control center at headquarters. (See the sample teletype messages in Exhibit 5.11.)

The Sanitation Department also maintains eighteen weather observation stations on the city's perimeter, from which periodic reports on the start of precipitation, snow depths, temperature, and rate of accumulation are telephoned to headquarters' snow office. After the initial report, condition checks are made and telephoned to sanitation headquarters every half hour.

Despite this battery of reports, there traditionally has been a 0.30 prob-

Exhibit 5.10
Communication links for citywide mobilization

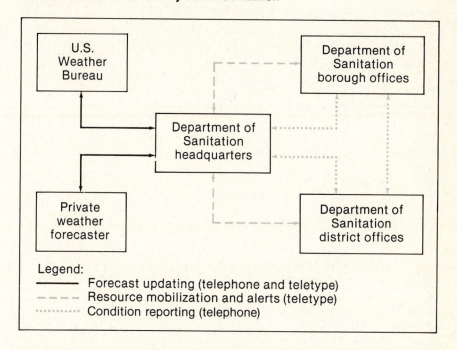

Legend:
———— Forecast updating (telephone and teletype)
‑ ‑ ‑ ‑ Resource mobilization and alerts (teletype)
············ Condition reporting (telephone)

ability that forecasted weather will not materialize. Snow forecasting is particularly difficult in the vicinity of New York. The east-west snow-rain line often crosses through the metropolitan region and a slight shift in meteorological factors will cause the line to shift a few miles to the north, producing rain, or a few miles to the south, producing snow. Under these circumstances, a forecast of precipitation is likely to be correct, but whether the precipitation will be rain or snow is more difficult to predict. During the 1968–69 snow season there were twenty-three snow alerts; yet snow materialized in only thirteen instances, of which five had only traces of snow and another five had less than two inches.

When snow is forecast by any one of the available sources and a storm has developed, the control center, under the instructions of the Chief of Operations, teletypes alerts to the borough and district offices. Resources are mobilized in progressive stages as weather conditions worsen. A complete list of snow alert commands is provided in Exhibit 5.12. Given the current accuracy of snowstorm forecasts, snow alert decisions proceed on a worst case assumption until the situation is proven to be other-

Exhibit 5.11
Sample weather forecast received via teletype
by Department of Sanitation from private weather service

FCST FOR NYDS   1-6-69   2 P.M.

THURS AFT	P/A
TEMP	30–34
WIND	N 7–14
THURS EVE	INC CLDNS
TEMP	34–30
WIND	LITE
THURS NITE	M/CLDY, PERIOD OF SNOW DEVL.
TEMP	30–27
WIND	NE 6–12
FRI MORN	M/CLDY, SNOW ENDING
TEMP	27–30
WIND	NE 7–14
FRI AFT	M/CLDY
TEMP	30–32
WIND	NNE 10–20
FRI EVE	VAR/CLDNS
TEMP	32–26
WIND	NNW 12–22
FRI NITE	P/CLDY
TEMP	26–20
WIND	NW 8–16
SAT MORN	M/S
TEMP	20–27
WIND	N 8–16
SAT AFT	P/S
TEMP	27–30
WIND	NE 8–16

NO PRECIP THRU THIS EVE. PERIOD OF SNOW DEV AROUND MIDNITE AND ENDING TOMORROW MORN. PATH OF STORM IS STILL UNCERTAIN SO IT IS DIFFICULT TO PREDICT ACCUMULATION, BUT PROB NO MORE THAN 2″. CHC OF SNOW SUNDAY. TEMPS WILL BE MAINLY BELOW FREEZING THRU MON.

wise. Thus, a forecast for two or three inches of snow receives the same preliminary action as does a forecast for a major blizzard, until actual weather conditions warrant different consideration.

In addition to its teletype system, the Department of Sanitation operates, on a twenty-four-hour basis, a network of 140 two-way radios for communications among supervisors' cars, districts, and headquarters.

Exhibit 5.12
Snow alert commands

Four alert instructions (*) are precut on tapes before the beginning of the snow season and are communicated via teletype when snow is forecast, starts to fall, etc. As conditions worsen, additional commands are issued, depending upon relevance. Should snowfall occur without an alert being issued, mobilization begins when snow is observed.

Snow Alert

A. *When snow is forecast:*
   1. Call operations advisor, follow instructions.
      Notify alert officer.
      Order office force to 5 workers (4 hours lead time).
      Take spreader and front-end loader report, take personnel report.
      Maintain snow watch; report to operations advisor as directed.
      If ordered to duty, notify chiefs.
      Notify chiefs' chauffeurs.
 *2. Load spreading machines with cinders or salt, fuel and have ready for a prompt start.
      Garage and field officers: check each spreading machine before assignment or dispatch from loading point; set rear gate of each spreader to allow an opening wide enough to prevent small stones from jamming between conveyor chain and rear of spreader hopper (prevents damage to conveyor).
   3. Inspect deflectors, which guide width of spread, for proper setting. Report spreaders, inserts, and front-end loaders by district—"assigned," "up," or "down." Continue report for duration of storm.

B. *When snow starts:*
 *1. Field Supervisor: inspect bridges, express highways, and parkways under your jurisdiction and report conditions to borough office.
   2. Borough Office: transmit reports to Bureau Operations Office on Extension 6874 or 5461.
   3. Continue to report precipitation every hour until ordered otherwise. Depths must be measured with a ruler every hour, to the nearest 1/8".
   4. Report number of spreaders loaded. Continue report each hour until all spreaders are loaded.
   5. Report number of officers and able-bodied sanitation workers available for snow duty on off shifts and Sundays and holidays.
   6. Attach plows. Report number attached each hour until terminated by Bureau Operations Office or all plows attached; report number of new type collection trucks "up" or "down" and "with plows attached."

C. *Snow falling:*
 *1. Assign spreading machines *where necessary.*
   2. Garage and Field Officers: check each spreading machine before assignment, etc. (same as A2).

D. *Snow continuing:*
 *1. Assign full spreading operation.
   2. Assign plows *where necessary.* Report number assigned by district; report each hour until full plow operation. (3" or 4" of snow)

Exhibit 5.12
Snow alert commands (continued)

    3.   Assign full plow operation.
        Cancel alternate-side-of-street regulations.
        Plow streets in priority order; assign crosswalk plows.
        Assign all front-end loaders and power wagons to clear crosswalks.
        Assign blower-type flushers and "V" plows.
        Assign tow trucks and wreckers to move stalled and abandoned vehicles.
        Sewer as much snow as possible.
        In drifts, raise plow of lead vehicle to take half the accumulation; follow-plow will remove remainder.
        Keep catch-basins open.
    4.   Inspect waterfront snow disposal locations.

Supplementary commands: Not precut, but selected from commands of prior storms and added as conditions worsen:

Extend all day personnel 2 hours to 6 P.M.
Cancel days off scheduled for following day.
Assign snow-hauling auxiliary field force battalion to report at 7 P.M.
Extend midnight shift from 8 A.M. to 11 A.M.
Open hired equipment measuring stations at 6 A.M.
Issue orders to employ emergency driver laborers and to hire registered hired
   trucks and front-end loaders, bulldozers, and winch trucks.
Assign other city trucks to sanitation hauling gangs.
Assign emergency truck drivers and motorized patrols.
Employ snow removal contractor.
Plow snow into piles so that snow won't impede traffic, etc.
Assign snow melter gangs to predesignated routes.
Schedule refuse collection on limited basis.
Scatter as much snow as possible when temperature permits.
Field officers and special patrol workers: enforce regulations relative to removal of
   snow and ice from sidewalks.
Assign limited duty Sanitation workers who have light sweeping tissues and who
   cannot use panscrapers to pick litter and remove debris from sidewalks, snow
   ridges, and roadways.

Discussion questions

Mayor Lindsay has received many constituent complaints concerning the snow removal crisis following the February 9, 1969, storm. As he prepares to campaign for reelection he has asked you, The Commissioner of Sanitation, to prepare a memo outlining the current situation and recommendations for change. Specifically, Lindsay wants to know:

1.   How unusual was the overall situation created by the February 9, 1969, snowstorm and the resulting snow removal difficulties? Should he be concerned that another storm will create similar problems in the

near future? If he should be, what specific proposal steps should he take before June when he will begin his campaign for reelection?

2. What is the current snow removal production system, including the inputs, process, and outputs? What specific input or process changes could be made to improve the City of New York's ability to respond to a major blizzard?

3. Did the city have sufficient snow removal capacity for this storm? For less severe snow storms? Mayor Lindsay needs specific information on the time it takes to plow and salt primary streets, the allocation of equipment throughout the city's boroughs and the scheduling of staff for snow fighting. What specific changes could be made to improve the capacity of the system? What are some of the costs of the alternatives that you suggest?

4. Finally, the Mayor wants to review the street priority plan that was devised to facilitate the clearance of major streets first. Does this approach make sense in all storms? What are some other assignment rules that might be more effective in different circumstances? Do you recommend any changes to the existing definitions of primary or secondary streets? Why?

Notes

* This case was prepared by Stephen R. Rosenthal. Funds for its development were provided by a grant from the Duke University/Rand Graduate Institute's Public Policy Curricular Materials Development Project which is sponsored by the Ford Foundation. The case is intended to serve as a basis for class discussion, not to illustrate either effective or ineffective handling of a managerial situation.

Chapter 6
Personnel planning and work measurement

The field of public personnel administration is well established and has generated a considerable literature dealing with questions of staff recruitment, compensation, motivation, development and conduct. (see, for example, Stahl, 1962). The U.S. Civil Service Commission (now the Office of Personnel Management) has existed for over thirty years as a central policymaking entity for these aspects of personnel administration. Only recently, however, have the personnel experts in government turned to questions of forecasting and planning.

In contrast, during the past twenty years, industrial firms have grown increasingly sophisticated in projecting their requirements for operating personnel.[1] Government has followed a different path, stressing the improvement of budgetary processes with the faith that better program planning and incremental budgeting will encourage more reasonable estimates of staffing requirements.[2] The budgetary route to improved personnel planning hasn't worked well for government. Agency management may attempt to make rational decisions on overall program levels, but the associated staffing changes from expanding—or, more recently, cutting back—program levels are usually highly subjective. A more refined capability for the planning of government staffing levels is generally needed. This chapter discusses techniques for investigating current workload requirements and for planning future personnel needs. A basic premise of the chapter is that public managers and planners often need a systematic view of existing organizational policies, processes, structures, roles, tasks, and demand levels as a basis for estimating future personnel requirements.

Chapter 3 presented a systems model of an organization in which services are produced in response to demands from the outside environment. The part of this system addressed in chapters 4 and 5 was the technology of production: the allocation of resources in prescribed patterns in accordance with organizational policies and procedures. In this chapter we concentrate on exploring how personnel participate in the production process. We begin by identifying the roles of those who hold the key production jobs. Roles are defined operationally, in terms of the processes through which the organization conducts its business. We then attempt to identify implicit norms which have evolved through time for the performance of different elements of key production jobs. These norms provide measures of the effort required to accomplish essential work elements. If the personnel, on average, perform their roles in accordance with these norms, then it is a straightforward matter to calculate the size of the work force needed to handle different work loads. Thus, through norms, staffing requirements can be related to the production capacity needed to meet external demands, using the existing technology of production. Changes in staffing requirements follow from changes in demands, technology, or norms.

In service organizations—public or private—the major inputs are human resources. Effective allocation and integration of human resources are critical to the successful delivery of services. This chapter presents two methods for projecting the level of staff needed to meet organizational goals and objectives, subject to the constraints on the system. The first, a traditional work measurement system, is discussed briefly, as much has been written on this approach since Frederick W. Taylor's (1911) initial use of task analysis as a basis for production standards and manpower requirements. The second method estimates baseline personnel requirements by adapting traditional task analysis and work measurement techniques within a framework of modern organization theory. It is particularly useful for public sector organizations which have large numbers of professional personnel. This method promotes the efficient allocation of staff across an agency, given aggregate constraints on the number of authorized personnel positions. The approach was developed and tested for managerial use at one specific federal agency. Other government agencies, which will probably differ in significant respects from the example, may nevertheless benefit from the proposed structural view of government as a system for producing services.

The proper application of these two approaches can help operations managers, at all levels of government, to plan their personnel requirements in a wide variety of functional responsibilities. It is important to appreciate the characteristics of each approach and the situations in which each can be employed effectively. The basic difference is that the traditional work measurement approach concentrates on direct observation of workers, with no broad conceptual framework, while the systems

approach begins with an overall model of the productive function of the
organization.

Traditional method of work measurement

This method involves several steps: (1) the definition of work tasks for a
particular job; (2) the measurement of the time needed to perform each
task; (3) a comparison of actual work times with standards or norms set by
management; and (4) a determination of staffing needs based on those
norms. This classic approach to work measurement has been successfully
applied to some government work settings, but its assumptions and limitations should be understood. In structurally simple production settings,
where each job is conducted independently of others, task analysis
techniques can be used to provide accurate and meaningful estimates of
the personnel requirements for each job. In an industrial assembly line,
for example, it is a fairly routine matter to establish the sequence of tasks
and the production time required for each task. In service production
settings this analytic step may be somewhat more complex, but the same
procedure can be followed. In recent years some municipalities have
successfully applied the traditional approach to productivity improvement
projects, for example, in parks or automotive maintenance (San Diego
Program Evaluation and Productivity Improvement Project, 1975, 1976;
United States Office of Personnel Management, 1981). A closer examination of the traditional method and discussion of an example will help to
identify appropriate applications in government.

Identifying work tasks

The traditional method of work measurement begins with the identification of all the distinct tasks performed by the personnel in the position
being examined. The specification of the elements to be measured is
determined by the level of detail required in the work measurement process and by the operations analyst's ability to divide a task into smaller
segments. Once the tasks have been identified, the (various) actual times
to perform them are measured and, based on the observed range, standard
times are established. It is especially important to spend sufficient time
defining the elements of the job so that each element is a measurable
segment of the entire process. When combined in the proper sequence,
these elements must satisfactorily complete the job in an accepted
method. To reduce timing errors, the analyst must be able to determine
the beginning and ending point of each job segment. Furthermore, each

element should be a repeatable portion of the task. Timing a segment only to find it is a unique occurrence is of little value in setting standards.

Consider an example from the normal operations of a Department of Motor Vehicles. If the department wanted to determine the staff needed to process license applicants, it would need to specify the tasks required in this processing. Elements of the processing could include assisting the applicant in filling out the application, conducting a vision check, administering a written test, and giving the actual driving test. It is possible that each of these tasks is a discrete element of the licensing process and that further refinement is unneeded. However, further breakdown of one or more of these tasks may be warranted. For example, it might be valuable to subdivide administration of the written exam into smaller elements such as distributing materials, explaining directions, collecting papers, and scoring.

Measuring work times

In order to establish standards for production under the traditional industrial engineering approach, it is necessary to measure the actual time taken in completion of a task. Analysts are advised not to ask employees for reports of the time taken to perform specific work tasks, since the reliability of given data could easily be questionable. Instead, analysts are encouraged to observe at least one employee at work and to record the time needed for each task. It is important to record times for several cycles of the process for each observed employee to eliminate the bias of one unusual event. For example, if the Department of Motor Vehicles wants to set a work-measurement standard for grading the written test, the time taken to correct the test would be recorded over many cycles. The actual number of cycles to be counted would differ, depending on the variability of the employee in grading the tests, the actual length of the task, and the importance or effect of unexpected events that interrupt the task. (In some instances a single extraordinary observed time, caused by a unique outside occurrence, may be excluded in the computation of the average time for the task.) A series of observed times can then be used to determine an average time for that task for the observed employee: Average time = time worked/number of units produced. One possible risk in the conduct of time studies, the so-called Hawthorne effect, is that observations may be contaminated by the very process of their acquisition. The analyst must try to ensure that employees do not change their regular work pace as a response to being observed. Other technical aspects of determining a sample size and timing a work activity are discussed in detail in traditional operations management texts such as Barnes (1968) or Chase and Aquilano (1981).

Establishing standard times

Management has the prerogative to determine the standard time acceptable for the completion of a task. It is generally assumed to be the time
needed by an employee who works at a normal pace to complete a task.
Management must determine if the times obtained by direct observation
fit these assumptions or whether adjustments must be made to the average
of the observed times to arrive at a normal time. If the times are accepted
by management, they can be used as a standard against which staffing
needs are determined. If it takes a normal grader an average of six minutes
to correct a written exam, this figure can be used for purposes of establishing a work standard. If a worker takes eight minutes but the manager
believes that worker's "performance rating" to be 25 percent slower than
normal, then $8 (1 - .25) = 6$ minutes would be the normal time (NT) for
the task. The standard time (ST) for a task is calculated as $ST = NT(1 +$
allowances), where allowances are the sum of expected interruptions in
work for personal breaks, unavoidable delays, or fatigue. If allowances,
on average, require 15 percent of an employee's time during the course of
a day's work at the Motor Vehicle Bureau, then the standard time for
exam grading would be: $ST = 6 (1 + 0.15) = 6.9$ minutes.

Determining requirements for staff

Once the tasks to be measured have been identified and timed and appropriate standards have been set, management can use this information to
assess the staffing required to produce the needed service at the level
demanded. Returning to the example of the Motor Vehicle Department,
we find that once standard times are set for each discrete activity, the
total time needed to issue a license can be computed and a staffing level to
meet projected demand can be determined. This calculation is simply:

$$\text{Required staff level} = \frac{\text{projected daily demand} \times \text{standard time (minutes)}}{\text{length of work day (minutes)}}$$

To illustrate, if an average of 122 drivers are expected to arrive each day
to take a written exam, the standard time for grading an exam is 6.9
minutes, and each employee works a 7-hour day, then two graders are
needed:

$$\frac{122 \times 6.9}{7 \times 60} = 2$$

Limitations

Use of these classical work measurement techniques in organizations such as a public works department (to determine the manpower needed to repair city streets) or a sanitation department (to determine manpower needed to collect trash at specified times) are legitimate and appropriate. Attempts to apply this approach to more discretionary services—such as criminal court cases or building inspections—are less likely to produce satisfactory results. It is in such situations that an alternative method of staffing and workload planning is needed.

A systems approach

The operations of many government agencies require that different patterns of tasks be performed depending on the nature of the work at hand. (One such class of activity is "case processing" which is described in chapters 11 and 12.) In situations characterized by extensive discretionary activity, the traditional task analysis technique does not provide a solid foundation for the determination of staffing needs. As the job develops from a routine line activity to one that requires professional judgment and decision making at various points in the production process, the need for a systems approach to personnel planning becomes apparent.

The systems approach provides a broader context for the analysis of any single job. The definition of work tasks, following the proposed approach, is logically derived from the total job under study. This focus on the functional roles of different kinds of personnel ensures that both the essential aspects of individual jobs and the important interactions among persons holding related production jobs are included in the analysis. Such interactions are often overlooked in the traditional work measurement approach which focuses only on a single job.

This approach will be described in terms of its application to a federal agency responsible for the solicitation of grant proposals, allocation of grant funds, and monitoring of funded programs. This agency was required by a formal request from the Office of Management and Budget (OMB) to perform a systematic analysis of its staffing needs as part of its budgeting process.

The Agency should undertake a comprehensive study of its staffing needs, addressing such matters as comparability of work load among organizational units and development of quantitative work standards and time budgets particularly as these are affected by the volume of work processed by the agency. Consideration should also be given to possibilities for reducing work load by means of policy changes and to means for increasing the productivity of current staffing resources. Results of the initial phase of this effort should be available to OMB by August 1 to be considered in reviewing the staffing needs in the FY 1980 budget.

In response to this request from OMB, the agency launched a project to develop a formal, fair, and clear presentation of its staffing needs.[3] The project's immediate objective was to establish a preliminary set of baseline estimates for current staffing requirements for each division of the agency. A more fundamental objective was to develop the techniques and procedures for conducting annual reviews of personnel needs and associated operating budgets. OMB wanted rigorous procedures which would explain, in terms of the way business was conducted, precisely what could be accomplished by the existing staff level, and how the requested marginal changes to the base level were derived from shifts in work loads.

Due to the large amount of discretion available to many staff members, the traditional work measurement approach to staff analysis appeared infeasible. The alternative method developed consisted of the following steps, which are subsequently discussed.

1. Conceptualize the organization as an operating system and identify its central productive process—the "core technology."
2. Classify the formal units or offices of the organization into groups with similar operational structures.
3. Identify the various roles performed in the productive process and describe the major functional activities associated with each role.
4. List the operational tasks required to perform the major job activities for each production role.
5. Develop norms to estimate the current standard time allocation for conducting the operational tasks.
6. Estimate the current production staffing needs.
7. Estimate the current staffing requirements for supervision and administrative support.

Identifying the "core technology"

The most common graphic form for representing an organization is the chart of its formal authority structure. A formal organization chart depicts authority relationships and is useful in presenting the overall scope of activities, but it does not explain the activities of any part of the agency or its personnel needs. Instead, operational descriptions are needed.

As discussed in chapter 1, a government agency is likely to produce more than one kind of output. An analysis of staffing requirements should

Exhibit 6.1
An open system

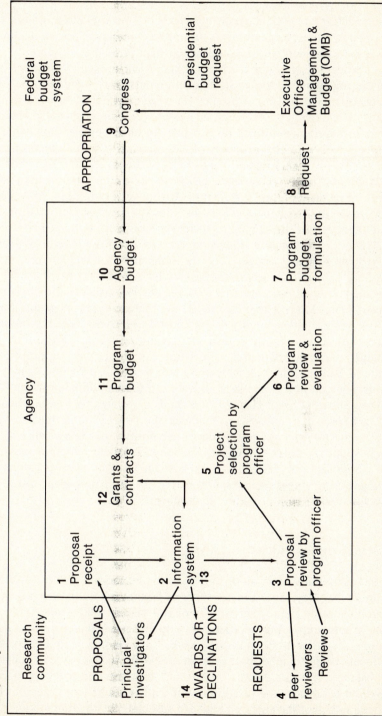

concentrate on the particular output most central to the purpose of the organization. The mechanism by which organizational inputs are transformed into these key outputs is the core technology. The core technology must be examined within its particular institutional environment.

A process chart, such as that in Exhibit 6.1, presents a systems model of the organization whose staff requirements were under study. The receipt of a proposal for a project (1) is acknowledged through a formal entry in the agency's information system (2). The proposal itself is then sent to a program officer responsible for the specialty into which the project falls (3). The program officer sends copies of the proposal to reviewers for them to rate the feasibility of the project (4). Based on these advisory reviews, the program officer assesses the merit of the proposal and, with consideration for the program budget available in this specialty, recommends whether to award funds for the proposed project (5).

Other parts of the agency's service environment, also shown in Exhibit 6.1, are the executive and legislative branches of the federal government which provide the budget. The development of a budget request is an elaborate annual process at the agency level. Professional staff and management in each program area examine current projects and likely trends consistent with objectives (6). They then prepare program budgets (7) which are subsequently integrated into an overall agency budget request (8). This request, in turn, is transmitted as part of the president's budget request to Congress (9). Congress passes laws appropriating a federal budget, which includes an operating budget for the agency (10). This aggregate budget is then allocated to the individual program for use during the next fiscal year (11). As funds are obligated for specific grants (12), appropriate entries are made in the agency's information system (13), and the principal investigators are notified of the awards (14).

In summary, this systems diagram identifies the production activities of the organization. Program proposals and budget appropriations from Congress are inputs to this productive process, and grant awards and declinations (nonawards) are its outputs.

Classifying the offices

The functional units in an organization can be classified with respect to its core technology. Two general types of functional units were identified in the illustrative agency: grant administration and staff support. The various grant administration offices directly determine which grants and contracts will be awarded in their specialty areas and program funds are then allocated accordingly. Staff support offices provide a range of centralized subsidiary services, such as personnel management or data processing. Exhibit 6.2 shows the distribution of staff in these two types of offices. Roughly half of the agency's staff are associated with grant administration

Exhibit 6.2
Personnel distribution by category of
office and type of position (1979 fiscal year)

Category of Office	Supervisory Positions	Technical[a] Positions	Administrative Positions	Total Authorized Positions	Percent
I. Grant Programs[b]	91	277	283	651	51
II. Other Programs, General Management, and Staff Support	123	344	157	624	49
Total	214	621	440	1275	100

[a] Includes all program officers.
[b] Includes a small number of positions (a total of thirteen) for external facilities management.

activities, while the remaining half are in the various staff support offices. In industrial accounting terminology, one might say that about half of the personnel are direct production workers and the rest provide indirect labor and overhead.

This agency has several grant administration departments, each of which has a number of offices. All such offices have the same operational structure. The staff support functions, in contrast, are organized within a number of separate offices each with its own unique structure. Therefore, in this case it was natural to focus initially on an analysis of the grant programs. Classifying the offices of an agency is a prerequisite for developing reasonable comparisons among their various requirements for personnel. This step should be followed whether or not many offices in an organization turn out to have structural similarities and can be treated together as a single class.

Analysis of major functional activities by personnel types

The determination of core technologies and the related classification of office units facilitates the definition of roles for the associated production personnel. Role definition consists of listing the major activities performed by any person holding the job of interest. People are critical elements of any agency's core technology and roles should be described in terms of the production process within which they work. If this is done properly, a comprehensive and meaningful assessment of staffing requirements may follow.

In the illustrative agency the program officer is the primary production worker. A list of the activities performed by staff holding this job was developed from in-depth interviews with several program officers from different areas. Several versions of this list were developed before the program officers agreed that the generic list was essentially complete. This list of activities was further categorized into three major groups: program management (obtaining budgets), project management (spending budgets), and administrative management. Exhibit 6.3 lists each group's activities. Further elaboration of these roles clarified the nature of the core technology and how the program officer makes it operational.

The Program Officer must participate in several tasks before a budget request for OMB and for Congress can be formulated and internally approved. Those program management activities include: identifying program goals; monitoring program performance; planning budgets; and explaining goals, performance measures, and budgets to the program officer's superior. Performance of these tasks requires that a program officer participate in two formal budgeting exercises annually: long-range program planning and preparation of the next year's budget request. Program

---

Exhibit 6.3
Major activities of program officers

A. *Program Management*
   1. Program Objectives & Domain (Maintain knowledge of field, read journals, attend scientific meetings, etc.)
   2. Program Budgets
      a. Long-range planning and preliminary budget estimates
      b. Budget to OMB
      c. Budget to Congress
      d. Testimony and budget responses
   3. Program Initiative and Research
      a. Program guidelines, announcements and responses to requests for program information
      b. Workshops and conferences
      c. Site visits
   4. Program Coordination
      a. Internal coordination with other programs, divisions, directorates
      b. External coordination with other agencies
      c. Official U.S. delegation and representational activities
      d. Review proposals for other programs
   5. Program Review and Oversight
      a. Program review
      b. Advisory committee

B. *Project Management*[a]
   1. Proposal development
   2. Proposal review and selection
   3. Project monitoring
   4. Project evaluation and dissemination of results

C. *Administration (General)*

D. *Center Facilities Management*[b]
   1. Grant/contract planning and funding and administration
   2. Site visits, studies, and evaluation
   3. User scheduling or monitoring

Note: A comprehensive list. Each program officer does not engage in all of these activities.
[a] These are almost entirely extramural projects (grants and contracts), although some programs occasionally have intramural projects (conducted by staff).
[b] A very specialized set of activities involving only a small number of program officers.

officers must also read journals and attend seminars and other meetings in order to maintain knowledge of their specialties. The other major program management activities are participating in recruiting and personnel matters, allocating and supervising clerical work, responding to requests for information, and receiving visitors.

    Project management, in brief, involves selecting the projects to fund and monitoring project performance. After the review process is completed, proposals are ranked by the program officer according to the reviewers' ratings. Highly rated proposals are funded, subject to the availability of program funds. Several processing tasks, to be performed by the program officer, are associated with these reviews and recommendations. Also, although the program officer position is not primarily supervisory, some participation in administrative matters, such as weekly staff meetings, is required. In summary, it is important that all significant activities be identified and organized around major functions of the job being analyzed.

List of operational tasks

The project management work load of the program officer depends directly upon the number of proposals received by the program. Work standards for these project management activities should therefore be expressed per unit of input (for example, hours per proposed project). Such estimates require the identification of a sequential series of tasks which together result in the award decision. Exhibit 6.4 is a comprehensive list of functional tasks for the program officer.[4] The task list is a refinement of the corresponding functional activities in Exhibit 6.3. While management is usually able to identify the broad activities of subordinate production workers, it may not be able to itemize the individual tasks; in government, it is quite common for operations managers never to have held the lower production positions in their agency. The task list must be constructed, or at least reviewed, by those who have held the job of interest.

Estimating norms for work activities

After the tasks for each of the key productive roles have been listed, the next step is estimating the normal time required to complete each task. As in the traditional method of work measurement, the concept of a norm is grounded in current practice. A *norm* is not an ideal target or standard of excellence, but rather, it is a reasonable time estimate, given the prevailing situation and caliber of personnel.

Estimating norms for work activities requires greater participation and takes more time and energy than all the other steps in the analytic process. First, a sample of personnel is used to create initial sets of estimates. In our illustrative agency, representatives from each division analyzed the original estimates and constructed a table of program officers' work norms for each kind of program. It is critical that the initial time estimates are reasonable for competent, qualified personnel. If the established norms do not accurately measure the time needed to perform a task, they will be of limited value in predicting staff requirements. Furthermore, this

---

Exhibit 6.4
Sample list of work tasks of the program officer:
proposal review and selection and project monitoring

Read proposal

Select reviewers or panelists

Communicate with reviewers or panelists
   letters and phone calls
   assemble review materials

Monitor reviews
   read and file reviews
   decide on need for additional reviews

Perform site visits (occasional)
   arrange and schedule
   prepare material
   conduct visit
   prepare report

Attend meetings (same kinds of tasks as site visits, also occasional)

Coordinate decisions
   with other programs
   with other federal agencies

Formulate award recommendation (support, decline, hold)
   analyze reviews received
   communicate with proposed investigators (occasional)
   document recommendations for the most and least competitive proposals
   decide on accumulated "hold" proposals
   prepare final recommendation

Prepare materials for award review board meetings (occasional)

Participate in award review board meetings

Monitor grant after award

Note: Refer to B2 and B3 in Exhibit 6.3.

---

analysis should not be conducted in small offices, which tend to be structured so that each person is solely responsible for certain activities. It is generally not worth the effort to try to set norms for a job in which only one person is employed, since the purpose of the norm-setting analysis is to plan overall staffing levels for the agency by creating average estimates of productivity for entire groups of personnel performing the same tasks.

In our illustrative agency, the norms for each grant program office were assumed to be similar unless a strong case was made that notable differences existed. It was agreed in advance that the ultimate arbiter of any unresolvable difference of opinions would be the agency director. This process of negotiation, though awkward at first, was very effective once the participants became familiar with the nature of the exercise. Participants commented that this step in the staffing planning exercise was extremely informative as it brought to light a number of fundamental differences in the way that various divisions were conducting the same business of awarding grants.

Standardization of the production process across the agency is necessary to predict accurately total staffing needs. Exhibit 6.5 is a table of sample work norms for the tasks performed by certain program officers. A few elaborations may help to illustrate the level of analysis required at this step in the personnel planning exercise. Program management tasks, it will be recalled, are based largely on an annual cycle of planning and budgeting events and have little to do with the size, scope, and content of the particular grants program itself. This is also largely true of the administrative tasks. Project management, in contrast, can vary from one program to another, depending on the volume and type of proposals, number of active grants, and the relative availability of new program

Exhibit 6.5
Sample of work norms for program officer:
management and project management research support

Activity		Norms
Program Management		(days/year)
planning, budgeting, interagency coordination		13
seminars, program officer's meetings		15
staff operations		8
other (special requests, office visits)		22
	Subtotal	58
Project Management		
site visits, project monitoring		20
strategic knowledge of scientific field		50
panel meetings		8
proposal review, selection and postawards actions[a]		91
	Subtotal	169
Total Days Required Per Year[b]		227

[a] Calculated as follows:

Item	Last Year's Quantity	Estimate of Unit Time Required
reviewed proposal	132	6 hours/proposal
unreviewed proposal	90	1.5 hours/proposal
active grant	136	3.3 hours/year/grant
board review package	2	40 hours/package

Total Time Required   = 1455 hours
Number of Program Officers =   2
Time/Program Officer   =   91 days/year

[b] This is a "balanced" set of work norms as there are 227 days available/person year (261 working days less a total of 34 holidays and leave days.)

funds. The project management estimates in Exhibit 6.5 resulted from task-by-task estimates of the tasks listed in Exhibit 6.4.

The initial estimation of norms should be done on a program-by-program basis until a pattern begins to emerge and a consensus can be reached, as described above, that certain average estimates are realistic for specified groups of programs. In the descriptions which follow, note the differences between this systems approach and the traditional work measurement technique described earlier in this chapter.

Most of the estimates of the normal time needed to complete tasks are handled on an aggregate annual basis: for example, staff operations account for all efforts regarding the acquisition and use of staff by the program. This would comprise many individual actions such as recruitment of new personnel, allocation of work, and supervision of secretaries or administrative assistants. The aggregate figure would be a "best guess" of those program officers who work in the program under investigation. It would not be compiled from a rigorous time study in which random samples of program officers' activities were measured throughout the year.

Estimating the normal time needed for project management activities is more complex. It requires separate consideration for the different kinds of tasks that fit within this broad job category. Even then, the separate components are estimated "on average": no two proposal reviews require the identical amount of effort. The norms, as explained above, represent professional judgments on how the program officer's time should be spent. The implication is that a qualified and diligent program officer who spends more than ninety-one days on proposal review, award selection, and monitoring is considered to be "overworked" on these tasks. That is, either the quality of review and decision making will be less than desired (if all grant actions are forced to stay within the ninety-one-day aggregate) or other tasks will suffer (if the ninety-one-day aggregate is exceeded and norms for other tasks are thus unmet). The possibility that a program officer may be unacceptably incompetent, careless, slow, or lazy is not excluded. However, this is a matter for supervisory concern and is separate from the planning of aggregate staff levels.

The method of calculating the aggregate time for the project management tasks is essentially a weighted sum based on the mix of tasks in the actual program work loads. This approach allows for comparisons of aggregate norms across programs. When projections of future work loads are considered, a manager can generate annual work requirements and see how they differ from the present. Differences reflect changed requirements for personnel, given current work norms.

Comparisons of work requirements for different parts of the agency help to identify programs which are likely to create more or less pressure on the program officers. This comparative analysis provides quantitative inputs to the critical planning question: How many more (or less) personnel should be requested for each division in the upcoming budget? Given a fixed number ("a ceiling") of personnel slots available to the agency as a whole, how should staff resources be allocated? In answering these questions, management from across the agency must meet and review the various norms and work load projections. They may decide to reevaluate the norms for various work tasks, a matter which is tied indirectly to agency policy.

In summary, norms are established in order to estimate the staff levels needed to perform all required production tasks at an acceptable level of quality. Other operational issues may arise in practice, but more detailed discussion is beyond the scope of this chapter.

Estimating production staffing needs

Once the norms for all operational tasks are developed, managers can begin to assess staffing needs for the agency. However, norms alone are not sufficient to make this decision; an estimate of demand is an integral part of the staffing decision. After the various program managers have projected the likely demand for these services in the coming year, the required staff levels can be calculated.[5]

Estimating supervisory and administrative support

Work standards for support staff can be assessed using a process similar to that used to determine the production staff level. In addition to setting work norms, management must decide what support activities are consistent with program objectives. The calculation of support staff requirements is similar to the method used to figure the production staff needed.

A note on implementation

Implementation of this systems approach to personnel planning proceeds in stages: the initial development of new techniques; their preliminary use in actual decision making; wide participation in their refinement, testing, and implementation; and finally, institutionalization of procedures and data bases for formulating, maintaining, and controlling future staff allocations. The elaborate procedures for accomplishing these ends are dictated by the highly interactive technical approach that was developed. Even before implementation was completed at the illustrative agency, a noticeable conceptual shift had occurred within the agency's debates about staff levels. Generalizations about needs for staff yielded to specifics about norms and priorities of tasks and the impacts of alternative policies on task definitions. Such changes in bureaucratic discussion may signal the emergency of new perspectives on efficient use of personnel. Although the illustrative agency may have been particularly ripe for this approach, it still took time before one could establish whether meaningful institutionalization had occurred. The first cycle or two of such a planning exercise are bound to be instructive.

Reflections on the systems approach to personnel planning

Any organizational planning model involves making prior assumptions about the significant features of the organization, especially establishing the relative importance of different aspects of performance.[6] The proposed method for developing disaggregated staffing plans in government agencies is no exception. Several general reflections emerge on the nature of the personnel planning problem, this methodological approach, and the significance of these kinds of projects.

First, consider the setting in which this kind of analysis occurs. Government organizations and operations rarely develop according to comprehensive plans. As mentioned in chapter 2, in the discussion of operations life cycles, public programs usually start chaotically, in response to a sudden legislative or administrative mandate that a particular service "shall be provided" or that a new set of regulations "shall be enforced." Initial program operations then develop incrementally until a steady state is reached. After reaching steady state, actual operations reflect many informal and undocumented work practices. Through the stages of development, group cultures and stylistic differences emerge as operating practices, and procedures evolve for various subdivisions of the agency. Procedural manuals will usually be prepared only for those operations which are repetitious or legally delicate. It is in this typical organizational setting that personnel planning procedures must be established.

Management scientists and policy analysts are quick to point to the triad of multiple performance measures for public agencies. Efficiency, effectiveness, and equity (defined in chapters 3 and 4) have become familiar terms in our national rhetoric. A natural question, therefore, is the extent to which a staff planning exercise should address these three concepts. The approaches presented in this chapter aim directly at the notion of efficiency—the relationship between organizational inputs (specifically staff resources) and outputs (the services which the agency produces in response to its actual objectives). This approach is particularly appropriate when the personnel planning exercise is designed to be part of an annual budgetary cycle.

In the wake of Planning-Programming-Budgeting Systems (PPBS) and zero-base budgeting (ZBB) experiences in the late 1960s and 1970s, it is naive to expect an agency to examine the effectiveness and equity of each of its organizational components whenever it submits a budget request. Efficiency, in contrast, is more appropriate as a continuing concern of management throughout an agency, especially in the prevailing mood of fiscal scarcity. If legislatures demand tighter staffing budgets, management must first look at the relative efficiency of its various operations, with an implicit acceptance of effectiveness and equity. This is not to say that effectiveness and equity are unimportant, but there are strong political and bureaucratic forces at work encouraging independent assessment of efficiency. Therefore, in the design and implementation of the staff planning process, staffing requirements are determined through a detailed examination of the efficient allocation of staff across the agency, without explicit analysis of the relative effectiveness and equity of the agency's outputs.

It should be clear, however, that this method is only one short step away from dealing directly with notions of effectiveness or equity. After preparing a map of current organizational practices and estimating the prevailing norms for executing the tasks associated with these practices, managers examine the differences in norms for completing the various work tasks. Comparisons of these norms across divisions of an agency— or even intensive scrutiny of the norms for a single program—lead directly to examinations of the quality of the service being delivered and issues of effectiveness and equity inevitably arise.

A major contribution of the proposed technique is its ability to link management knowledge to actions relating to personnel allocation. The analytic methods define the required personnel needs as a function of operational tasks and demand levels. Their use discourages top management from yielding to the "squeaky wheel," where supervisors with the loudest and most frequent complaints about "overworked staff" get the greatest personnel increases. In contrast, the proposed approach to establishing norms is designed, based on prior steps in the technical approach, to be comprehensive. All tasks performed by those working in the key productive roles are specified. This explicit analysis helps managers to explain in complete operational terms what their personnel actually do. Thus, the common tendency to construct unrealistic, partial stereotypes of organizational roles can be avoided. The resulting data and perspectives promote more rational discussions of personnel requirements.

The direct experience and operational intuition of a good supervisor provide a legitimate understanding of personnel needs. The proposed methods force supervisors to make their knowledge more explicit within a comparative operational framework. This is a valuable opportunity for discussion, reflection, and compromise. Top management's direct contact with daily operations and current practice tends to be both rare and random, although these officials are responsible for agency-wide personnel allocation decisions. Since total resources are never sufficient to satisfy all the supervisors' staffing wishes, policymakers need routine analytic procedures to help establish which department's personnel needs are more critical to the overall organization. The proposed methods provide a planning capacity which encourages top management to examine existing alternatives and to assess the competence of supervisors advocating their personnel requests. In short, while all managerial decisions, including staffing allocations, are ultimately judgments based on the particular experience of those who participate, analytic procedures can facilitate a more systematic process for making such judgments.

Summary

In assessing the value of the systems approach to staff planning, we must understand what is *not* accomplished by this method. To avoid some possible misconceptions, consider these concluding observations:

☐ This chapter has not dealt with short-term scheduling of operations but rather with strategic resource planning.

☐ Work norms are not to be used for performance appraisal of individual staff members but rather for the allocation of aggregate staff resources.

☐ The measurement of work activities does not directly lead to the redesign of jobs but rather accepts the existing job scope and contents.

☐ These analytic procedures, accordingly, are descriptive rather than prescriptive: they are not aimed primarily at productivity improvement.

☐ The emphasis on describing staffing requirements leads to an examination of actual work tasks (not overall responsibilities) and of specific existing work norms (not general statements of organizational priorities).

The planning of personnel requirements for the various divisions of a government agency is a prerequisite to the preparation of reasonable operational budgets. Sometimes traditional work measurement techniques can lead to estimates of particular staff requirements within a single program of an agency. However, the systems approach to personnel planning presented in this chapter is likely to be more appropriate for public sector agencies with large professional staffs. Successful application of the systems approach will lead directly to the efficient allocation of personnel, given prevailing agency policies, procedures, and budgetary limitations.

Perhaps equally important, the process of conducting periodic agency-wide personnel planning exercises can promote more basic inquiries about the policies and performance of the agency.

Discussion questions

1. Public managers are often pressured by public employee unions to increase staffing levels and wages. On the other hand, legislatures are concerned with reducing costs and eliminating unneeded positions. As a public manager faced with this conflict, what value would the systems approach to staff planning have in developing support for your personnel requests as you negotiate with both unions and the legislature?

2. Chapter 2 discussed the general characteristics of a production system. The approach to personnel planning presented in this chapter is a special kind of production system. Outline the necessary inputs and processes to produce the desired output (determination of the needed staff to adequately provide required services).

3. In the establishment of work norms, the use of competent, qualified personnel is central to the development of accurate norms. What criteria can a manager employ to ensure that the analyst observes appropriate employees? What information would help a manager determine which employees should be used to establish these norms?

4. The implementation of any work measurement program—using either a traditional or a systems approach—can have unexpected negative consequences, such as reduced employee morale, active or passive resistance, or loss of productivity. What cues of these problems should a manager look for when implementing work measurement techniques? Can such problems be avoided? How?

Notes

[*]This chapter is adapted from "Planning for Governmental Efficiency Through Staffing Allocation" by Frederick W. Betz and Stephen R. Rosenthal, *International Journal of Public Administration* 3 (2) 1981, 157–188. Copyright © 1981 by Marcel Dekker, Inc. Reprinted by permission of Marcel Dekker, Inc.

[1] The management science literature on production planning includes this focus. See Peterson and Silver (1979) for a recent survey. Applications naturally lag behind research contributions but are widespread for the less sophisticated forecasting and planning models.

[2] Many writings on Planning-Programming-Budgeting Systems (PPBS) appeared during the late 1960s and early 1970s. A statement of the hopes for PPBS is contained in Schick (1966); its reality is summed up in Schick (1973). The development of zero-base budgeting (ZBB) is more recent. See Phyrr (1973).

[3] This request and the agency response illustrate the importance of the budgetary process as a natural mechanism for forcing improved planning of staffing levels. See Wildavsky (1964) for general arguments along these lines.

[4] The actual list that was developed and used at the subject agency was somewhat more detailed in two respects: it contained a more refined list of tasks and it identified four

different types of proposals. In practice, the list should be as detailed as possible, to the point where separate estimates of work processing norms still have a practical significance.
[5] This assumes that all efforts will be made to satisfy the projected demand. If, however, initial demand projections exceed the maximum capacity likely to be achieved, a strategy of demand management (the subject of chapter 7) is advisable.
[6] It is important to note that in the absence of mechanisms for personnel planning and productivity measurement, there is little likelihood of being able to conduct rigorous performance appraisals of management, as prescribed in the U.S. Civil Service Reform Act of 1979.

Bibliography

Barnes, Ralph M. *Motion and Time Study: Design and Measurement of Work*. 6th ed. New York: John Wiley and Sons, 1968.

Chase, Richard B., and Nicholas J. Aquilano. *Production and Operations Management*. Homewood, Ill.: Irwin, 1981.

Churchman, C. West. *The Design of Inquiring Systems*. New York: Basic Books, 1971.

Hatry, Harry P.; Louis H. Blair; Donald M. Fisk; John M. Greiner; John R. Hall, Jr.; and Philip S. Schaenman. *How Effective Are Your Community Services*. Washington, D.C.: The Urban Institute, 1977.

Katz, Daniel, and Robert L. Kahn. *The Social Psychology of Organizations*. New York: John Wiley and Sons, 1966.

Peterson, Rein, and Edward A. Silver. *Decision Systems for Inventory Management and Production Planning*. New York: John Wiley and Sons, 1979.

Pyhrr, Peter A. *Zero-Base Budgeting*. New York: John Wiley and Sons, 1973.

San Diego Program Evaluation and Productivity Improvement Project. *Automotive Maintenance Unit of the San Diego Police Department*. San Diego, Calif., 1975.

Schick, A. "The Road to PPB: The Stages of Budget Reform." *Public Administration Review*, December 1966, pp. 243–58.

———. "A Death in the Bureaucracy: The Demise of Federal PPB." *Public Administration Review*, March–April 1973, pp. 146–56.

Stahl, O. Glenn. *Public Personnel Administration*. New York: Harper and Row, 1962.

Taylor, Frederick. *Principles of Scientific Management*. New York: Harper Brothers, 1911.

Udler, A. "Productivity Measurement of Administrative Services." *Personnel Journal*, December 1978, pp. 672–75.

United States Office of Personnel Management. *The New Jersey Public Works Performance Standards Study*. Washington, D.C.: U.S. Government Printing Office, 1981.

Wildavsky, Aaron. *The Politics of the Budgetary Process*. Boston: Little, Brown & Co., 1964.

Chapter 7
Demand Management

The management of a public service delivery system can be viewed as the task of achieving a successful balance between demand and supply, given prevailing constraints on alternative actions.[1] To an operating manager, in government, demand for a public service is more than an aggregation of people or dollars. It is a set of requirements that particular responses be made at a specified time and place. The kind of "demand" that is of primary interest is often implied in statements of organizational goals which identify desired program outcomes.[2] Service "supply" refers both to the ways in which resources are allocated to establish the service and to the resulting patterns of service delivery. Effective management of service system operations requires the identification of patterns of service demand and supply, the specification of related service delivery "problems," and the formulation of strategic interventions throughout the life of the service. This chapter presents a conceptual framework and some managerial approaches for assessing service demand and supply. A heightened appreciation of these concepts will help policy analysts and program directors to improve the management of public operations.

The concept of demand management

The basic premises of this chapter are:

☐ Program performance in government is often largely determined by the public demand for the program;

☐ Public officials may be able to affect the demand for service through policies and procedures that define the supply of the service.

To improve the performance of a public service system, managers should attempt to identify ways in which supply and demand interact. For some public services, the standard market mechanism of altering the price may be employed intentionally to manipulate demand. Transit systems, for example, may try to boost ridership by offering special off-peak fares. Service delivery may also be characterized by its relative availability or attractiveness. Changes in the availability of a service (for example, the schedule of clinic hours for walk-in preventive health care) or its attractiveness (for example, the physical and social environment in such clinics) are other common ways to affect service demand in desired directions.

Sometimes the effective demand for a service may seem essentially independent of the way in which it is supplied. Managers, however, should seek practical exceptions to this general impression. A program which is set up to provide relief to victims of natural disasters, for example, cannot influence the number or severity of floods or earthquakes by improving its ability to respond with needed emergency support. But the availability of disaster relief funds can influence the demand for its use: any particular natural disaster is more likely to lead to requests for aid if a program of relief with substantial available resources exists. Furthermore, such a program is more likely to consider a request to be "legitimate" if indeed there are surplus resources.

Similar examples readily come to mind. Consider the demand for a public health service such as an immunization program established to protect citizens from an impending flu epidemic. If anyone potentially vulnerable to the flu is considered eligible for immunization, the demand for a special flu vaccine will rise in direct response to an outbreak of that disease. The effective demand may be restricted, however, by declaring—perhaps in response to a limited supply of available vaccine—that only certain population groups are eligible for immunization. Demand may also decline, less directly, if the available vaccine turns out to induce a dangerous side effect and if eligible recipients choose to ignore the offered treatment.[3] An understanding that decisions on the supply of a public service may lead to changes in the demand for it is a first step toward developing a strategy for demand management.[4]

Management-relevant dimensions of demand

Public managers need to ask several questions about the demand that they seek to satisfy. Who are the current and potential clients (or users)? Do the clients all require the same standard service? Or are their needs different either in degree or in kind? Where are these clients (or users)? Location is important, since the service will either have to be brought to the clients (or users) or they will have to be transported to the service (refuse collection is an example of the former, and neighborhood health clinics of the latter). The timing of demand is also likely to be of interest, since this will affect schedules and capacity requirements. In short, the relevant attributes of service demand are related to: *Who* wants *what* service? *Where*? And *when*?

The degree of attention to be paid to such questions will vary from one service delivery system to another and will also depend upon the kinds of managerial decisions to be made. Two organizations providing trans-portation-related services—a state department of highways and a munici-pal emergency ambulance program—provide an illustrative contrast. A state department of highways needs to develop statistical forecasts of the peak capacity that is likely to be required along particular sections of an existing or planned highway link. Planners must construct traffic projec-tions which are partially derived from broad considerations of travel be-havior (work versus shopping trips). In defining the number of lanes re-quired, highway planners need not collect detailed information on the exact purposes of each highway use or personal profiles of those who use the highway system. A municipal emergency ambulance service, in con-trast, requires a much more refined knowledge of the needs of its users. Some users may represent a life-or-death situation and need specialized forms of service (on-site treatment), while others who request service do not require it (noncritical calls). For the ambulance system, quality of service depends on the ability to respond to each particular event as it occurs, and very specific information is required on the time, the place, and (probably) the situation regarding each incoming call.

Policy-relevant dimensions of supply

Public managers may affect the supply of a service through their selection and control of facilities, equipment, personnel, and sources of funding. To make reasonable choices, they need to understand the ways in which the supply of the service may affect its subsequent demand. Public statements in the form of promises for (or simply information on the existence of) a service can greatly stimulate demand, as can a successful demonstration program. Curtailment of demand can result from poor information, in-adequate performance, or restrictive practices. For example, in the early years of the national food stamp program, there was confusion and con-flict about whether the program was primarily a public support system for farmers or a welfare program for the poor. As a result, the original pricing structure inadvertently excluded participation by those at the lower end of the income scale. During that initial period, clients of the program were perceived to be farmers, rather than the lowest income consumers; sub-sequently, however, the poor came to be considered the primary source of demand. However, as public officials refine their appreciation of the demand for a service, they can develop and maintain a compatible service delivery configuration: food stamps were subsequently priced so as to be more accessible to the lowest income citizens.[5]

The supply of a public service is characterized by its quantity, equity, and quality as well as by its "price" (which is often complicated by the extent and source of subsidy). Each of these attributes needs to be analyzed for its operational significance. Service quantity is distributed in particular temporal and geographical patterns and may be offered in different forms. These are the production outputs discussed in chapter 3. Also, as described in chapter 4, the public sector is obliged to be equitable in its supply of services: if a police emergency phone number exists, it must be available to all citizens, not just to selected groups, and access to it cannot depend on callers' ability to pay. Perhaps the most complex attribute of public service delivery is its quality. Timeliness, accessibility, convenience, and reliability are important indicators of service quality. Remember that for most services (for example, mass transit) more than one indicator will have some significance; the important question is which ones tend to affect demand most (for example, ridership decisions). The balancing of service demand and supply calls for careful attention to these multiple dimensions of supply.

Responding to mismatches

A mismatch between service demand and supply occurs when there is evidence that the quantity or quality of the program outputs are either excessive or inadequate. When such mismatches are perceived, a managerial (and/or policy) response is needed. Perhaps demand can be altered by pricing innovations, reservation systems, or the offering of new related services. Or, supply might be controlled by reallocating manpower, equipment, or facilities. Often there will be more than one way to respond and a choice will have to be made. The transportation-related examples cited earlier offer some illustrations of such alternatives. A traditional solution to excessive peak hour highway demand is to alter the actual supply of highway facilities by constructing additional lanes for the highway link in question; a more recent energy-efficient strategy is to alter the effective peak hour demand. This can be accomplished by policies which affect the allocation of existing facilities, as when one lane is designated for restricted use (express buses or car pools), thereby encouraging commuters not to ride alone in their autos. Other policies, such as flex time or staggered shifts, exert direct impacts on demand patterns during the day, thereby reducing congestion without expanding existing highway facilities.

The director of a municipal ambulance program might try to reduce the effective service demand by ordering that incoming calls be screened more thoroughly to determine whether the situation requires emergency response; other methods of improving the supply of this service include changing the ambulance districts or the dispatch procedures, or upgrading or expanding the fleet of vehicles (Savas, 1969). In any particular situation, a public manager should respond to demand/supply mismatches in ways that reflect the structure of the service delivery system as well as the kinds of actions that are considered feasible at the time.

Perceiving "problems" as demand/supply mismatches

Policy analysts, program designers and public managers who are likely to discover opportunities for demand management pay attention to the questions and concepts outlined above. In particular, the collection and analysis of demand and supply data must be adequate for probing beneath superficial indicators of program success or failure. Unintentional and indirect relationships between supply and demand must be identified and described, as must those which are more obviously intentional and direct.

Consider once again the example of the national food stamp program. In assessing the success of the food stamp program, one must do more than tabulate how many stamps are being sold in different regions of the country. Such facts will not suffice to answer the questions: Is the program too small? Is it too large? Does it need to be redesigned? If food stamps are supposed to ensure that everyone is able to achieve a diet of adequate nutritional value, then those concerned with the performance of the program would be better served to learn the following: the extent to which those who need food stamps for this purpose are eligible for them, the extent to which those who are not eligible for food stamps are actually participating in the program, why some choose not to participate, and perhaps even the extent to which the purchase of food stamps leads to the provision of nutritional diets.

Strategic interactions through time

The proposed strategy of matching demand and supply must be implemented throughout the life of the program. It is of little value to make a good decision at one point, only to fail to adapt when conditions change. Most public service delivery systems will require modifications. In part this is due to shifts in environmental conditions, such as altered public values and norms and new constraints on governmental resources. Furthermore, at various points in the life of a government program, elements of the demand for and supply of a service may be expected to change.

A manager of a new program is likely to be concerned with achieving a particular quantity of services supplied in order to demonstrate the existence of a market: a new drug abuse program, a legal assistance project, an equal employment opportunity office, or a community health center often will act quickly to develop an adequate clientele. This is an understandable first step when those responsible for a program feel the need to justify newly provided resources. Subsequently, as the program matures, it is typical and appropriate that public managers initiate a more refined examination of who is being served (equity) and how well (effectiveness).

As time passes, relationships between the demand for a service and its supply will shift. Policymakers, managers, and planners must expect that changes in the scope, distribution, and content of demand will alter the perceived performance of the program. A delivery system which has long been stable may suddenly experience a gap between the available capacity and the desire for service. For example, the National Park Service is a recent dramatic case in which a relatively fixed set of facilities is becoming subject to more intensive usage by broader segments of the population, creating the potential for extensive damage to those facilities.

Conversely, changes in the capacity, procedures, and quality of the supplied service may affect the subsequent demand. Such impacts often occur in unintended directions. Mandatory sentencing, for example, is directed to law enforcement goals but may also result in increasing the population of already crowded correctional facilities, since inmates who have received such sentences are ineligible for early parole. The lack of prison space, in turn, may lead to a widespread pattern of convictions for lesser offenses that do not carry fixed penalties, a result which is in contradiction to the original notion of mandatory sentencing. Consider also the possible effect of inadequate program performance on subsequent demand. An equal opportunity agency, for example, may consistently fail to settle charges of discrimination against certain employers. Because of such problems in quality of service delivery, other employers may not take voluntary affirmative action to eliminate discrimination in their own employment practices. This, in turn, is likely to result in an increase in the number of new charges of discrimination brought to the equal opportunity agency.

Chapter 2 outlined how the scope and contents of a public program may be shaped by actions that were taken at prior stages of the life cycle of an operating system. Hence it becomes particularly important that current decisions be consistent with plans for the future. The concepts of demand management presented here can help to provide an overall coherence to program management through time. Then, as time passes, shifts in the scope, distribution, and content of demand will stimulate deliberate changes in the supply of a service delivery system. Meanwhile, changes in the quantity, quality, and (perhaps) price of the supplied service will, in turn, affect subsequent demand. Use of this management strategy requires an organizational capability for identifying the available options and for acquiring the relevant diagnostic information in time to stimulate corrective action.

Guidelines for developing a diagnostic capability

The balancing of service demand and supply within existing constraints is not easy to achieve. The major operational tasks likely to be involved are: bringing assumptions to the surface; creating and updating appropriate demand profiles; and identifying how changes in supply tend to affect demand. These tasks are outlined below in terms of the kind of issues that may arise and the alternative strategies that may be pursued. These guidelines, however, are only a first step. For any particular program application, analytic and managerial judgments will be required from the major participants in order to achieve the design, development, and implementation of the proposed diagnostic capability. Note that these guidelines assume that the key actors want to eliminate mismatches between service demand and supply. Before launching such an initiative, top management must first consider whether the problem of excess demand may originate with operations managers and their staff. Especially in times of fiscal crisis, some managers may try to market their programs as vigorously as possible as a device for raising future operating budgets. Any such attempts must be stopped if the proposed guidelines are to be effective.

Bringing assumptions to the surface

The design and operation of any service delivery system reflects a series of assumptions about the potential and actual demand for the service and the ways in which that system will satisfy it. Premature program failure can easily result from leaving basic assumptions and judgments implicit and creating an early situation in which demand and supply are critically mismatched. Throughout the life of a service delivery system, public managers should articulate and review prevailing assumptions and judgments in an attempt to signal needs and directions for subsequent policy or program investigations. Naturally, political and bureaucratic forces will impede complete openness and explicitness, but in most situations there is probably already much more being said or implied about the expected development of an ongoing program than is currently being codified for subsequent examination. It is unlikely that a coherent set of consistent assumptions and judgments will emerge, but it is still feasible and fruitful to identify those which are already evident to the major participants.[6]

In attempting to make more of these items explicit, one should attempt to distinguish factual matters from those which are value based. Assumptions of fact include characteristics of the population being served or relationships between different program activities and the output of the delivery system. The design and development of the Bay Area Rapid Transit System (BART), for example, assumed that automobile commuters could be enticed into using a different method of transportation (Webber, 1976). Value-based judgments, in contrast, would include the relative priorities among different potential client groups, minimum acceptable service quality standards, or definitions of what is considered to be a legitimate demand. A recent issue in some states is whether currently unemployed but employable persons should be denied certain general assistance program benefits. Though different in kind, factual assumptions and value judgments should be considered together, since they often interact in their impacts on program design and performance. Even when it becomes difficult to differentiate factual and value-based assumptions, public managers who make the effort may gain an improved understanding of the kinds of information needed to test those assumptions.

To the extent possible, such assumptions and judgments should be acknowledged when the program is initiated. Doing so will establish what the program originally was intended to accomplish and why certain approaches were taken. At a minimum, these assumptions and judgments will serve as a set of hypotheses for subsequent review and modification. If conditions permit a more deliberate approach, a carefully targeted market research effort to explore certain key assumptions might be included in the early stages of the program. For example, under what conditions will members of various potential market segments be likely to use the new service if it is delivered in the intended manner? Such research can be especially important at early stages, before new legislation or administrative directives, specifying how the new program will be organized and delivered, are formulated. Current policy analysis efforts, however, rarely address this level of operational feasibility (Williams, 1975). And needs assessments based on questionnaires or interviews are often divorced from operation realities such as client behavior and current constraints on service delivery.

Sometimes a program must begin on short notice, and there is no time for preliminary market testing. Under such conditions, it could be strategically wise to avoid making many program specifications (procedures, job definitions, staffing constraints) before the service is launched. A more attractive alternative could be an extensive (or delayed) start-up period, during which basic assumptions would be subject to an appropriate level of analysis and debate. In this spirit, "demonstration programs" of limited scope and experimental procedures and practices, coupled with an evaluation component, are a form of "action diagnosis" that has become increasingly common (Riecken & Boruch, 1974). In general, the examination of various options for delivery provides an opportunity to test a range of assumptions about how a new service might operate and how the market is likely to respond to those options. Technical skills in operations analysis, such as those discussed in chapters 3 and 4, are likely to be particularly useful in such ventures.

Creating and updating appropriate demand profiles

Program evaluation is becoming increasingly common throughout government. In the more sophisticated areas of public management, evaluations are performed throughout the life of a public service program to provide policymakers and managers with indications of the program's impact. User or client profiles are important indicators of this impact—such profiles identify who is being served. Demographic cross tabulations and statistical summaries are becoming familiar ingredients in ascertaining the equity of a program. The extent of information that should be included in any particular demand profile will depend, as mentioned earlier, upon the factors that have managerial significance.

The manager of an emergency ambulance service, for example, will want to know the hours during which requests for service are received, the locations from which those requests came, the reasons for requesting service, and the actual need in each case as discovered by the ambulance drivers when they arrived. Such demand-based statistics are necessary inputs for calculating the spatial and temporal distribution of the apparent demand and determining the differences between anticipated and actual requirements for on-site treatment. These are crucial inputs for assessing how well this service system is being managed, specifically its responsiveness to peak demands and spatial disaggregation, and the accuracy with which incoming calls are screened.

For some service delivery systems, a profile of "frequency of use" might be of particular value. The knowledge of how often and for what reasons a given building comes to the attention of a housing code enforcement program provides an indication of the overall condition of the building and the likely extent of negligence of its owner. Such measures are important in developing an appropriate program response. Sometimes investigations of nonusers of the service can be especially significant; understanding the major reasons people choose not to use available mass transit facilities (for example, poor access, discomfort, or unreliability) will help transit managers to select meaningful improvements to the service.

The specifications of what should be included in a demand profile is a trade-off decision between the potential usefulness of the information and the dollar and social cost of acquiring that knowledge. A major indicator of the usefulness of a demand profile is the extent to which it may signal needed adjustments in the supply of the service. In the emergency ambulance example, several types of actions might be taken. First, reallocation of ambulances within a district (or redistricting) could bring supply more in line with the geographic distribution of demand. Second, reallocation of ambulance crews between the day and night shifts could serve the same function in the temporal dimension. Third, improved screening of incoming calls could reduce the number of nonemergency responses. Demand profiles maintained during the entire life of the program can provide useful indicators of the need for such program revision. Such profiles are likely to indicate patterns of use or need that the program in its current form is ill-equipped to handle. These profiles may even make it clear that termination of the program is advisable, for example, when it turns out to be serving mainly "illegitimate" or nonpriority demands. Additional considerations in the cost/benefit trade-offs from new information systems is presented in chapter 9.

Identifying how changes in supply tend to affect demand

The supply side of a service delivery system must also be monitored and related to service demand. It is not sufficient to stay within budget; it is just as important to strive to deliver a greater quantity and quality of service within that budget, or even to figure out how to run an adequate program on a decreased budget.

Policymakers, program managers, and planners who seek to learn from service demand profiles need an up-to-date and accurate picture of the supply side of their operations. As discussed in chapter 3, public managers need meaningful measures of the output and performance levels of their programs. Inspections made, miles of streets plowed, court cases processed are examples of the outputs (though not necessarily the performance levels) of some different services. Such outputs must be combined with measures of the associated inputs: inspector-hours available, plow shifts available and plows requiring repairs, or police hours spent in courtrooms. The difficulty in measuring performance levels by comparing a program's achievement with its target standards, has already been discussed. Nevertheless, developing such monitoring systems for supply operations may be less problematic than doing so for demand, since a considerable emphasis is typically placed on these types of measurements by those who develop and review program budgets.

Monitoring the supply of a service delivery system is only part of the necessary diagnostic capability. Program managers must also learn how changes in supply tend to affect demand. What difference will it make to the demand for a public service if its price is lowered, if it is made more convenient, more reliable, or more accessible. What will happen to demand if these supply attributes shift in the opposite direction? Can a public official begin to think in terms of possible "elastic" relationships between service supply and demand. Can one begin to understand how the public perceives supply characteristics such as price (under subsidy conditions), reliability, and accessibility?

Theoretical insights along these lines must be grounded by specifying particular options for modifying the service delivery system. As program managers strive to bring program assumptions to the surface, they will become more sensitive to prevailing political, social, and economic views of service requirements and alternative actions that might be taken. At the same time, they should begin to understand how such broad environmental factors might affect service delivery options through external constraints such as public opinion, union work rules, and judicial interpretations. Managers must also seek creative alternatives for allocating resources subject to these constraints. The purpose of such efforts is to identify strategies which can help to manage the demand for that service—recognizing that "the service" is being changed in the process.

Anticipating performance problems (demand forecasting)

It is easy to say that anticipation is important. The difficulty is knowing when it is worthwhile to try to anticipate a future phenomenon and how to attempt to do so. To a limited extent, anticipation is a technical problem; one of the most highly developed areas in the field of operations research is demand forecasting. There are various statistical approaches to examining data on past and current demand for a product or service and generating historical patterns and likely future tendencies.[7] Relationships can be estimated between the demand in question and explanatory factors, which are either controllable or more readily predictable. Similar models can be developed to forecast trends in key supply parameters, especially costs (for example, the costs of maintaining public housing as a function of trends in building deterioration, costs of building supplies, and the wage levels of laborers who repair the buildings). To a large extent, use of these kinds of anticipatory devices is a matter of *technology transfer*: taking forecasting techniques which have proved useful in one context and trying to apply them to other situations.

Overreliance on such technology-based approaches for anticipating program performance is a constant danger. A large part of the mystery in anticipating future service delivery problems derives from the ebb and flow of social values and public expenditures. Intuition may therefore be more reliable than statistics when trying to predict the future. Convening knowledgeable people to speculate on alternative trends in the public need or desire for the service in question is one method of harnessing intuition. Structured approaches for conducting such sessions and creating collective predictions have been developed under the general label of

"Delphi" techniques (Dalkey, 1969). Such techniques can be used to incorporate the views of a program's users or clients as well as those of more detached experts.[8]

Regardless of the particular techniques used, the purpose of such forecasts and predictions is to signal warnings of an impending demand/supply mismatch. Such analyses should be pursued and refined throughout the life of a public service delivery system. The operations management life cycle model described in chapter 2 indicates the several stages when a manager or policymaker might intentionally alter the supply of the service or redefine the demand at which it will be directed. The types of signals that should be helpful have already been suggested. On the demand side: demand for a service begins to grow faster or slower than was expected at the time the program's capacity requirements were established; spatial, temporal, or demographic distributions of demand develop unexpected peaks and valleys; or illegitimate kinds of demand start to require disproportionate amounts of available resources. On the supply side: productivity begins to fall below planned levels; service quality shows signs of becoming unacceptable; or the program's methods and procedures seem either too rigid or too flexible to cope with the range of situations being experienced. The range of responses to such signals, also outlined above, will depend on the current policies and status of the program, planned directions for its further development and constraints on innovation. Given adequate warning, a program manager can attempt to avoid the identified problem.

As described in chapter 2, the time may come when termination of a program is the most reasonable action. A variety of imbalances can be envisioned when termination rather than revision would be appropriate: when demand for the service declines to an insignificant level; when it becomes clear that a private sector response to the original need for the service is more effective than a public one; when another public program demonstrates a better ability to meet the existing demand; or when the current demand is so different (in form, scope, distribution, size, or intensity) from its earlier status that the existing program requires more revision than is feasible (economically, politically, or socially). The occurrence of any of these imbalances between demand and supply is a signal that policymakers should seriously question the value of trying to maintain the program.

Summary

The management of demand is especially valuable in government where normal market mechanisms are often absent. It is essential, particularly in an era of cutbacks in government resources, that public managers become skilled at applying the concepts presented in this chapter. These concepts apply to all levels of government and different types of public programs. The basic skills are:

☐ Understanding the relationships between supply choices—how a public program is designed and executed—and the resulting demand patterns.
☐ Appreciating how different demand patterns will affect program performance.
☐ Responding to mismatches between service demand and supply.

This chapter presents a series of guidelines for developing the diagnostic capability which is essential to successful demand management.

Discussion questions

1. At a public university the delivery of many services are constrained by supply factors: dormitory space is limited; classrooms hold a fixed number of students; and there is a finite number of faculty members. Using these examples, and others drawn from your own experience, discuss what a university can do to manage the demand to meet the constraints of supply. If demand exceeds supply, what options does the university have to increase the supply of services? How would you decide whether these options should be pursued? Be specific.

2. As an organization develops through the operations life cycle, initial forecasts of demand and subsequent revisions to such forecasts are needed. Choose a public service with which you are familiar and describe the kinds of information that would assist a public manager in making this sequence of demand forecasts. How might estimates of demand affect the planning and design stages of the operations life cycle? How important is an accurate estimate of service demand before start-up?

3. The National Park Service was mentioned as a current example of a supply/demand mismatch. Why do you feel this problem has developed? Could the National Park Service have anticipated this problem before it occurred? If so, what actions might have been taken to prevent the current crisis? What specific actions could be taken now to alleviate the overdemand on the park system? Consider the costs of any actions you recommend. What groups of people are likely to be hurt or to benefit from such demand-management initiatives?

4. A public manager is often faced with unexpected changes in supply because of legislative reductions in program funding. Statements such as "the library budget must be cut by 20 percent," "three schools must be closed to save money," and "we must lay off 25 percent of

the fire fighters due to funding cuts'' are becoming more and more common. What information would an operations manager need to support service delivery decisions made in the face of these supply cuts? Can demand always be reduced by the same amount as supply? What actions can a manager take to continue to provide high quality and equitably allocated service, if faced with an overall reduction in supply?

Notes

*This chapter is an adaptation of ''Managing the Demand for Public Service Delivery Systems: Anticipation, Diagnosis and Program Response'' by Stephen R. Rosenthal in *The Journal of Urban Analysis,* 1979, Vol. 6, pp. 15–31.

[1] Although economists' vocabulary—service *demand* and *supply*—is used throughout this chapter, these terms have special operational meanings to managers (Sasser, 1976).

[2] The concept of demand for a public service, as used here, is different from the need for it. Need for a public service varies with perceptions and expectations of individual citizens and is often far removed from the operational world of the public manager. Demand is largely established by price and, when subsidies exist, by categories of eligibility. Ideally, demand would rationally reflect need, but in practice this is not necessarily so.

[3] In December 1976, the federal government issued a moratorium on influenza vaccinations because of the possible risk of a rare form of paralysis called Guillain-Barre syndrome.

[4] This phenomenon is readily translated into the language of the economist. Service demand functions may shift up or down based on changes in social, economic, or environmental factors. But even when such exogenous factors are constant, a public manager can stimulate a move up or down along the slope of a stable demand curve by changing controllable supply measures such as price or eligibility criteria. Despite this analogy, the construction of quantitative estimates of elasticities of demand and supply functions are beyond the scope of what is being called for here, especially considering the complex causal chains of interest to the public manager.

[5] For an account of the politics of the food stamp program in later 1960s, see Kotz (1971).

[6] For a specific method of conducting related strategic management processes, see Mitroff and Mason (1980).

[7] A classic text on forecasting is Brown (1963), and most introductory books on operations management techniques include a chapter on this topic.

[8] For a critical evaluation of Delphi techniques, see Sackman (1975).

Bibliography

Brown, Robert G. *Smoothing, Forecasting and Prediction of Discrete Time Series*. Englewood Cliffs, N.J.: Prentice-Hall, 1963.

Churchman, C. West. *The Systems Approach*. New York: Delacorte Press, 1968.

Dalkey, N. C. *The Delphi Method: An Experimental Study of Group Opinion*. Santa Monica, Calif.: The Rand Corporation, RM-5888-PR, 1969.

Kotz, Nick. *Let Them Eat Promises*. Garden City, N.Y.: Doubleday, 1971.

Michael, Donald N. *On Learning to Plan–And Planning to Learn*. San Francisco: Jossey-Bass, 1973.

Mitroff, Ian I., and Richard O. Mason. ''A Logic for Strategic Management.'' *Human Systems Management* 1, 2 (September 1980): 115–26.

Riecken, Henry W., and Robert F. Boruch, eds. *Social Experimentation*. New York: Academic Press, 1974.

Sackman, Harold. ''Summary Evaluation of Delphi.'' *Policy Analysis* 1, 4 (Fall 1975): 693–718.

Sasser, W. Earl. ''Match Supply and Demand in Service Industries.'' *Harvard Business Review*, November-December 1976, pp. 133–40.

Savas, E. S. ''Simulation and Cost Effectiveness Analysis of New York's Emergency Ambulance Service.'' *Management Science* 15, 12 (August 1969): B608–B627.

Webber, Melvin M. "The BART Experience—What Have We Learned?" *The Public Interest* 45 (Fall 1976): 101–22.
The Urban Institute and International City Management Association. *Measuring the Effectiveness of Basic Municipal Services: Initial Report*. Washington D.C.: The Urban Institute, February 1974.
Williams, Walter. "Implementation Analysis and Assessment." *Policy Analysis* 1, 3 (Summer 1975): 531–66.

Chapter 8
"Housing code enforcement"

The Office of Code Enforcement (OCE) of New York City is responsible for enforcing housing regulations related to repair, maintenance, and occupancy. The obligations to repair and provide housing to meet code regulations are imposed by government and enforced for the general welfare. Besides defining standards for occupancy and maintenance of residential buildings, these codes prescribe criminal and civil proceedings to be followed in cases of violations of standards; they also specify administrative action to be taken for cases in which buildings are to be repaired, vacated, or demolished.

In 1968, 2.8 million housing units were under the general purview of the OCE. These included about 800,000 one- or two-family dwelling units, of which 150,000 were occupied by renters. Of the remaining 2 million units in multiple dwellings, most—nearly 1.8 million—were renter-occupied. These units, located in 148,000 multiple-dwelling structures, account for most of the city's code enforcement activity. Approximately 40,000 of these buildings are "old law" tenements, built before 1901, and contain more than 300,000 apartments. About 49,000 "new law" tenements, built between 1901 and 1929, contain over 800,000 dwelling units. Buildings constructed after 1929 fall under the Multiple Dwelling Law. Numbering approximately 8000 buildings containing 650,000 units, these are the largest structures and generally are in the best condition. The remaining multiple-dwelling structures consist of various types of buildings including converted single-family dwellings (brownstones) and miscellaneous rooming houses, hotels, and other buildings.

Legal basis of housing maintenance code enforcement

Housing maintenance codes, as they have developed in New York State, enforce two different classes of standards. On the one hand, they specify that every building must meet certain physical standards that the law deems necessary to the public welfare. Standards of what is minimally necessary change over time. For example, in 1895, the courts upheld a regulation requiring one water outlet per floor in tenements that previously had none but warned that it was "reasonably apparent that one such place on each floor, fairly accessible to all the occupants of the floor, would be all that could usually and reasonably be required, and anything further would be unreasonable." Standards have, of course, changed since that time, and courts are no longer loath to uphold laws that require running water in individual apartments. As a second type of standard, housing maintenance codes may also require that building owners keep their property in good repair. This means that all parts of the building, whether or not specifically covered by maintenance, building, health, or other codes, must be maintained in good condition.

In 1968 three broad classes of action could be taken against owners who violated the codes. First, the city could apply punitive sanctions through the criminal or civil courts. Second, the city could take direct action by arranging for emergency repairs, vacate orders, or rent reductions. Third, tenants could bring civil or criminal proceedings against owners directly. Of these sanctions, only city-initiated criminal prosecution and rent reductions were used extensively.

The office of code enforcement

OCE is part of the Housing and Development Administration (HDA), one of the superagencies created by Mayor John V. Lindsay in 1967 through consolidation of several independent housing-related departments. More specifically, OCE is one of the three principal divisions of HDA's Department of Rent and Housing Maintenance, the others being the Office of Rent Control and the Office of Special Improvement Programs. Exhibit 8.1 is an organization chart of HDA. Within the OCE there are centralized divisions for receiving complaints; for processing complaints, violations, and inspections data; for scheduling emergency repairs; for accounting and management; and for overseeing the five borough offices (from which the bulk of inspections and other field activities emanate) and a series of local offices of the city's Emergency Repair Program.

During the 1960s, in response to both the rising incidence of housing deterioration and to new and transferred responsibilities for OCE, the OCE work load increased substantially. In the early 1960s, the Housing

Exhibit 8.1
Chart of New York City's Housing and Development Administration (HDA), 1969

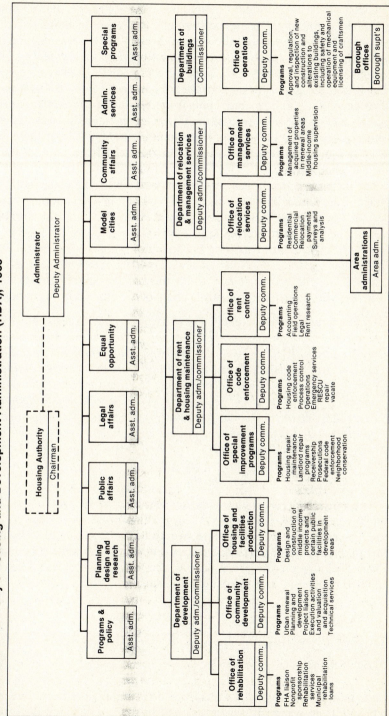

Division of the Department of Buildings received about 100,000 housing complaints annually. During the 1967–68 fiscal year, an estimated total of 500,000 complaints entered the system through the several existing channels. This fivefold increase in housing complaints undoubtedly signaled increased housing problems. Some of this growth, however, could be traced to three important organizational changes: (1) the transfer in 1965 of responsibility for heat complaints from the Health Department to Housing; (2) the formation in 1965 of the Central Complaints Bureau and widespread promulgation of its telephone number; and (3) the establishment in 1966 of a direct Emergency Repair Program (ERP) to operate through special local offices.

The increase in work load was accompanied by an increase in the OCE budget from $3.3 million in 1963 to $10.6 million in 1969. During the same period, the total OCE staff grew from 626 to 1315, and the number of housing inspectors rose from 485 to 641.

By 1970, OCE was receiving considerable public criticism for its lax enforcement of the Housing Maintenance Code. While some critics charged the city administration with mismanagement of the Code Enforcement Program, one large-scale study of the city's housing concluded:

Widespread undermaintenance of the City's rental housing stock is the result of economic and social forces too powerful to be overcome simply by attempts to enforce the Housing Maintenance Code. The increased rate of deterioration in the latter part of the 1960s is due to a combination of overly rigid rent controls, rapid increases in costs of operating rental housing, tenants unable to afford rents adequate to cover these costs, and social pathology reflected in a rising incidence of burglary, vandalism, and fire. Landlords unable to see present or future profits from their buildings cut their losses by undermaintenance and abandonment. As deterioration has increased, so has the demand by tenants for code enforcement.

Key officials at OCE and at higher levels of HDA agreed with these general perceptions. Yet they felt a growing pressure to identify what could be done to make OCE more effective. The first step, they believed, was to assess the performance of current code enforcement operations. Exhibit 8.2 depicts the process by which code enforcement cases were initiated, executed, and (ultimately) closed.

Tenant complaints: intake and preinspection processing

Code enforcement activity was initiated by complaints from tenants, by referrals from other city agencies, and by internal agency decisions to

Exhibit 8.2
The code enforcement pipeline: tenant complaint, inspection, and violation placement

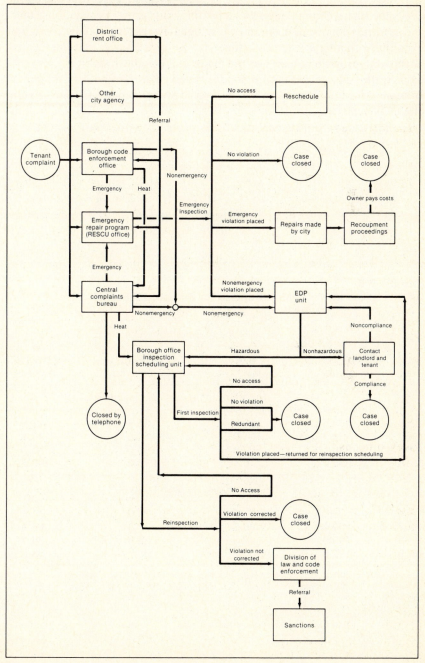

carry out intensive area-wide enforcement through cyclical inspections. As a result of violations noted during these inspections, reinspections were made to monitor the correction of violations.

Tenant complaints accounted for most of OCE's intake, and during the 1960s the relative importance of such complaints grew. Tenant complaints and referrals from HDA or other city agencies entered OCE through at least three channels: borough offices; local ERP offices, and the Central Complaints Bureau, which was the major entry point. Exhibit 8.3 presents data on the volume and nature of calls received at the Central Complaints Bureau since its establishment in 1965. The existence of these several channels permitted duplicate complaints to be received. One OCE manager, particularly concerned about this problem, remarked:

We've created a real mess here. If a tenant calls Central Complaints and isn't satisfied that his problem is being taken seriously, he may call the same number again later. Lots of times a tenant will begin to exaggerate his complaint to make it sound more like an emergency. Or he might call his local ERP office or borough office as well as Central Complaints. We think that duplicate complaints account for up to 20

Exhibit 8.3
Calls received at the Central Complaints Bureau, 1966–1969

Year	Total Calls	Type of Telephone Call		
		Heat Complaints	Housing Complaints	Information Requests[a]
		Number of Calls (in Thousands)		
1966	453.5	209.6	131.4	112.5
1967	521.2	191.0	183.8	146.4
1968	646.1	260.4	165.5	220.2
1969	593.2	179.4	218.0	195.8
		Percentage Distribution[b]		
1966	100.0	46.2	29.0	24.8
1967	100.0	36.6	35.3	28.1
1968	100.0	40.3	25.6	34.1
1969	100.0	30.2	36.7	33.0

Sources: New York City Department of Buildings, *Annual Report*, 1966; Central Complaints Bureau, *Statistical Summaries*, 1968 and 1969.

[a] Many of these requests are referred directly to other agencies.
[b] Percentage distributions may not add to 100 because of rounding.

percent of the Central Complaint volume. And probably even more in borough offices. Usually we discover this duplication only when we send out more than one inspector for the same situation.

The city response: call-back, mail contact, and inspections scheduling

Complaints were classified into three categories: emergency, heat, and nonemergency. Each type could be received through any intake channel. After receipt of a complaint, the Central Complaints Bureau followed certain preset procedures, the first of which was an attempt to telephone the owner. If the owner was reached and agreed to attend voluntarily to the complaint, the bureau subsequently checked back with the tenant to see whether the cause of the complaint had been corrected. For heat complaints, the tenant was called on the day following notification of the owner; for other complaints, more time might be allowed for corrective action. If the tenant verbally reported that the condition was corrected, the case was closed; otherwise, the complaint was processed for further action. In 1969, more than 60 percent of all heat complaints and 18 percent of other housing complaints were closed by telephone.

Deteriorating housing stock and overload in the Central Complaints Bureau were claimed to be the major reasons that only a small fraction of total housing complaints were closed by telephone contact. The bureau was hard pressed to handle its intake, especially during the cold months when heat complaints were most frequent. Faced with a large number of incoming calls, operators did not have time to make the several calls needed to locate a building owner—a sample study of nonemergency complaints disclosed that the Central Complaints Bureau tried to contact the owner in only 23 percent of the cases. Even when operators had enough time to call owners, they often failed to make contact. An assistant to the deputy commissioner of OCE described this problem:

We do our best to update the list of owners' emergency telephone numbers. Twice a year we get the latest numbers from the owners' registration files. But our list is incomplete. We only have numbers for about 80,000 of the 148,000 multiple dwellings in the city. Owners are failing to register. We expect things to improve though because we're cracking down on them. Last November we placed 2000 registration violations and filed suits against thirty owners. Successful civil actions usually result in $500 fines.

Nonemergency complaints were classified at the time of their receipt into noninspection-generating (N) or inspection-generating (G) types. Nonemergency complaints were sent to the Electronics Data Processing (EDP) unit of the OCE. For all G complaints, multiple copies of the inspection form (the 1036) were prepared and sent to borough offices for daily scheduling and routing. When telephone contact could not be made for N complaints, a written notice of complaint was sent to the owner and tenant allowing thirty days for correction of the alleged violation. If the tenant reported that the owner had failed to take action within that time, an inspection was scheduled. During the late 1960s, there were about 40,000 N complaints annually, of which 75 percent were cleared without inspection.

Exhibit 8.4
Distribution of inspection visits by type[a] of inspection, 1962–1969

	Type of Inspection			
Year	Total Inspections	Housing[b]	Heat[c]	Emergency[d]
	Number of Visits (in Thousands)			
1962	274.0	274.0	—	—
1963	221.0	221.0	—	—
1964	288.2	288.2	—	—
1965	310.5	283.7	26.8	—
1966	349.0	272.9	64.3	11.8
1967	443.3	329.5	57.3	56.5
1968	399.7	275.9	56.9	66.9
1969	388.7	267.5	55.8	65.4
	Percentage Distribution[e]			
1962	100.0	100.0	—	—
1963	100.0	100.0	—	—
1964	100.0	100.0	—	—
1965	100.0	91.4	8.6	—
1966	100.0	78.2	18.4	3.4
1967	100.0	74.3	12.9	12.7
1968	100.0	69.0	14.2	16.7
1969	100.0	68.8	14.4	16.8

Source: OCE *Summary Statistics,* 1962–1969.

[a] Inspections do not imply that access was gained to an apartment.
[b] Housing inspections include nonheat and nonemergency cases after 1965 and also include reinspections; before 1966, emergencies are included. Figures for 1967 include a large number of OCE-initiated inspections for door lights.
[c] Heat inspections became the responsibility of the Buildings Department in 1965.
[d] Emergency visits include those from Emergency Repair Program offices and special night emergency visits.
[e] Percentage distributions may not add to 100 because of rounding.

Inspection activity

Housing code enforcement inspections took several forms and served several purposes. Aside from those which responded to tenants' complaints, inspections were also initiated by OCE either in response to referrals from other city agencies or as part of a larger effort to improve housing in selected neighborhoods (cycle inspections). Results of all inspections were reported to the EDP system.

Inspections might focus narrowly on problems of immediate health and safety or cover the broad spectrum of provisions of the Housing Maintenance Code. When inspectors observed a condition that conflicted with these provisions, they placed an appropriate violation against that building. Existing violations could be removed only by reinspection, which was triggered when an EDP printout of an updated Form 1036 showed the existence of outstanding violations on a building. Exhibit 8.4 indicates trends in the number of inspections, categorized by type of problem. Complaints accounted for a continually increasing share of total inspections, as shown in Exhibit 8.5.

The central importance of the inspection activity was explained by a borough office supervisor:

Exhibit 8.5
Code enforcement activities, by type, 1962–1969

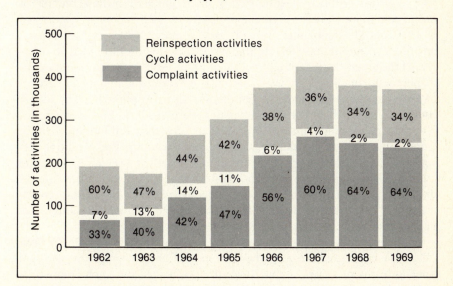

Source: OCE *Summary Statistics,* 1962–1969.

Our violation placement and removal statistics tell us how well OCE is doing. Individual violations establish the legal basis for taking action against delinquent landlords. And the total number and composition of outstanding violations tells us about the condition of the city's housing stock. But placing and removing violations is a costly activity for us. OCE had a staff of 640 inspectors in 1969. In many areas of the city, inspectors travel in pairs, rather than alone, for safety's sake. At the beginning of each day, borough office supervisors give a set of about eight Form 1036s to each inspector or pair and they make up the route they intend to follow for the day. The inspectors tend to know their neighborhoods quite well since we try to let them work in the same neighborhood for a year or so. Eventually we have to rotate them to another area. You know, after awhile, people may begin to worry about the inspectors getting too friendly with the local landlords. In fact we've had some problems along these lines and have had to reassign some inspectors rather suddenly. Still, field inspection is the guts of code enforcement and we always have to worry about the inspectors' morale. Morale seems low now and turnover is high. Lots of inspectors move over to the Buildings Department as soon as they qualify to be construction inspectors. Pay and promotions aren't any better there, but the men find that job to be more attractive. Probably because it gives them more responsibility.

Unfortunately, many inspections turned out to be nonproductive. One source of this problem was the lack of discrimination in the screening of initial complaints to determine the appropriate OCE response. Operators in the Central Complaints Bureau were supplied with a list of typical emergency conditions. Despite this guideline, operators tended to over-report the emergency nature of complaints. In 1968, inspectors sent out to inspect reported emergencies found valid emergencies in only 23 percent of the observed cases and no violation at all in 33 percent. (The latter, however, included cases where repairs were made before inspection.) Nonemergency complaints also presented screening difficulties. Central Complaints Bureau operators had to decide whether the condition described by the tenant merited an inspection or only a warning letter to the building owner. The operators had no written instructions for making this distinction. Comparisons between nonemergency complaints recommended for inspection and those recommended for warning letters revealed no significant substantive differences.

Emergency complaints were received either directly at a local ERP office or were routed there by phone from the Central Complaints Bureau. Special teams of inspectors at ERP offices checked out such complaints by conducting field visits as soon as possible. (They did not wait for a Form 1036 but proceeded based on the complaint description alone.) If emergency conditions were indeed observed, a violation was issued at

Exhibit 8.6
Results of inspection visits made in response to complaints received in 1968

Type of Complaint	Total Inspection Visits[a]	Result of Inspection Visit			
		Violation Reported	No Violation	Violation Previously Placed	No Access[b]
		Number of Visits (in Thousands)			
Noninspection-generating (N)[c]	13.1	2.2	5.2	0.7	5.0
Inspection-generating (G)	54.4	11.1	18.6	1.9	22.8
Referral (R)	31.2	4.9	14.4	1.0	10.9
Emergency (S)	24.1	8.4	8.6	0.8	6.3
Total	122.9	26.6	46.8	4.5	45.0
		Percentage Distribution[d]			
Noninspection-generating (N)	100.0	16.7	39.7	5.3	38.3
Inspection-generating (G)	100.0	20.4	34.2	3.5	41.8
Referral (R)	100.0	15.7	46.0	3.3	35.0
Emergency (S)	100.0	34.7	35.7	3.4	26.2
Distribution for all types	100.0	21.6	38.1	3.6	36.6

Source: OCE, *Statistics of Complaints Received,* 1968.

Note: Includes only complaints processed through EDP.
a Total visits made through November 1969 in response to complaints received in 1968.
b Reflects the fact that many complaints required multiple visits. Actual distribution of complaints for which the last inspection visit resulted in no access: N = 0.8 complaints, G = 2.4, R = 1.3, S = 0.4. (Figures in thousands.)
c Inspections scheduled on N-type complaints following tenant confirmation that complaints had not been remedied.
d Percentage distributions may not add to 100 because of rounding.

once and telephoned to the ERP Contracting Unit. Then ERP moved into action and tried once again to contact the owner by phone to gain immediate voluntary compliance or—failing to get that response—ordered repairs to be made at once, using city-hired contractors. Telephone calls and telegrammed bids were substituted for the normal, time-consuming procedures usually used for city contracts. After a repair had been made, the city instituted recoupment proceedings against the owner to recover the amount of the repair plus a charge for the city's time and effort. ERP inspection services were available around the clock (with a reduced central office staff at night) seven days a week. OCE attempted to assign enough inspectors to handle the winter peak loads that arose when, during severe cold spells, heating systems would break down and frozen plumbing lines would crack.

Inspections made in response to complaints had one of several outcomes: a violation was reported, no violation was found to exist, a violation was found but it had previously been reported, or the inspection could not be completed for lack of access to the premises because the tenant wasn't home when the inspector arrived. (This last outcome necessitated a rescheduled inspection.) Exhibit 8.6 provides statistics on the results of such inspection visits.

Removal of violations resulted from action by owners to remedy housing deficiencies (previously recorded as violations), followed by an inspector's confirmation that the violation no longer existed. Trends in violation placement and removal are shown in Exhibit 8.7. Information on the distribution of outstanding violations is in Exhibits 8.8 and 8.9. All violations are expressed in terms of order numbers which relate to a particular aspect of the Housing Maintenance Code. The meaning of violation statistics was subject to interpretation, even within OCE. As one program analyst put it:

> *It's hard to know what these statistics really mean. In general, we believe that almost half of the outstanding violations are "cosmetic"—you know, things which might inconvenience or annoy tenants, but don't really threaten their health or safety. Maybe another 40 percent of the violations could be potential hazards . . . like leaks that could cause serious problems if not corrected or doors that don't meet fire safety requirements. Real emergencies . . . conditions which are really hazardous probably aren't much more than 10 percent of the total violations. The reason we're not more certain of these statistics is that some of "general orders," like 501 and 505, include a wide range of actual situations. We've given the inspectors these order book categories to help take care of the code's general requirement for "good repair." Fortunately, most of the code lists specific conditions which are easily included as separate understandable items in the order book.*

Exhibit 8.7
Housing code violation placement and removal, 1960–1969

	Number of Violations (in Thousands)		
Year	Placed[a]	Removed[a]	Uncleared at Year End
1960	204.7	221.9	127.0
1961	198.4	222.6	102.8
1962	195.6	201.0	97.4
1963	302.3	154.4	245.4
1964	425.5	411.3	264.3
1965	386.4	365.9	282.9
1966	777.8	467.4	592.9
1967	602.7	506.5	683.1
1968	458.0	391.3	742.3
1969	283.9	404.6	619.5

Sources: OCE *Summary Statistics,* 1963–1969; New York City Department of Buildings, *Annual Report,* 1966.

Note: Reported backlogs are not always consistent with annual totals of violations placed and removed owing to adjustments made at the end of each year. Uncleared violations for 1960 and 1961 have been computed on the basis of differences between violations placed and removed. For 1962–69, the figures are as given by the OCE data processing system.
[a] Variations from year to year in the rate of violation placement and removal are complicated by special factors. For example, the requirement for peepholes partly accounts for the very high volume of violations in 1966. But overall patterns and implications remain unchanged by such variations.

Exhibit 8.8
Distribution of violations by building, May 1, 1969

Number of Violations per Building	Buildings		Total Violations		Average Violations per Building
	Number	Percent	Number	Percent	
0	56,600	38.3	0	0	0
1–2	34,700	23.5	48,900	6.7	1.4
3–10	39,300	26.5	208,200	28.3	5.3
11–30	12,500	8.5	210,300	28.7	16.8
31 or more	4,800	3.2	266,000	36.3	55.3
Total	147,900	100.0	733,400	100.0	5.0

Source: New York City Master Building File (May 1, 1969).

Note: All statistics were estimated by expanding proportions from a random sample of 2000 buildings.

Exhibit 8.9
Violations placed in 1969, by violation order number

Rank by Frequency of Use	Order Number and Description	Number of Violations Placed	Percent of Total Violations
1	508. Repair the broken or defective plastered surfaces and paint in uniform color the . . .	37,845	13.3
2	501. Properly repair the broken or defective . . .	26,587	9.4
3	556. Paint with light colored paint to the satisfaction of this department the . . .	17,742	6.3
4	510. Abate the nuisance consisting of . . .	17,542	6.2
5	505. Replace with new the broken or defective . . .	16,770	5.9
6	506. Replace with new the missing . . .	13,707	4.8
7	502. Properly repair with similar material the broken or defective . . .	9,918	3.5
8	670. Provide hot water at all hot water fixtures.	9,747	3.4
9	552. Remove the accumulation of refuse and/or rubbish and maintain in a clean condition the . . .	6,802	2.4
10	579. Repair the leaky and/or defective faucets.	6,348	2.2
11–20	10 violations occurring between 6328 and 3391 times	42,897	15.1
Total, 20 most frequent violations		205,905	72.5
All other violations[a] (198 different orders)		77,989	27.5
Total, all violations[a]		283,894	100.0

Source: OCE tabulations.

[a] Includes 25,824 violations placed as order No. 851 that are referred to other agencies for action.

Criminal court prosecution

Once a violation had been reported by an inspector, elimination of its cause did not remove the building owner's criminal liability under the code. Prosecution in a special housing section of the criminal court was the principal sanction against housing code violations. Procedures existed to prepare a case for criminal court action, to present it to the court, and to record the results. First, the Electronics Data Processing Unit matched buildings having violations with a registration file of parties responsible for each building's upkeep. Computer-generated legal complaint forms and related documents were forwarded to the Legal Processing Unit. A single criminal case against a building owner might cover any number of violations placed against a building. Before a case could be docketed for court action, the Electronics Data Processing Unit had to obtain a sworn signature of the inspector who had originally noted the violations. The date for arraignment was then set, and the responsible party was notified by mail to appear before the court. On the scheduled date of appearance, the complaint and other forms were sent to the criminal court in the appropriate borough.

The mailed notice cannot be legally binding, so if the defendant failed to appear (which happened about 80 percent of the time) the summons control section had to serve a personal summons. If a defendant who had been personally served did not appear, an arrest warrant could be issued by the court. In 1968, 29 percent of the violations which were brought to the attention of the court actually appeared in court cases within ten months following their identification by inspectors. For 35 percent of the violations, twenty-three months elapsed between their placement by inspectors and their first court appearance.

Once the defendant appeared, case disposition was under the control of the criminal court. Initial arraignment took place before a criminal court judge who was supplied a list of the violations in the case (Form 1036). Adjournments were routinely granted upon request of the owners for a variety of reasons including their inability to appear on the scheduled date. Sometimes the court would request a reinspection before sentencing and would then receive reports on these inspections directly. Most cases were terminated with a plea of guilty and the imposition of a fine. "Not guilty" pleas, based on the contention that the violations did not exist or that the defendant was not responsible for them, were deferred for trial, at which the prosecuting attorney was an assistant corporation counsel. This entire cycle might begin again—even before the original case had been disposed of by the court—if the violations were not removed and another case was initiated by the Legal Processing Unit. Exhibit 8.10 shows trends in the number of cases prosecuted to termination in the criminal court, the number of cases which resulted in fines, and the amount of the fines imposed.

Exhibit 8.10
Criminal court cases and fines resulting from
code enforcement, 1960–1969

Year	Number of Cases		Amount of Fine (in Dollars)	
	Terminated in Court	Resulting in Fines	Total, All Cases	Average per Case[a]
1960	23,853	20,384	543,606	26.67
1961	21,307	18,273	420,041	22.99
1962	16,917	14,479	329,428	22.75
1963	15,917	13,657	299,341	21.92
1964	21,790	19,719	332,508	16.86
1965	27,317	25,384	348,750	13.74
1966	27,345	25,307	373,508	14.76
1967	30,346	27,058	337,905	12.49
1968	30,200	26,755	306,824	11.47
1969	23,471	21,041	265,564	12.62

Source: OCE *Summary Statistics*.

[a] A court case covers all violations pending against the building at the time the case is filed. Although violation counts are not available for all cases from 1960 to 1969, fragmentary evidence indicates that the average fine per violation would be about a tenth of the average fine per case.

Rent reductions

For certain types of particularly serious violations the inspector might recommend rent reduction as a penalty against building owners. Each such case was referred directly to the Office of Rent Control from the borough office. No information on this referral was given to the Electronics Data Processing Unit or the Legal Processing Unit. The Office of Rent Control then decided whether rents should be reduced and the amount of the decrease. Such a case might be simultaneously referred for criminal prosecution.

Rent reductions imposed by the Office of Rent Control generally resulted in compliance with the Housing Maintenance Code. In three fourths of the cases for which a building owner was threatened with a rent reduction if the violations were not corrected, the owner chose to take positive action. But when rents were actually reduced by this mechanism, only in 6 percent of the cases were rents restored to the original level within the subsequent year.

City-initiated remedies: vacate orders and civil court action

When extremely hazardous conditions were noted by an inspector, the borough office had the power to issue a vacate order. If the condition of a building warranted such an order, the HDA's Office of Relocation Services was asked to assist in finding alternative housing for the tenants of the building to be vacated.

Occasionally, cases were selected by HDA's Deputy General Counsel, for special or unusual city action, such as prosecution in the civil court by the staff of the corporation counsel. Some observers believed that civil court action provided a promising approach to code enforcement since it required less stringent proof of guilt than did the criminal court. HDA's experience, however, was that case preparation and coordination with the Office of the Corporation Counsel were too time-consuming to allow a high-volume operation to be feasible.

Discussion questions

1. A study team appointed by the mayor recommended that the following standards be established for the operations of the Office of Code Enforcement (OCE):
    a. Emergency complaints will be inspected within one day.
    b. Heat complaints will be inspected within two days.
    c. Nonemergency complaints will generate an immediate warning letter to the building owner and an inspection, if necessary, within forty-five days.
    d. Buildings with outstanding violations will have automatic "public parts" (for example, boiler, cellar, stairs) inspections every six months.

    The implementation of these standards obviously impinges on the inspection requirements of the department. As Deputy Commissioner of OCE, what do you consider the likely resource implications of adopting each of these standards? Do you believe that these standards can be met? Should OCE try to implement them? Assume that demand levels are the same as those of 1969.
2. The mayor's study team also recommended that steps be taken to improve the inspector's rate of access to buildings and to reduce the number of duplicate inspections. Finally, it proposed that OCE management improve the overall efficiency of the inspection process (in-

take, complaint screening, inspection, closure). As a borough office supervisor, what changes would you recommend that could be adopted within the current OCE structure to accomplish the above goals? Consider specific bottlenecks that now occur and how they could be resolved.

3. Another operational problem in OCE is handling the large number of "no heat" complaints received during the winter months. This results in delayed responses to other complaints, both emergency and non-emergency. From your perspective as the borough office supervisor, describe the current operational responses to heat complaints. What alternatives exist for improving this response? Specifically, are there ways to reduce the supply/demand mismatch that exists during these months?

4. In an attempt to evaluate and improve the integration of the overall housing code enforcement program, the Administrator of HDA has asked you, the Deputy Administrator of the Department of Rent and Housing Maintenance, to assess if the OCE processes fit well with the processes available through Office of Rent Control, relocation services, or the criminal courts. Can OCE really enforce the housing code in New York City? Why or why not?

Notes

*This case was prepared by Stephen R. Rosenthal. It draws on material in Michael B. Teitz and Stephen R. Rosenthal, *Housing Code Enforcement in New York City*, R648-NYC (New York: The New York City Rand Institute, 1971). Funds for its development were provided by a grant from the Duke University/Rand Graduate Institute's Public Policy Curricular Materials Development Project which is sponsored by the Ford Foundation. The case is intended to serve as a basis for class discussion, not to illustrate either effective or ineffective handling of a managerial situation.

Chapter 9
Information systems for operations management

Information is a necessary component of any production system. In chapter 3 we outlined how information should flow through the production process (recall Exhibit 3.1). In other chapters of this book we noted that specific information of one type or another is required by the operations manager to support the selection, design, operation, control, and updating of a production system. Furthermore, managers need information systems to support their decisions at all levels of the production process and at all stages of the operations life cycle. The information needed and the form in which it should be presented depend on such factors as the sophistication of decision making, the stage of the operations life cycle, the extent of technical staff support, and the cost and benefits associated with data processing. This chapter explores how information systems can help operations managers and identifies critical issues in the design, development, and implementation of such systems.

During the 1980s, corporate decision makers are likely to view information systems as prerequisites for operations management. Many firms have progressed rapidly over the past twenty years and have improved their capacity for handling information. It is probably obvious at all levels of such organizations that adequate understanding of an operating system—its past, present, and future trends—requires significant investment in the collection, storage, and retrieval of data. In addition, the analytic concepts, procedures, and other necessary information discussed in earlier chapters are familiar to most operations managers in the private sector. In manufacturing organizations, for example, accurate and up-to-date records of orders, production levels, inventories, shipments, and billings are vital to the maintenance of a profitable enterprise. Most successful manufacturing organizations routinely maintain product line records which include historical statistics on input levels (labor, raw materials, energy); production problems (equipment breakdowns, maintenance costs, unplanned overtime, quality control findings); and output levels (actual volume produced, forecasts of future demand). Successful firms in service industries, such as fast food franchises, retailing, hotel chains, banking, and insurance have comparable information systems.

In the public sector, information at the operating level is less well developed and progress has been more gradual. Inadequacies in the management of information hinder successful operations in many public programs. In this chapter we will examine the major issues underlying the need for and implementation of information systems in government. We will not, however, discuss how to acquire computer hardware and software, how to use computer specialists, and how to integrate such resources into an existing organization. These matters are well covered in texts such as Kraemer and King (1977).

An introduction to management information systems

Today, the subject of information management often provokes pictures of sophisticated computer systems manipulating huge data files to produce complex statistical analyses as output. Thanks to media documentaries, most people are aware that managers can sit at TV-like screens and communicate directly with a computer on questions of organizational well-being. Today, in fact, much information processing is accomplished by computers, but the basic concepts of information management are equally applicable to manual systems. Operations managers in government traditionally work in paper-processing environments with extensive clerical, rather than computer, support. To include manual approaches within the discussion of "information systems" is essential if one is to address the issues faced by most public managers.

A management information system (MIS) is a special kind of production system. (See Exhibit 9.1.) Data is the raw material of an MIS. Data becomes information after it has been manipulated and presented to managers in ways that are potentially useful for making decisions. Purists may argue that an organization does not have a management information system if the MIS output does not lead to improved decisions. However, it is probably more pragmatic to consider that an MIS exists if competent and motivated managers draw on it for assistance.

There are many types of data, including numeric results of operations, lists of names of users, specific characteristics of users, and a combination of numeric and nonnumeric features (such as students' names and

Exhibit 9.1
The production system for operational information

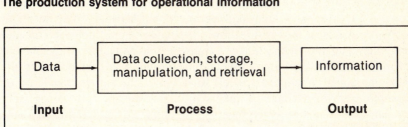

test scores). A simple listing of data in a specified format (highest score to lowest) can be considered information if it leads to a decision which could not have been made without this output (for example, students with scores below X require special tutoring). The information requirements of managers vary with their organizational responsibilities and with the degree of sophistication of the organization being managed. These requirements, in turn, determine the requirements of an MIS. This chapter identifies the various kinds of information that may support operational decisions and the costs and benefits of generating such information.

Manual versus computer systems

All organizations have some minimal capability for managing information. Even a file cabinet containing individual folders for clients of a social service program is the start of an MIS. An MIS is any formal, systematic approach to the collection and manipulation of data and the preparation of information in a usable format. Computers are not an essential component of an MIS. In deciding whether to use a computer, managers must assess the organization's needs relative to its current capability for handling information.

Public managers often bring a strong bias of optimism to any decision involving the development of a new or improved information system. Ironically, this occurs despite the fact that skepticism about ''management misinformation systems'' has been voiced for well over a decade (Ackoff, 1967). Public officials and administrators often tend to ''think big'' regarding the development of an information system. Frequently, they are called upon either to approve purchases or leases of expensive equipment or to allocate funds for system development activities, without understanding the broad implications of such decisions. Since they generally lack technical expertise in this area, public managers sometimes fail to realize that computers just may not be necessary. In organizations with limited information management experience or ability, simple manual techniques may meet short-term (and even long-term) needs.

As an organization expands, the demands for timely and accurate information usually grow as well. When a manual MIS no longer seems to serve the needs of an organization, a manager should consider the development and implementation of a computer-based system. If the current manual system is functioning well and has provided adequate support for decision making, it is often possible to automate the existing system. For example, data on welfare payments to clients can be transferred from written files to computer storage. Straightforward automation of these files would facilitate rapid retrieval of information and data manipulation to obtain summaries or comparisons among clients.

Too often, however, the decision is made to automate a manual system that has proved unsatisfactory for reasons unrelated to growth. Mere automation will not correct the earlier problems. Consider the case of a public health hospital with several independent clinics. Traditionally, each clinic in this hospital scheduled its own patients' visits, and the existing appointment processing system could not coordinate appointments among clinics. In an attempt to reduce the total number of trips each patient would need to make to the hospital, a computer-based MIS was implemented which allowed multiple appointments to be made sequentially on the same day. At first, this sytem was just an automation of prior methods; it allowed each clinic to input the new appointments exactly as had been done under the manual appointment book system. Consequently, coordination was not improved and many patients (each of whom needed more than one clinic appointment) were still forced to make extra trips to the hospital. If the computer-based appointment system was to be better than the manual system it would have to be designed with the capacity to batch all appointments for a given patient. This would have minimized the patient's hospital trips. To achieve this capacity required a new, more sophisticated, computerized management information system.

An organization's demands for information will determine the specific nature of the appropriate computer-based MIS. The technological sophistication of recent computer hardware and software capabilities is awesome, and costs are dropping each year. If, as for medical treatment purposes, responses must be immediately available, data or inquiries must be input directly into the computer from an on-line terminal, and required information must be displayed on an on-line output device such as a cathode-ray tube (CRT). The use of such advanced system capabilities facilitates rapid decision making based on new information. Some government agencies have been the recent recipients of even more advanced decision support capacities. In some cities, law enforcement officers now can obtain information to aid in tactical decisions by drawing on the capabilities of advanced computer systems: patrol officers using two-way car radios, can communicate with headquarters staff, who can immediately access information stored in computer files.

When speed of response is not vital, less expensive "batch processing" systems may suffice. In these cases, requests for information are accumulated, processed together as one batch (often at night, when there are fewer demands on the computer than there are during the day), and the results are returned at a later time. For example, a state civil service director may need to know the names and salaries of employees in several different job categories. Batch processing is a sensible approach in this instance since such a routine request for information does not require an instantaneous response.

It is often a particularly complex matter to decide how frequently information is needed and how up-to-date it must be. Many public service delivery programs need a system that can produce daily, weekly, and monthly reports, each requiring different information system capabilities. The more varied and extensive the information requirements, the more likely it is that some type of computer-based MIS will be required.

In summary, then, the decision whether to leave the current system (either manual or automated) intact, to make small modifications to it, or to upgrade it from manual to computer, is not a simple one. The size of the organization, the amount of paperwork processed, the impact on staffing, the cost of any changes, and the level of management support are some of the factors that must be considered. It is essential, in any event, to understand how the handling of information might be improved.

Improving decisions with an MIS

Managers must be aware of how an improved MIS can change their organization's decision processes. Consider the allocation of classrooms in a university, an activity which occurs during registration periods. The job is to assign each class to a room large enough to accommodate all students, without wasting scarce space by using unnecessarily large rooms. If the registrar responsible for classroom allocation does not have timely access to anticipated enrollment figures, room assignment mismatches can occur. When there is a time lag between classroom scheduling and student registration, such errors are especially likely. If all registration information were collected and updated daily and a master class list prepared, appropriate room assignments could be made. If this process were automated so that registration data was input, on-line, into a computer, the registrar could obtain up-to-the-minute counts for each class and could automatically adjust classroom assignments as needed.

As more information becomes available for use, the quality of associated decisions should improve. With a sophisticated MIS, managers can ask more "what if" questions and obtain the information needed to identify future options and operational issues. Consider the planning needs of a superintendent of schools. A comprehensive MIS for personnel could help answer questions such as:

☐ If enrollment drops 5 percent for the next three years, how much of a staff reduction can be made?
☐ If all reductions are based on seniority, who will be laid off?
☐ Given the special skills of those laid off, will it still be possible to provide all the needed educational programs?

Similarly, an MIS could assist a community hospital in planning for a disaster:

☐ If fifty emergency cases arrive at one time, how many nurses and physicians will be needed?
☐ Does the hospital have sufficient blood supplies for this crisis?
☐ Who could be called upon to donate blood in an emergency?

A major challenge for any operations manager is to identify the key questions that are likely to arise and then to take steps to provide the required data and processing capacity.

Types of decisions and associated information requirements

Any decision process eventually can be hampered by too much information. A manager deluged by sheets of computer printouts may be overwhelmed and turn out to be no more effective at decision making than the manager with no information. There must be a balance between the quantity of information needed and the quantity provided. The specific types of information provided must meet the needs of the decision maker. For example, a production manager who needs to know the current availability of a specific part would find little value in statistical reports of last year's average inventory. Conversely, the director of a public welfare agency would want aggregate supply and demand projections to help support a decision on next year's budget, rather than an hourly count of welfare applicants. In short, different levels of management responsible for making different kinds of decisions require different kinds of information. However, no system can provide information for all conceivable decisions. Public managers frequently need to respond to specific and unanticipated requests for information. Having the staff capacity to handle such ad hoc requests will ensure that some information can be brought to bear on policy decisions even when a formal MIS is not available for this purpose. An MIS for operations managers may be more limited in scope and content than the information ideally needed for policy analysis.

Ultimately, it makes sense to develop an MIS that has the capacity to serve multiple operations management needs—short-term and long-term, detailed and aggregate. In practice, however, information management capabilities are likely to develop sequentially, first serving one level of management, then the next. It is important to understand the substantive differences among three traditional types of management decisions: operations, evaluation, and planning. As described below, each of these requires different kinds of information support.

Operational decisions

Managers concerned with day-to-day activities make decisions that will have an immediate impact on the production system. Regardless of whether the system that provides the information is manual or computer based, certain informational requirements must be met. Consider the needs of an assembly line manager in a manufacturing facility who must decide when to reduce production of a particular product. One logical decision rule is to cease production when the existing finished goods inventory of that product exceeds a specific level. A report from the storeroom clerk that more than that number of units are in inventory would then trigger the decision to cut back production. Exhibit 9.2 lists some other common operational decisions and the associated information that is likely to be required.

In general, managers responsible for operating decisions are likely to seek the following qualities in an MIS:

☐ *Information must be reported rapidly and accurately.* To effect a timely change in operations, information provided to management must be based on data that has been collected and analyzed recently. Furthermore, this information must be reported to management in time to affect decisions. For example, if air traffic controllers are to reroute aircraft around storms, a precise and timely account of the locations of planes and storm fronts is essential. A computerized MIS with on-line, real time capabilities will usually provide information more rapidly and accurately than a manual system. However, computers are not always required to meet the information needs of operating managers.

☐ *The information must be presented concisely in an easily under-standable format.* Since many operational decisions require quick response, managers must be able to assimilate the needed information without the distraction of irrelevant data. Presentation of information in a standardized format often helps a manager focus on the

Exhibit 9.2
Illustrative operating decisions
and associated information requirements

Decision Area	Type of Decision	Information Required
Inventory	Is enough fuel on hand to operate all public works vehicles if there is a major snowstorm?	Current inventory of fuel, fuel capacity of vehicles, number of miles to be driven, mileage of vehicles
Personnel Selection	Are there any skilled electricians available to repair the electrical system in city hall?	City employees listed by skill, technical specifications of the system
Capacity	How many motor vehicle clerks are needed each hour?	Number of registrations to be processed, rate of arrival of applicants, time needed to process each application
Personnel Dispatching	The arrival of the governor's plane has been delayed and several police are needed for overtime. Which officers should be required to stay? What will be the additional cost?	A list of available police officers with amount of overtime currently on the books, wage scale for each officer

needed information. On a hospital chart, a patient's vital signs are often listed together in a specific order so that a physician can see them all at a glance. Visual displays of information are particularly valuable to those who make decisions involving spatial relations. Visual displays for air traffic controllers are likely to be computer based, while for city planners, hard copy maps may be appropriate.

□ *The data used as a basis for information must be updated regularly.* Consider again the air traffic controllers. As weather patterns shift, the last information report will need to be updated so that flight patterns can be adjusted accordingly.

□ *At an operational level, aggregate data is of little value.* Information on the current status of the operating system is vital. Air traffic controllers do not need to know that on average the wind blows from the north at twelve knots, but they do need to know that at the moment the wind is from the south at twenty knots.

To further clarify the unique informational needs at the operational level, consider the needs of a fire chief and fire department officers to respond rapidly to fire emergencies. Information such as the current location and availability of fire equipment (that is, whether in use, available but unassigned, being maintained or repaired and therefore unavailable) and personnel will allow a dispatcher to select the optimal combination of units to fight a fire. If such data are to be reliable for life-or-death decisions, they should be maintained and updated constantly as changes occur. Other data needed for operational decisions, for example, hydrant location, structural characteristics and contents of buildings, and locations of high priority buildings (hospitals and schools) may be collected at greater intervals since such information is less likely to change. Finally, in general, data on the best route for appropriate fire units to reach any potential fire location will be collected just once (with updating as needed) to provide adequate information for all subsequent routing decisions. As this fire protection example indicates, some of the data for operational decisions must be collected during the design and start-up stages of the operations life cycle and will remain constant throughout steady-state. Other data must be updated regularly throughout the life cycle.

Evaluation decisions

Periodically, all public managers looking for areas to improve will have to evaluate their current operations. As discussed in chapter 3, operations managers should be concerned with the efficiency, effectiveness, and equity of a process. Such performance measures require the existence of some kind of information system. The information required for evaluation decisions differs from that needed to execute day-to-day operations. The objective of such information is not to effect an immediate routine operational change in the production process, but rather to point to any program area needing substantial revision. Exhibit 9.3 outlines the major decisions accompanying an evaluation of program operations and related information requirements.

Managers who are responsible for evaluation decisions have the following requirements for information:

☐ *Recent aggregate operating information should be presented in comparison with standards or trends.* The operating information is generally aggregated over the evaluation period: weekly, monthly, or even annually, depending upon how often program performance is reviewed. Such information is often compiled from daily data but reported only as summary information. Tabulations of trends in key performance indicators and indications of accepted standards provide the comparative basis required for evaluation decisions.

☐ *Evaluators do not usually require the on-line real time capabilities needed for operational decisions.* Although the data used cannot be

Exhibit 9.3
Illustrative evaluation decisions
and associated information requirements

Decision Area	Illustrative Decision	Information Required
Capacity Utilization	Is the utilization of trash collection trucks equal throughout the city?	Number of tons of trash collected per truck by district, time taken to collect a ton of trash by district
Effectiveness Assessment	Are the arrest rates in the second precinct up to the standards set citywide?	Number of arrests and crimes in the second precinct, number of arrests and crimes elsewhere in city, manpower available in each precinct
Opportunities for Demand Management	Is there a difference in fire damage between buildings with and without smoke detectors?	List of fires in buildings with and without smoke detectors, estimates of damage in each fire
Cost Performance	Which departments are adhering to the budgets established by the city council?	Budgeted spending limits for each department, actual spending for each department

out-of-date, decisions are often based on last week's or even last month's data. Furthermore, decisions resulting from an evaluation of performance usually do not require immediate action, so a manager has more time to assimilate information. Under such circumstances, it is possible to provide extra backup information without causing a decline in the quality of the decision. A manager also has the flexibility to determine what is the most useful information before making an evaluation decision. For example, when deciding which of several long-term treatment plans to recommend for a nonacute patient, a physician may want to review an entire medical record, selecting the most pertinent information to support a full diagnosis.

□ *Environmental information, drawing on data beyond the production system in question, may be needed.* The manager of a local unemployment office may wish to compare trends in monthly claims processed from year to year to assess the utilization of the office's staff. For example, if it is discovered that the number of processed claims has fallen this month, as compared with a year ago, information on external issues is needed before the manager can make an informed decision. Simply knowing the rate at which claims are completed does not permit the manager to determine whether the staff's performance is falling or the number of initial claims has dropped due to an economic upturn.

☐ *If a government agency operates multisite programs, it may want to collect the same kinds of data from each site to facilitate comparative performance.* A chief of police, for example, might review a semiannual summary of the supply of and demand for patrol officers in each precinct. Using statistical comparisons of the number of officers, crimes reported, and arrests made, the police chief would be able to suggest periodic shifts in resources to meet changing demand patterns among the precincts. Such occasional adjustments, based on program evaluations, will help maintain the efficiency, effectiveness, and equity of the multisite production system.

To appreciate the range of typical evaluation decisions, consider again the example of the municipal fire department. Statistical data on response time, the severity of fires, the average readiness of apparatus and manpower, and the number of runs made would all be useful in an assessment of the effectiveness of a fire department. If, in addition, the department were required to inspect buildings and to educate the public, periodic statistical summaries of these activities would also be valuable input to an evaluation. Although such information does not affect day-to-day operations, it is needed to assess utilization of manpower and equipment and often to support requests for additional funding.

The ability to monitor the overall fiscal performance of a state or local government jurisdiction is becoming increasingly important in today's economy. The value of a computer-based MIS capable of such analysis now often outweighs the costs associated with its implementation. An MIS that provides information support for evaluation decisions may also support such fiscal analyses by promoting periodic comparisons of current spending and budgeted allowances. The International City Management Association (1980) has pioneered in the development of such fiscal management information systems.

Planning-oriented decisions

Another level of decision making that may be supported by an MIS involves the planning function of an organization. Planning is the set of analytic activities designed to answer the question "Where do we go from here?" The operations management functions of selection, design, and updating require the act of planning. In general, public officials must plan to provide resources which are consistent with program mandates. To do this, they must project program requirements under different policy and environmental assumptions.

An MIS may be used as the input to sophisticated production planning or scheduling exercises. Computer simulation models, for example, can be developed to assist managers in assessing different operational strategies. Such models explicitly incorporate the uncertainty in key variables, such as levels of demand and required production times, and project the resulting pattern of system outputs. The nature of these uncertainties is established through statistical analyses of historical data. As the cost of computer hardware and software continues to decrease, simulation models become feasible analytic tools for more and more organizations. For further discussion of the simulation technique and examples of public sector applications, see Stokey and Zeckhauser (1978).

Planning-oriented decisions traditionally are made at the top management level, although information support originates at the operating levels of the organization. Some typical planning decisions in government, and associated information requirements, are shown in Exhibit 9.4. The char-

Exhibit 9.4
Illustrative planning decisions
and associated information requirements

Decision Area	Illustrative Decision	Information Required
Manpower Planning	Given that next year's budget has not been increased over this year's budget, what effect will that have on city employees?	Actual personnel expenditures this year, budgeted expenses for next year, projected inflation rate for wages, layoff sequence list, list of critical jobs
Facilities Planning	Over the past five years there has been a 15 percent annual growth in a town's population. When will the town need additional waste disposal sites for trash collected? Where should it be located?	Amount of trash collected over past five years, estimated space still available in landfills, other sites within the town suitable for landfill
Real Property and Fiscal Planning	The city is considering selling a large parcel of land either to a nonprofit university or to a real estate developer. What will be the impact on property tax revenue compared to costs to the city over the next five years? ten years?	Current tax rate, tax revenue collected, potential value of property, time needed for development of university or private structures, cost of annual services required by each use

acteristics of information to support successful planning, in contrast to successful operations and evaluation decisions, are as follows:

☐ *Planners require highly aggregated internal information and extensive external information.* An analysis of different external trends—such as population shifts, changes in income, or construction practices—are needed for most long-term planning decisions. Knowledge of current operations is also needed, but it must be derived using highly condensed measures such as annual trends in hospital admissions, crimes committed, or school enrollments. Examining trends in program operations in light of external factors allows decision makers to plan for the future, whether "future" refers to the birth, design, steady-state, revision, or termination stages of the operations life cycle.

Many unique questions are asked in planning exercises; these require data manipulations that previously had been untried. For example, in the face of a gradual but constant shift of population from urban centers to suburban communities, a change in the location of available public services may be required. In assessing this need, public officials must know the rates of population shift as well as associated changes in service demands (both city and suburban). Only then can they properly anticipate upcoming requirements for municipal personnel and equipment in these two different kinds of locations.

☐ *Planning is normally a long-term, ongoing activity that requires many independent analyses of related information.* Planning exercises do not normally require rapid retrieval and processing of information, but the ability of the information system to respond to a wide range of requests is essential. Traditionally, comparatively slow, batch process, systems have been developed for planning purposes. Unique managerial requests lead to further delays when reprogramming of conventional systems is required to provide the desired information. To enhance the speed and flexibility of strategic planning, decision support systems, which use sophisticated techniques for interaction between managers and computers, are being developed. See Alter (1980) and Keen and Morton (1978). Such systems are rare in government.

☐ *The information desired for planning may be unavailable.* Once an information system is in operation, many top level managers erroneously assume that it can be used to answer any and all questions about the program. An MIS that can provide adequate operational and evaluation support may lack the historical data needed to aid in planning decisions. If, for example, data on program input, output, and costs had not been collected prior to the implementation of a (manual or computer-based) MIS, the system could not comply with a request for a long-term trend analysis.

Upgrading a fire department's present information system to include planning capabilities might require extensive additions. Data on shifts in population, building materials and construction techniques, the current age and expected life span of equipment, and the current length of service and projected retirement dates of personnel are some of the likely additional requirements. Data on the current cost of new equipment, comparisons of features of new and old equipment, projections of new technological developments in fire protection, and estimates of the rate of inflation would also be needed for effective planning in the fire department. These additional kinds of data probably would be stored in different forms and in different places. It would be essential, however, to bring them together, as needed, for use in support of various planning-oriented decisions.

Development of a management information system

The first issue to be considered in the assessment of information systems for operating management is whether a completely new MIS is required. If a reasonable base MIS system already exists in an agency, it might be expanded. Or another agency might already have an MIS that could be adapted for use by the second organization. The existence of such a system might be discovered through a brief survey of similar organizations. If this "transfer" option is chosen, extreme care must be taken to ensure that the adapted MIS is suitable for the new application; slight differences in organization demands can create dramatic contrasts in requirements for information support. The relative cost of transfer, compared with the cost of a new design, also must be a consideration.

In any event, the development and implementation of an MIS is often determined by the source of available funding. Federal contracts often provide funds for state and local government agencies to develop information systems that furnish statistics and reports to the funding agency. However, such external funds are rarely available to subsidize the continuing costs of operating the new MIS. In such situations uncertainty over the likelihood of future state or local support may argue for a more modest information system design. These economic realities are further strengthened in jurisdictions where the MIS design and development costs are funded through a capital budget, independent of the "tight" operating budgets needed for day-to-day operational support of an MIS. In summary, the decision to develop an MIS must consider information on both technical options and their associated costs. One costly error would be to construct a sophisticated system only to find that it has little operational value because users cannot afford to maintain it.

Assuming that it seems appropriate to develop an improved information system, a manager may choose to follow one of two basic paths: a step-by-step approach or an integrated system approach. The selection of either of these alternatives will lead to a distinct set of development, implementation, and operating issues. In the following sections, we will examine the costs and benefits associated with choices at these several stages.

The step-by-step approach

The step-by-step approach consists of the development of an MIS with intentionally limited capabilities and its subsequent expansion to serve additional management requirements. This approach may begin with operational support followed by planning and evaluation support, or it may initially provide planning and evaluation support, while offering operational support at a later date. The nature of the organization and its information priorities will determine which sequence is adopted. For example, the benefits to a fire department from improved information at an operational level are clear: fires will be put out more rapidly, resulting in less loss of property and lives. Therefore, it would seem most reasonable for a fire department to begin by developing the operational capabilities of an MIS. The subsequent development of planning and evaluation support would be a logical next step, assuming that such capabilities would then be used.

A major benefit of the "operations first" strategy of MIS development is that it may naturally lead to the consideration of the future development of a planning and evaluation MIS. An operations manager who grows accustomed to receiving useful information on day-to-day program processes is likely to become interested in being able to prepare future program plans based on historical projections and periodic evaluations of recent program performance. If a manager begins to ask sensible questions related to program planning or evaluation, future MIS development may naturally move in these directions. Eventually, an integrated MIS is likely to evolve. If, however, the existence of an operations MIS does not prompt management to raise such questions, then the planning and evaluation phases of the MIS may never be developed. The cost of this oversight may not be readily apparent until a demand for unavailable information is placed on the organization. The need to provide adequate reports to outside funding sources or to justify current and future expenditures to a legislature requires the use of the planning and evaluation capabilities of an MIS. Failure to provide information could result in the reduction of funding or even the termination of a program or agency. As an organization develops specifications for an MIS, such real, though indirect, costs must be weighed.

The alternative step-by-step approach is to develop planning and evaluation support first, followed by operations support. This is the approach often adopted by organizations that must provide detailed, periodic reports to funding agencies or other governmental bodies. Federally funded human service and health care agencies strive to develop a planning and evaluation MIS to meet the reporting requirements imposed on them. They are naturally less concerned initially with the operational support an MIS might provide. In fact, the visibility of traditional reporting capabilities at the operational (service delivery) level can have a negative impact on a program: failures, as well as successes, become apparent to all who have access to the data.

The "planning first" approach can also be costly to an organization. First, there is a tendency to develop a system that collects too much data "just in case it's needed." Data collection is a time-consuming and costly venture. Second, much information produced for external reporting purposes has little value for program managers; however, it is often these same managers who must collect the data used in the MIS. Such managers are likely to question the value of an MIS developed on a planning first basis. It is natural that they subsequently fail to encourage the development of the capability to provide operations support. Development of an MIS with only planning and evaluation capabilities may well serve an organization in the short term, but an MIS which also includes operational support features is desirable in the long run.

An integrated system approach

An integrated system approach to MIS development eliminates the possibility that limited information-support functions will be served. This approach is intended to meet the various information needs of operations managers and their staff by providing efficient flows of information from data collection, through storage, retrieval, and manipulation, to the output of usable reports. An integrated design can also avoid potential problems of system incompatibility that can result from step-by-step MIS development. Furthermore, this approach also permits early discovery of data processing requirements and options which are unrealistic, considering the capabilities and resources of the agency.

The development of an integrated MIS is time-consuming and requires extensive coordination throughout an organization. Delay by any single group of agency personnel will affect the progress of the project as a whole. The common tendency to try to accommodate all potential users, regardless of their need for information, can result in an unwieldy system that contains much unused and unneeded data. Furthermore, an integrated MIS results in greater costs for design, development, and implementation. If these up front costs get out of line, management might become discouraged and withdraw support before the MIS is operational and any return is seen. Because the integrated system approach takes so much time, the enthusiasm present at the start of a major MIS project may disappear; proponents within an agency, waiting for a major integrated system to be designed before it can be implemented, may either lose interest in the project or leave their original jobs.

Implementation and operation of an MIS

Following its development, an MIS must first be implemented and then operated on a regular basis. The choice of developmental process (either step-by-step or integrated) will affect directly the subsequent costs and benefits during the implementation and operation stages. Under a step-by-step development approach, implementation involves only those organizational units directly involved with the MIS. Meanwhile the rest of the organization continues to function as before. In contrast, the integrated approach affects everyone at the same time.

The step-by-step approach may lead to information mismatches across an agency. If a fire department implements an MIS to improve fire-fighting capabilities, its changed data collection practices may affect other nonoperational units in the department such as budget, personnel, or maintenance. Care must be taken to ensure that implementation of one phase of an MIS will not cause unexpected repercussions elsewhere in the organization. Although step-by-step implementation is generally less expensive than integrated system implementation, savings may be short-lived if subsequent attempts to expand the MIS require conversions of the original system. Furthermore, additional organizational disruptions will occur whenever a new capability of the MIS is added; staff will require training to use the new system, errors will be created as a result of unfamiliarity with the new system, and employees whose jobs are changed will naturally become concerned. If a computerized system is installed, the potential for disruption grows, as does the need for management support during implementation. The choice of the operations first approach can overcome some of these problems if managers begin early to realize the value of an MIS. Managers who appreciate the operations support of an MIS are more likely to favor future planning and evaluation applications. In contrast, the initial implementation of a planning and evaluation system may create long-term problems, if operating managers do not appreciate the potential value of such a system. Widespread resentment of the whole idea of information systems development may arise when key managers feel that a new MIS has little effect on day-to-day operations.

Now consider the implementation and operation of an integrated information system, an approach which offers great benefits but also has the potential for considerable costs. Following this strategy, public managers intervene in their agency's information-related activities. While this intrusion initially lasts longer than would be experienced in a step-by-step implementation, normal operations will resume once the initial uncertainties are resolved. Management must be prepared for these disruptions and support the MIS if it is to receive a fair evaluation during its early stages. Confusion over the use of new data collection techniques and information storage is to be expected at first. The receipt of needed information may be slower and less reliable during the early phase of MIS implementation. These are normal disruptions, and once they are resolved, information management of the agency will be improved. Ideally, personnel at all levels of an agency will work together to support the MIS through improved data collection, storage, manipulation, and information production. If an integrated MIS is implemented successfully, gradual but widespread acceptance of the system may be expected. Operations management at all levels will reflect the new information resources, especially when multiple payoffs (in operations, planning, and evaluation) are associated with a single new MIS. A successful integrated system will provide information support for a range of managerial questions. Data needs of operations and planning will have been coordinated so that output will be usable throughout the organization.

Unfortunately, the decision to implement an integrated system can severely damage an organization's MIS plans when serious, unanticipated problems arise. For example, personnel resistance and related sabotage, either overt or covert, is not uncommon in the face of this all-or-none approach to information system development. Personnel who fear loss of their jobs, when a sophisticated MIS is being installed, may be tempted to destroy the system. Improper submission of input data, delay in reporting of output, expressions of confusion over operating the MIS, and sabotage of hardware are some of the most likely types of opposition. In the face of such resistance, any future attempt to implement an MIS may be doomed. In recognition of the possibility of these barriers to change, managers should take care to prepare the staff, both psychologically and professionally, for the installation of an MIS. Without such efforts, implementation of an integrated system may be impossible.

Summary

In many organizations, operating problems can be eased simply by determining who has certain kinds of information and who needs it. Proper use of paper, pencil, calculators, and telephones may allow small government offices to collect and process most of their operational data. From direct cost considerations alone, it is a mistake to install a sophisticated, automated MIS in an organization that is neither prepared for nor interested in using such a capability. A less obvious shortcoming, though possibly more serious in the long run, is that such an initial failure may leave an organizational bias against any future information systems development. Therefore the decision to modify a current information system—either by upgrading a manual process or by installing a computerized system— should receive careful attention by managers, operating personnel, and technical staff.

In this chapter, many of the choices and issues inherent in developing a new MIS were discussed. Several concluding observations must also be kept in mind. In designing an MIS for a government agency, one should begin by examining the service currently provided and then seek to identify weaknesses in the existing support. Furthermore, the designer must take care that any new or revised MIS match the culture and competence of the organization; in many small governmental operations complex computer-based systems are not needed.

The depth and breadth of top management's commitment to improved decision making are critical factors in the successful strengthening of information systems throughout an agency. A genuine belief by management that an MIS is needed must be echoed by the wholehearted support of key staff during the development and implementation stages. Conversely, mixed signals about the MIS from top management will quickly lead to resistance from the system's potential users, almost guaranteeing the eventual failure of the system. The full range of managerial support includes financing, personnel, training, and realistic evaluation at key stages of design, development, and implementation. It is particularly important for a manager to allocate sufficient resources to develop a complete and clear set of training materials explaining how (and why) all data are to be entered and interpreted. An MIS developed with this commitment and support can become an integral tool in the management of public sector operations. The value of a well-designed, carefully implemented, and fully operational MIS ought to be apparent throughout the life of the organization.

Discussion questions

1. In chapter 8 we discussed the Office of Code Enforcement in the Housing and Development Administration of New York City. Current practices concerning inspection scheduling and violation coding were described. How might the current management information system be improved to make these activities more efficient and effective?

Do your recommendations require better management of current information or upgrading the system to provide additional information?

2. Assuming Mayor Lindsay would support the implementation of an additional computerized MIS, what recommendations would you make, taking account of issues and options discussed in this chapter? What new data would be needed? Who would provide such data? Which participants in the code enforcement program would benefit from the new information provided? What kinds of decisions—operating or planning—would be most affected by the system you are recommending?

3. Cost considerations often discourage managers from developing and implementing a computerized MIS. A common low cost alternative is upgrading an existing manual information system. For example, developing a central case file to eliminate duplication of effort (in maintaining multiple files on the same case) could improve the management of information in the offices of a mental health program. What other manual processes might be candidates for improvement(without computers) in government programs with which you have some familiarity? How would you implement these changes?

4. Major changes in information systems are likely to affect operating personnel and other program staff. As a recently hired manager of a public agency you have just learned that a new integrated computerized MIS will be installed throughout your agency in ninety days. What actions would you take to prepare your staff for the new system? Discuss changes in job assignments, staff reductions and additions, training, implementation, and any other personnel-related issues that you believe to be significant.

Bibliography

Ackoff, Russell L. "Management Misinformation Systems." *Management Science* 14, 4 (December 1967): B147–56.

Alter, Steven L. *Decision Support Systems: Current Practice and Continuing Challenges*. Reading, Mass.: Addison-Wesley Publishing Co., 1980.

International City Management Association. *Evaluating Local Government Financial Conditions Handbooks 1–5*. Washington, D.C.: ICMA, 1980.

Keen, Peter, and Michael S. Scott Morton. *Decision Support Systems: An Organizational Perspective*. Reading, Mass.: Addison-Wesley Publishing Co., 1978.

Kraemer, Kenneth L., and John Leslie King, eds. *Computers and Local Government: A Manager's Guide*, Vol 1. New York: Praeger Publishers, 1977.

Stokey, Edith, and Richard Zeckhauser. *A Primer for Policy Analysis*. New York: W. W. Norton & Co., 1978.

Chapter 10
"Transit maintenance"

Late one afternoon in the fall of 1976, Jack Herringer and Paul Westlake prepared to leave their office. The two consultants unplugged the computer terminal, carefully packed away their latest set of numerical output, and locked the door marked "UMTA/MBTA Project." "Well, MASSTRAM's almost completed now," Jack said. "All that's left is to prepare the final user's manual. This project sure has been a lot of work. I hope the MBTA will make use of our model."

"Me too," said Paul. "But they've got so many problems, even in the maintenance area, that I wonder whether they'll consider MASSTRAM's implementation as a high priority? And even if they want to, I wonder if they can take all the right steps to make the best use of it? Guess we'll have to wait and see what they do, now that they have MASSTRAM over there to play with."

Background

The Massachusetts Bay Transportation Authority (MBTA) is an independent state agency that provides mass transit service to seventy-nine cities and towns in the Boston metropolitan area. In 1975, the MBTA was beset with severe problems in virtually every area and showed all the characteristics of a dying enterprise: declining ridership and fare revenues, deteriorating service, and deferred maintenance. The existence of powerful unions and weak management further contributed to the bleak outlook for this major transit operator.

In April 1975, in an attempt to reverse the fortunes of the authority, Governor Michael Dukakis appointed Robert R. Kiley, former deputy mayor of Boston, to the post of chief executive officer (CEO) of the MBTA. The post, created in 1975 by combining the roles of chairman of the board of directors and general manager, was designed to provide strong leadership and direct accountability for costs and the quality of service. Kiley, with a reputation as a competent and politically skillful manager, was strongly supported by the state and municipal leaders responsible for paying the authority's deficit, and was committed to a major overhaul of all levels of the authority.

Among Kiley's most severe challenges was the revitalization of the rail vehicle maintenance department, the major bottleneck in MBTA service. Although weaknesses in all operating departments were readily apparent, the drop in the quality of service during the previous decade could be attributed primarily to the deterioration of car maintenance. As one scheduling manager put it:

Back in the Boston Elevated days when we used to make a little money around here, we used to schedule the service for where the passengers were. Now we just schedule according to how many cars the maintenance departments can keep going. And every time we reduce the schedule to what we think they can produce, vehicle availability drops some more. I tell you—we talk about increasing ridership—we're driving them away with bad service.

Services

In 1975, the MBTA served 79 municipalities with a total population of 2.8 million. It operated 37 route miles of heavy rail rapid transit, 43 miles of light rail streetcar lines, 3538 route miles of bus service, and 8 route miles of trackless trolley. Over these routes, it operated three heavy rail rapid transit lines (the Red, Orange, and Blue Lines), a light rail streetcar-subway line with four surface branches (the Green Line), over 200 bus routes, and four trackless trolley routes. In addition, the authority contracted with 17 private bus carriers for the operation of routes throughout the metropolitan area and subsidized passenger service along 10 railroad routes owned and operated by the Penn Central and Boston & Maine railroads.

The quality of service depended largely on the available equipment and varied widely over the system. Exhibit 10.1 shows the composition of the MBTA's fleet of transit vehicles. In the rapid transit section, service was

Exhibit 10.1
Rail transit vehicles of MBTA, 1976

	Number of Vehicles	Year Purchased
Green Line: 291 vehicles	7	1941
Pullman Co. Presidential	80	1944
Conference Cars (PCC)	94	1945
	36	1946
	50	1951
	8	1958
	16	1959
Orange Line: 100 vehicles	50	1957
Pullman Co. Standard	50	1958
Red Line: 167 vehicles	91	1963 (Bluebirds)
Pullman Co. Standard	76	1969 (Silverbirds)
Blue Line: 75 vehicles	32	1923, refurbished 1951
Pullman Co. Standard	6	1924, refurbished 1951
St. Louis Co.	37	1951

most reliable on the Blue Line, although its cars were the oldest. The Red Line had the newest cars and provided the swiftest and most comfortable rides, but the MBTA had trouble maintaining axle assemblies and a new signal system, so the Red Line often broke down during storms. The Green Line, the most heavily used, was the worst in the system. New cars expected in 1971 had not yet materialized, and the line's maintenance record was terrible.

The quality and reliability of bus and commuter rail service similarly varied. Some bus runs were slow and filled to capacity, while others ran quickly and were almost empty most of the day. Political interference in MBTA service planning had, over the years, led to the creation of a number of runs which could not be justified on the basis of ridership.

Organization

The governing body of the MBTA was the five-member board of directors chaired by the CEO. Board approval was required for the hiring of top level department heads, the disbursement of major contracts, fare changes, bonding, and for the submission of the final budget to the MBTA's appropriating body, the advisory board.

The only major statutory check on the MBTA's power to spend was the advisory board, made up of representatives from each of the seventy-nine communities served by the MBTA. Each community's vote on the board was proportional to its share of the previous year's MBTA assessment. (In recent years, these communities had paid half of the annual fiscal deficit of the MBTA, while the remainder had been contributed at the state level.)

The MBTA's line and staff departments, as reorganized by Kiley in early 1976, are shown in the organization chart in Exhibit 10.2. The major operating and maintenance functions were handled by four major departments which included most of the authority's 6400 employees:

☐ The Transportation Department was responsible for scheduling, traffic control, and manpower to operate service. All motormen, drivers, car shifters, guards, collectors, station masters, and other operating personnel were part of this department.

Exhibit 10.2
Organization chart of the MBTA, January 1976

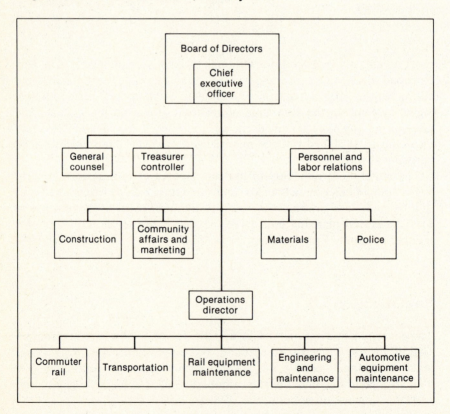

☐ The Engineering and Maintenance Department provided all maintenance to fixed property including buildings, tracks, structures, tunnels, power stations, transmission systems, and the like.

☐ The Automotive Equipment Maintenance Department provided ongoing repair for buses and trackless trolleys.

☐ The Rail Equipment Department was responsible for both light and
heavy maintenance of all rapid transit vehicles and Green Line cars.
Ongoing light repairs and inspection work took place at carhouses on
the lines, while heavy repair work was performed at a repair facility
located in Everett, Mass.

The 1975 budget and authorized manpower of these departments were:
Transportation—$54.6 million budget, 3440 manpower; Engineering and
Maintenance—$19.5 million budget, 1051 manpower; Automotive
Equipment Maintenance—$11.3 million budget, 662 manpower; and Rail
Equipment—$12.2 million budget, 594 manpower.

The major staff functions of the MBTA were handled by seven smaller
departments: Law, Treasurer/Controller, Personnel and Labor Relations,
Community Affairs and Marketing, Commuter Rail, Police, and Construction.

Unions

In 1975, the MBTA had collective bargaining agreements with 29 separate
unions representing all but 450 of the authority's 6400 employees. The
most important union, Amalgamated Transit Workers Local 589, represented over 60 percent of the work force. Local 589 represented only
the least skilled employees—the trades and middle management belonged
to other unions—but it set the basic standards for all other bargaining
agreements.

Outsiders described Local 589 as the strongest, tightest, most inured to
criticism, and most experienced in dealing with management of all public
unions in Massachusetts. The membership included a great many extended families and close-knit groups. As an organization with strong
internal bonds in a key service industry, Local 589 had been able to
extend its power considerably. Over the years, it had won contract settlements which included extremely generous wages and fringe benefits,
plus a host of restrictive work rules which were generally believed to be
costing the authority millions of dollars annually in productivity losses.
Furthermore, the fact that most of the MBTA's management personnel
had come up through the ranks contributed to the strong identification of
most employees with the company family.

Rail equipment department

In 1975, rail vehicle maintenance was handled by two separate departments, the Rail Equipment Maintenance Department and the Maintenance Shops Department. Rail Equipment Maintenance operated the rapid transit and streetcar carhouses located on each of the rail lines and was responsible for cleaning, routine inspection and servicing, and repair of defective vehicles. Minor repairs were performed directly on the vehicle involved. But since the number of vehicles available for service was limited, workers at the carhouses often quickly replaced an entire component system, such as an air compressor, with a working spare in order to rush the vehicle back into service. Maintenance Shops provided the components, and defective assemblies were returned to the major facility at Everett for overhaul. The Everett facility included the machine component shop and a body shop whose workers were responsible for all bodywork, whether it was performed at Everett or at the carhouses. Both the bodywork and the component overhauls in Maintenance Shops were critical to the Rail Equipment Maintenance Department's day-to-day operations.

Sometimes it was difficult to pinpoint responsibility for maintenance problems since the two departments had complementary functions. Mechanics at the carhouses complained that Everett did not keep them adequately supplied with usable spare components, while Everett workers complained that often there was sufficient stock at the carhouses and that the mechanics did not properly lubricate and service working vehicles.

In April 1976, Kiley's new director of operations, David Gunn, consolidated Rail Equipment Maintenance and Maintenance Shops into one unit, the Rail Equipment Department, headed by a new chief mechanical officer. Within the department, Gunn gave greater responsibility and authority to managers of each of the four lines to strengthen line management accountability. The structure of the new department is outlined in Exhibit 10.3

Vehicle maintenance and repair

Maintenance work was divided into two areas: (1) scheduled inspections and routine servicing and (2) breakdown repair. The removal and return of cars either for in-service difficulties or for scheduled inspections required coordination between the Transportation and the Maintenance departments and there was much telephone contact between the two. The Maintenance Department determined when serviceable cars would be used and where they would be stored. When cars were due for routine

Exhibit 10.3
Organization of the MBTA's rail equipment department, 1976

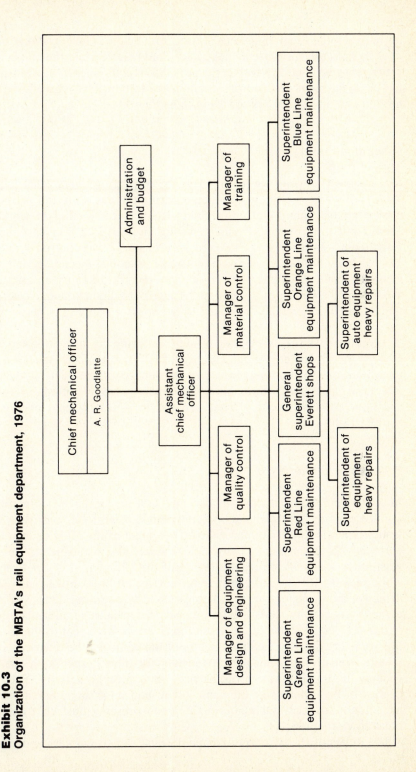

inspections, the Maintenance Department relied on Transportation to deliver them to the carhouse on schedule. Conversely, when the number of serviceable cars was fewer than the peak-hour requirement, the Transportation Department counted on Maintenance to complete its work on the needed cars in time to restore them to service.

Scheduled maintenance

Rapid transit vehicles were called in for inspection every 5000 miles. Inspections were normally conducted during the day shift and often included minor repairs and adjustments. Repair teams of eight workers carried out the inspections and servicing and covered four cars daily. Each team was made up of two truck mechanics, two control workers, one car-body worker, one grease mechanic, one axle mechanic, and one insulator block mechanic. The workers were supervised by an assistant foreman and foreman of inspections. These periodic maintenance activities required an average of twenty to twenty-five man-hours per transit car.

Additional workers were often brought in during the inspection process to perform scheduled "modification" work—the planned repair or replacement of specific components in all vehicles of the fleet. Occasionally, cars that required more extensive repairs were identified during inspection, but cars needing those repairs were usually held over until another shift.

Breakdown repair

In-service breakdowns were divided into four categories: (1) superficial problems such as a stuck hand brake, remedied at least temporarily by the vehicle operator without immediate involvement of the Maintenance Department, (2) minor breakdowns such as a defective windshield wiper, in which cars were able to reach the end of the line and, after brief repair work performed there, to continue in service, (3) breakdowns such as a defective motor generator, in which cars had to be towed directly to the carhouse for repairs, and (4) extreme instances such as derailments, fires, or major electrical failures, in which repair crews were sent to the scene. For some breakdowns, such as failure of the controls, the diagnosis of a required repair could be quite extensive; for others, such as a broken window, diagnosis was a trivial part of the total repair activity. The frequency of breakdowns of the same subsystem on a single car was one indicator of unsuccessful repairs. Exhibit 10.4 presents illustrative data on breakdown frequencies.

The duties of the two types of manpower—skilled workers and repair

Exhibit 10.4
Annual failure rate of selected vehicle subsystems

Vehicle Subsystem	Total Failures (Per car per year)	New Failures (Per car per year)	Repeat Failures[a] (Per car per year)
Air brake	5.8	4.4	1.4
Control	9.9	5.5	4.4
Motors	0.7	0.6	0.1
Auto Signal	2.0	1.7	0.3
Trucks	2.8	2.6	0.2
Door	3.9	3.2	0.7
Heat, Ventilation, and Air Conditioning	1.8	1.5	0.3
Other	11.6	11.4	0.2
Total	38.5	30.9	7.6

Source: MBTA Sample of forty-five rapid transit line vehicles for the year 1976.

[a] A repeat is a failure that occurs within two weeks of a previous repair of the same subsystem.

crews—were established separately, as the groups operated under different supervision and had separate unions. Skilled workers who were affiliated with the old Maintenance Shops Department became involved in direct repair on a vehicle only when their special talents were required in the carhouses or when damage to a car was sufficient to justify its removal to the Everett shops. The great bulk of their time was spent repairing damaged component systems for subsequent use as replacements for others which fail in service. Repair crews were part of the old Rail Equipment Maintenance Department and worked at the various carhouses.

Determining daily work priorities

The determination of daily priorities was the responsibility of the carhouse supervisor. Scheduled inspections had the highest priority, and, occasionally, workers were required to work overtime to avoid backlogs in scheduled inspections. Other carhouse work included scheduled repair of vehicles held over from previous days and unscheduled repair of newly arrived defective vehicles.

In-service breakdowns could not be anticipated, and, when only minor repairs were needed, were handled on a first-come-first-serve basis.

Major repairs (for example, those resulting from a fire in a car), were backlogged until workers were available. When there was a shortage of available cars for use during the next rush hour, cars requiring the easiest and quickest repairs were given top priority. When a line or carhouse faced a shortage, the use of overtime provided some flexibility, although in 1976 the MBTA faced strong external pressures to limit overtime.

Deferred maintenance

Despite this emphasis on car availability and huge overtime expenditures in 1976, the Rail Equipment Department was unable to maintain enough vehicles in working condition to cover scheduled service. Exhibit 10.5 lists statistics on vehicle breakdowns and service schedules. Vehicles that were placed in service frequently broke down, thus disrupting service and

---

Exhibit 10.5
Illustrative data for MBTA rapid transit lines:
service summary and equipment availability

Date: Friday, November 5, 1976

Service Summary		Reasons for Canceled Trips	
Trips scheduled	2078	Vehicle not available	66
Trips canceled	96	Crew not available	2
Trips added	4	Vehicle disabled	22
Trips run	1986	Accident	0
		Vandalism	0
		Weather	0
		Miscellaneous	6
		Total	96

Equipment Availability	6:00 A.M.	8:00 P.M.
Peak Requirement[a]	224	228
Over[b]	4	6
(Short)[b]	(14)	(10)
Available	214	224
Held[c]	110	100
Stored[d]	18	18
Total	342	342

Note: Includes the Orange, Red, and Blue lines.
[a] Peak requirement is number needed for rush hours: Red Line—104, Orange—76, Blue—44 (48).
[b] While one line is short on vehicles, another may have more than its peak requirement.
[c] Held signifies cars that are temporarily unavailable due to scheduled inspections or ongoing repairs.
[d] Stored signifies cars that are unusable but which have not been totally scrapped.

adding to the maintenance backlog. Behind this poor record was a long list of problems. C. W. England, superintendent of the Everett Shops, commented:

Ever since the mid-1950s, we have been robbing Peter to pay Paul— pulling people out of Maintenance and into Transportation. Above all, remember, this has always been a very political organization. Without strong leadership and with split factions, the outside political types have had a lot of influence. One result was that the MBTA would do almost anything to keep service from dropping because that was the visible, politically sensitive part of the operation. And if you drop a driver, you have to drop a route, so any belt tightening always came out of maintenance. Nobody really noticed immediately if there were 36 or 37 rather than 40 repairmen in one of the carhouses or one less machinist in the shops, but eventually, of course, it caught up with us.

Since the late 1960s the MBTA has been caught in a failure-maintenance spiral. We have no time for programmed maintenance— just for putting out fires and trying to stay half a step ahead of the Grim Reaper. We aren't able to plan and schedule work—you know—every year a third of the older Red Line cars should be repaired, there should be a systematized interior overhaul program, the lights should be changed on a regular basis—with manpower costs like ours, we have to get as much as possible out of every hour, and the only way to do that is through programmed maintenance. Otherwise, cars break down on the line, workers have to be shuttled from stop to stop at $10 an hour—it's a very costly business. Take right now, we've got an emergency request for gearboxes on the Green Line PCC cars. We always have an emergency request for something on the Green Line. As a result, among other things, we haven't been able to systematically overhaul the silverbirds on the C-D (Cambridge-Dorchester) Line. And now all their axles are breaking and the Red Line is a disaster, so now we've got an emergency for axle assemblies, and the overtime is going out of sight.

One of the chief reasons for this, and you may think this is crazy, is that we have too much capital money. At the same time that lines have been extended and rolling stock made more sophisticated, there has been a real decrease *in the number of maintenance man-hours—not money, but man-hours—available.*

Management's response to the failure-maintenance cycle generally involved attempts to attract additional resources. In past years, the MBTA had been very successful in securing support from its advisory board and the federal government for special maintenance programs on the grounds that if the MBTA were ever able to resolve its deferred maintenance problem, it then would be able to develop some long-term preventive maintenance programs. One manager remarked, "We've gotten some good things out of these programs. We would have had to do that work anyway, but we put it together in a special funding package and got some extra money. That's what really kept us alive.'' Some of the programs did produce—it was believed that maintenance work done in 1973 still accounted for Orange Line vehicle availability in 1976. But the Rail Equipment Department had limited preventive maintenance programs, overtime was out of control, and the carhouses were not meeting their schedules.

Work force attitudes and capabilities

Contributing to the failure-maintenance cycle was the inability of past MBTA management to deal effectively with labor. A host of union work rules locked into the contract with Local 589 interfered with the assignment of personnel, drove up overtime, and created inefficient jobs. For example, an employee who was unable to finish a job during regular working hours had to quit and turn the job over to the most senior repair worker who wanted overtime, even if that worker couldn't do the job properly. Foremen often hired two or three workers they didn't want in order to get down the seniority list to the one they needed. Other rules specified that two workers be used on jobs where one was likely to be adequate and carved out sharp ''jurisdictions'' for workers. In the trades, jobs were often delayed until an employee from a particular union could be sent over to perform a particular job.

The most damaging work rule, however, was the bidding system which provided the MBTA with car repairers who did not possess the necessary maintenance skills. Union contracts specified that repairers would be selected from the ranks of car cleaners, who were usually former bus operators. Seniority was the sole qualification for the job, and workers were never disqualified for failure to demonstrate skills or aptitude in the MBTA's modest training course.

The relationships among repair workers, the union leadership, foremen, and upper level management also contributed to the problem. The vehicle availability crisis guaranteed extra overtime earnings for the work force. Dealing with union leadership on this subject was difficult. One MBTA manager put it this way:

The union membership, especially the workers in the RTL carhouses, know they have a good thing going with overtime—they average over $4000 a year. They have come to think of it as a normal part of their pay. Many have quit second jobs or bought a boat or mortgaged their homes to buy cottages, and they are afraid to lose the extra pay. As a result, the union politicos try to outdo each other in virtually every area in ragging management to look as tough as possible.

The lengths to which union leaders and individual workers would go to support their interests were, at times, extreme. There were stories of intimidation of foremen and cooperative repairmen. At Everett, there were even rumors of "rat-holing" where components produced during the day were hidden to force overtime.

The foremen also had incentives to force overtime and often had stronger ties to labor than to management. Foremen were on the weekly payroll and received little extra pay for their supervisory responsibilities. They were usually appointed to supervise the same people they had worked with for years and usually retained their dues-paying membership and their seniority rights in Local 589 or a trade union. Many were "temporary charge" foremen who might be returned to repair duties at any time. And the foremen also received overtime pay at time-and-a-half rate with no competing incentive to complete work within normal working hours.

New technology

The Rail Equipment Department's problems were further complicated by the introduction during the late 1960s and early 1970s of complex technical improvements. Operations Director Gunn felt that differences between the federal government's perceptions of transit needs and the operational capabilities of transit systems had created severe long-term problems.

> *The trap is that the Feds pour all sorts of money into the development of new hardware and support systems, and insist that you have to buy it, so everyone has been planning castles and letting the stuff we're operating fall down. Take the new Light Rail Vehicles. We were supposed to have the LRV's three years ago, so maintenance on the old PCC Green Line cars was deferred. We now have equipment falling apart, we have a seniority personnel system that says we have to bid out all our repair jobs among the bus drivers, collectors, and porters—you know, what the hell do they know about cars, no technical qualifications at all—so the only way we get a qualified worker is by chance, and on top of that the Feds are coming down our backs with equipment that is fantastically complicated. It's here now—the LRV. To give you an idea of the problem: you can put the circuitry of a PCC car on one piece of paper, reduce it to one page, and it's legible. On an LRV the circuit book is 288 pages long. It is a maintenance nightmare. It's another case of sale's inventiveness exceeding the system's engineering capability—the lack of a realistic evolutionary approach to building a railroad. You don't go out and build a system that only 1 percent of your maintenance force can work on.*

On the Red Line, we have another story. We have a brand new shop in the wrong place and we can't get to it. It was put there because there was a lot of local resistance (in other places) and now the Red Line falls apart every time it clouds up. It's over behind South Station. You have to go down to Columbia Junction, go through a lot of reverse moves—because the newfangled signal system doesn't work, and we don't have enough qualified people to fix it, but that's still another story—to get to the shop. We've gone from a shop that was ideally suited for the line, albeit old, to one that is fantastic, modern, and jazzy but absolutely in the wrong place, with a signal system that ties up the whole line whenever you want to get in there. The problem is the Feds are parceling out grants to aircraft companies to develop sophisticated technology and requiring transit systems to include it in their specifications to get grant money. If the MBTA had strong operations input at the time, they would never have gotten into this mess. It's technology for technology's sake. You've got the motorman there anyway, who does a smoother job of running the train than the automatic signal system. In one step it obsoleted our whole maintenance force; the same with the LRV's.

Maintenance planning

The chaotic condition of rail equipment maintenance at the MBTA was not conducive to formal management analysis or planning. Limited staff capability and short-term operational crises constrained strategic planning in the maintenance area to occasional studies of facilities and equipment requirements. These studies were required to support requests for capital assistance from the Urban Mass Transportation Administration (UMTA) of the U.S. Department of Transportation. Even before the appointment of Robert Kiley as CEO in 1975, some managers believed that there was a need for ongoing planning at the MBTA.

Perhaps that's why these MBTA managers were so receptive when, in the winter of 1974, a team of consultants approached them to try to define a high-priority management science project which might be eligible for federal funding. Of the several options that were discussed, one clearly seemed to be of greatest mutual interest: the development of a computer-based model to aid MBTA management in evaluating the costs and benefits of different preventive maintenance schedules for rail rapid transit equipment. The purpose of the model was to relate preventive maintenance strategies to vehicle breakdowns (and associated loss of transit service). It would keep track of labor and material costs associated with repair and maintenance of the many different vehicle subsystems. The model was to be used by MBTA management to calculate the overall cost and transit service implications of altering current maintenance schedules. Or it could be used "in reverse" to calculate the most cost-effective changes to current maintenance schedules in light of altered budgetary realities such as overtime constraints. As originally envisioned, the model was to be programmed for interactive use on a computer terminal located in the offices of top management of the maintenance function. These managers hoped that the proposed model would allow them to plan for improved preventive maintenance on the several rapid transit lines. It was also believed that projections from this model could provide persuasive backup for the Rail Equipment Department's budget requests. The Red Line was selected for the development and testing of the model.

Armed with this idea for a joint research and development project with the MBTA, the consultants prepared a proposal to develop the model, which was named MASSTRAM. Exhibit 10.6 contains excerpts from the research proposal sent to UMTA in the spring of 1975.

Exhibit 10.6
Excerpts from consultants' proposal to UMTA

Statement of the problem
In general, equipment maintenance and repair work typically are of two interrelated types: *emergency* and *preventive.* Emergencies arise when equipment breaks down, causing direct disruption to the production of goods or to the provision of services. For transit systems such emergency situations are particularly undesirable since they lead to reduced public confidence in the reliability of the service, and naturally upset patrons, many of whom have chosen to use public transit rather than their own automobiles. (In contrast to emergency breakdowns of production facilities, transit system stoppage is immediately apparent to the system's consumers. Indeed such occurrences are often reported by the media, thus having an indirect and perhaps profound impact on future public acceptance of the system.) And yet it is unreasonable to expect that such system breakdowns can be eliminated entirely; older equipment and uncontrollable events will always result in the need for some emergency maintenance. Nevertheless, it should be possible to reduce the frequency of emergency breakdowns by the implementation of a sound program of preventive maintenance.

The design of a suitable preventive maintenance program for transit vehicles is essentially a matter of balancing two types of costs: 1. the cost of scheduling inspections and then repairing or replacing different equipment components at specified intervals and 2. the cost of experiencing an emergency breakdown between such intervals. The more thorough the preventive program (that is, the shorter the inspection intervals), the less will be the likelihood of emergency breakdowns. But a preventive maintenance program itself can be costly, and ongoing fiscal pressures on transit operators make it difficult to expand indefinitely the size of the equipment maintenance work force. The management problem, then, is to develop a cost-effective maintenance schedule, specifying for a fleet of transit vehicles, when the cars, the subassemblies, and the individual components should be overhauled or replaced.

More specifically, the problem is to 1. determine whether to use preventive maintenance on a component of a transit vehicle or wait until it fails; 2. evaluate alternative preventive maintenance schedules in terms of cost and number of disruptive failures; 3. determine when it may be economical to work on several subassemblies simultaneously; and 4. determine whether to replace an item or to repair it. . . . The purpose of this proposal is to develop a computer-based system to assist the management of urban transit systems in making (these) maintenance decisions.

To our knowledge there are no existing operational models which fulfill this function for transit maintenance managers today. Recent research and development activity in this general area has been restricted to the development of data processing systems which help to implement a predetermined maintenance schedule. The creation of such schedules at present is essentially determined by a combination of equipment manufacturers' guidelines and the experience of maintenance managers and engineers, tempered by the aggregate budgetary restrictions on the maintenance function. Although these maintenance schedules are sometimes partially based on the performance of existing transit vehicles, the use of such performance data is far from optimal. In fact, historical data of this sort are often too incomplete to provide a firm analytic base for such decisions. We know of no transit operator who currently develops preventive maintenance schedules by systematically estimating the likely costs and benefits of different alternatives.

For the Massachusetts Bay Transportation Authority (MBTA), this problem of rail vehicle maintenance is of particular current interest. Due to a combination of several factors—the age and condition of the equipment, very long lead times for delivery of replacement components, and the necessity of manufacturing in house certain components which are no longer available—there are currently substantial backlogs on needed maintenance and repair of existing equipment. Most importantly, the MBTA will be adding a substantial number of new vehicles (including the LRV) as well as some new maintenance facilities, thus requiring changes in the current maintenance operation. The proposed research is designed to provide this tool to the MBTA for their own use and to do so in a manner which could also be of value to other transit operators elsewhere who are faced with a similar need.

Technical approach
There are several different aspects of the technical approach we plan to follow in the proposed project: 1. model formulation; 2. use of the model; and 3. integration of the model within a transit operator's overall maintenance system. Each of these subjects is discussed below.

Model formulation   Although it is premature to specify the precise methodology to be used in developing the proposed model, the major features of such a model can be anticipated. Technically speaking, the problem addressed by this project does not fit neatly into any single well-established theoretical framework. It does, however, share similarities with several familiar areas of management science: renewal theory, job shop scheduling, and production smoothing. A brief introduction to the theoretical strands which are likely to be relevant to our problem is provided below . . .

Use of the proposed model: manager-machine interaction   In the absence of any significant changes to transit equipment usage, the proposed system would probably be used at periodic intervals (semiannually and annually) to reevaluate existing maintenance schedules. At this time all relevant statistical information, such as equipment failure rates and repair costs, would be updated. Naturally, the more differentiated the transit system (for example, types of vehicles, numbers of transit lines), the more extensive will be these periodic uses of the proposed schedule evaluation model. We would also expect our model to be used on an as-needed basis to help transit managers evaluate the maintenance implications of additions or modifications to the fleet of transit vehicles or to the nature of its service. A further occasion for using the proposed model would be to help a transit equipment maintenance manager assess the implication of external changes to the maintenance schedules, ones which might be imposed, for example, by modifications to operating budgets or to labor union agreements.

With these types of applications in mind, we propose to design a computer-based model which is "conversational" in format: a manager will be able to sit at a remote computer terminal (in the offices of the MBTA, for example) and work directly with this model, eliminating the need for an intervening staff of computer experts. Programming the model in "conversational" mode will facilitate the manager-machine interaction that is desired for a model truly to be a decision-aiding tool of management. To ensure that this conversational mode is successfully implemented, we plan to develop a prototype early in the course of this proposed project. Using this prototype, the project's researchers and key managers of the MBTA will jointly identify needed improvements to the computer system's design. Implementing these improvements will be a crucial task during the latter part of the grant period. Following this process, we hope to become quite knowledgeable on the more general problem of how to integrate modern computer-based tools with ongoing transit management activities that require different styles of decision making.

Integration of the proposed model within overall maintenance system   The evaluation of alternative equipment maintenance schedules, upon which this proposal centers, could serve as one piece of a larger system to aid transit managers in their maintenance activities. This overall system should be capable of scheduling the jobs, maintaining time and cost for each job, and automatically updating inventories and reordering spare parts. In our research project, we intend to explore the crucial questions of how to integrate the proposed computer-based system for establishing maintenance schedules with other state-of-the-art computer systems which support the ongoing function of transit equipment service, inventory, and maintenance (but which accept the schedules as given).

. . . we plan to work closely with managers and staff of the MBTA to ensure that the proposed model will successfully interface with the other portions of their system, specifically the Computerized Maintenance Records System (CMRS) now being developed at the MBTA, and with a computerized production and inventory control system that is to be developed by the MBTA.

A letter of sponsorship, signed by an official at the Maintenance Department of the MBTA, accompanied this proposal. The letter included the following passage:

I believe that (this) tool will be useful to us and will be pleased to cooperate in (the proposed) venture. I am especially interested in developing a schedule evaluation system which will make use of the Computerized Maintenance Records System (CMRS) now being developed at the MBTA. . . . It would be most helpful to be able to use the proposed model to help develop maintenance schedules for the new MBTA vehicles currently on order.

Several months later UMTA reviewed and approved the proposed project which was to be conducted over a twelve-month period. The consultants received a grant from funds that UMTA set aside for "research and investigations into the theoretical or practical problems of urban transportation." UMTA was especially interested in this project because it was designed to be of direct benefit to a particular transit organization in a key area of management. Maintenance managers at the MBTA were pleased with the launching of this project and promised their board of directors that the forthcoming model would help them to plan for more cost-effective maintenance of the rail car fleet.

Later in 1975 after the development of MASSTRAM was well underway, one of the consultants, Paul Westlake, was asked to review the project with the director of the budget office of the MBTA's advisory board. After describing the purpose of the project, Westlake reported on the progress of the consultant team and tried to distinguish MASSTRAM from other ongoing analytic efforts in the MBTA's maintenance area:

Our team has completed an extensive review of MBTA activities in the ongoing maintenance and repair of rapid transit vehicles. We've also begun to explore some of the activities by which "crippled" cars are taken out of and returned to service. . . . Most of our work to date has been on the Red Line, although we have also spent considerable time looking at the Orange Line. . . . This operation review has helped our model-building efforts. Now we're doing a very detailed assessment of the repair time and breakdown frequency of about twenty-five rail vehicle subsystems. These data are being assembled for the first time thanks to the cooperation of several key foremen and supervisors. We'll feed our initial computer model with these data as soon as it approaches a form that is suitable for operational use.

Are you aware of the forthcoming Computerized Maintenance Records System, which is being developed for the Maintenance Shops Department? Don't get confused about the different functions of that system and our model. The CMRS is designed to collect, store, and report data on MBTA rail vehicle maintenance activities as an information and control system. *It tells management day by day, week by week, what's been happening with regard to inspections, repairs, and breakdowns. Our model looks ahead to evaluate different potential maintenance strategies. It's a* planning or policy tool. *It requires as input the kind of information which will exist in the files of the CMRS. So these two activities complement each other. In fact, without the CMRS, our model would lack an adequate supply of timely input estimates.*

Another distinction is probably worth mentioning. I've heard that the MBTA is conducting a study of productivity of its maintenance operations. Our work has different immediate concerns compared with that study. We haven't attempted to evaluate current productivity. We just want to estimate actual current levels of effort required to accomplish various inspection and repair activities.

This spring we'll deliver the model to the MBTA. We're pleased with our progress so far. We're hoping the model can potentially serve a crucial managerial function. Between now and the end of our grant period, we'll do our best to help ensure that the model will turn out to be useful to the MBTA. Eventually, we're hoping that this model and the data base will be used in strategic evaluations for all of the MBTA's rapid transit lines.

The development of MASSTRAM required the consultant team to work closely with the MBTA staff and supervisors. Considerable time was spent at Cabot Center, the new Red Line carhouse. The researchers paid special attention to maintenance and repair practices and procedures. They also became familiar with the kinds of records that were kept at the carhouse (see Exhibit 10.7). All this information helped the team to develop a reasonable set of test data for use on the new model.

By the summer of 1976 MASSTRAM was fully developed. The consultants met with MBTA officials to review the model with them. Among the topics covered were: the definition of a rail vehicle in terms of its respective "subsystems" (see Exhibit 10.8); data requirements for using

---

Exhibit 10.7
Manual records available at MBTA maintenance carhouses

Log Sheets
The most informative repair and maintenance records are the daily log sheets which are filled out by the foremen. On these logs are recorded troubles reported and repairs made. The information gathered by the foreman is entered in chronological order.

Car Histories
From the log sheets a record of individual car histories is created. It includes information on troubles, repairs, and inspections, although it is less detailed than the original log sheet.

Trip Reports
A record is kept of the number of trips made by the cars as reported by the transportation department. These trip reports are posted daily by car on a sheet at the carhouse. The trip log is used for inspection-scheduling decisions.

Dispatcher's Summary Sheets
The Transportation Department is responsible for the Dispatcher's Summary Sheets, which report daily all incidents of vandalism and other troubles with cars. This list is distributed to carhouse supervisors, but there is no claim that it provides adequate detail or timeliness for guiding repairs. There is no comprehensive matching of items on this list with the condition of the cars that actually arrive in the shop.

Exhibit 10.8
List of subsystems included in an MBTA
application of MASSTRAM

Code	System	Subsystem
co01	control	motor generator
co02	control	compressor
co03	control	compressor motor
co04	control	compressor switch
co05	control	heat and fan
co06	control	d-bar cable and button banks
co07	control	cineston
co08	control	relays and switches
co09	control	grids and connections
tr01	trucks	truck frame
tr02	trucks	wheels
tr03	trucks	contact shoes
tr04	trucks	emergency trips
tr05	trucks	hand brake and cable
tr06	trucks	drawbar
tr07	trucks	brake shoes
tr08	trucks	suspension
tr09	trucks	operating unit
ab01	air brakes	cineston and d-man control
ab02	air brakes	batteries
mo01	motors	traction motors
mo02	motors	brushes
cb01	car body	general condition
cb02	car body	window glass
cb03	car body	destination signs
cb04	car body	door/light/crew signal equipment

MASSTRAM (see the list in Exhibit 10.9); and the need to view MASS-TRAM as part of an ongoing process of analysis, management, and control (see the chart in Exhibit 10.10). The presentation also covered some methodological points, especially the difference between data preparation for testing the new model and subsequent data needs for verifying the model. One of the researchers explained:

> *The availability of machine-readable input data is a fundamental assumption in the design and construction of MASSTRAM. Fully effective ongoing use of MASSTRAM requires an automated data collection and processing system. . . . To test MASSTRAM we pulled together some data for the Red Line from a combination of interviews, sampling of your manual records, and some special purpose studies that you had previously conducted yourselves. Interviews with carhouse foremen*

Exhibit 10.9
Data input requirements of MASSTRAM

General Operating Statistics
Total mileage for all vehicles on the line during a specified time period
Total number of serviceable vehicles
Number of vehicles required for peak service
Average time to move a vehicle to the repair shop when it breaks down in service

Maintenance and Repair Crew Characteristics
Average annual hours worked for each type of worker (straight time, overtime)
Number of workers available and average hourly wage rate for each type of worker
Overtime pay rate

Maintenance and Repair Related Activities and Events
(organized by subsystem)
Number of workers in each category required for maintenance or repair of each
   subsystem together with the average elapsed time per worker to perform the
   particular task
Direct material cost attributable to maintenance or repair activities
Held time, the average number of hours the car will be held if a subsystem must be
   repaired because of an in-service failure
Maintenance interval expressed in terms of the number of miles between the
   scheduled inspection of each vehicle subsystem
Failure rate (per 10,000 miles), related to the maintenance interval being used
Probability that when a subsystem fails the vehicle will need to be taken to the
   repair shop

*gave us subjective estimates for much of the required data. This is how
we began to calculate some relationships between maintenance intervals and failure frequencies for the different vehicle subsystems. And
we used these statistics to help us develop and test our computer programs. We believe these input data to be reasonably accurate and feel
comfortable that our findings are generally reliable. Still, MASSTRAM
will be much more useful when your new data system's functioning.*

At this point in the presentation David Gunn, director of operations,
asked for the status of the forthcoming information system, called CMRS.
He was told that the engineer who had been working for the past two
years on the development of that information system was having some
difficulty in completing the project. Recently, that engineer had been
temporarily transferred to another project involving the new LRV cars,
but he was to resume work on the CMRS as soon as possible.

The presentation concluded with the review of a set of sample output
from MASSTRAM. Exhibit 10.11 contains the materials that were distributed for this review. At the conclusion of the presentation Gunn
asked: "What's the most significant finding from your analysis of our Red
Line's maintenance schedules?" Paul Westlake answered: "This run of

Exhibit 10.10
MASSTRAM contribution to improved transit system management

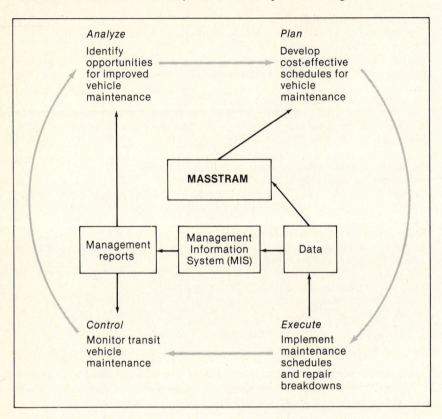

MASSTRAM shows that a savings of about 10 percent could be achieved by switching the maintenance frequency from its current rate of once every 5000 miles for every vehicle subsystem to the 4000- and 8000-mile combined schedule shown in our "optimal" run of the model. But you must realize that all this is based on the data we were using, which may not be completely accurate, even though it's the best that's available." Gunn then asked Chief Mechanical Officer Richard Goodlatte what he planned to do with the model. Goodlatte responded: "Let's send it over to Cabot Center where Frank Crowley, superintendent of Red Line Maintenance, can decide if he's interested in using it." James Burns, Goodlatte's assistant chief mechanical officer, suggested that Crowley ought to get better data by running some experiments. The group discussed this idea and it seemed reasonable to intentionally change the maintenance interval for selected subsystems on a number of Red Line rail vehicles. Experimenting with a shorter maintenance interval would involve some additional cost but no added risk. When a longer interval was attempted, the subsystem would be closely monitored so that even though the subsystem was not maintained at the old interval, when a failure appeared imminent, it could be tallied as a failure and repaired at once. In this way, it was agreed, longer maintenance intervals could be tested without increasing in-service failures during the course of the experiment. This experimental procedure would provide systematic data for refining the failure rate relationships and thereby improve the accuracy of a MASSTRAM analysis. The meeting ended with the consultants' promise to deliver MASSTRAM and a computer console to Frank Crowley at the Red Line's Cabot Center, and David Gunn's thanks to the outside team for contributing their skills to an important problem area of the MBTA.

Exhibit 10.11
Sample output from MASSTRAM

As an introduction to MASSTRAM, a sample set of model output is presented below. While realistic, these outputs are only illustrative.

Table 1 illustrates a comparison between the standard schedule, in which all subsystems are maintained at 5000 miles, and modified schedule that uses a maintenance interval of 4000 miles for some subsystems and 8000 miles for the others. The modified schedule is the least costly schedule provided that the schedule contains no more than two different maintenance intervals. In this comparison, the modified case shows an expected annual net saving of 2272 hours (about 10 percent) of maintenance labor. This modified case required 855 hours (14 percent) less per year for scheduled inspections and 1917 hours (8 percent) less for emergency repairs. The expected net annual savings of $34,000 (about 10 percent) in this illustrative comparison is due entirely to a reduction of overtime costs. (Parts costs which were ignored in these sample runs would tend to drive the system to more frequent maintenance.) The modified maintenance schedule not only costs less, it should also result in better service: there are 259 (8 percent fewer in-service vehicle failures expected during the year and annual "lost" vehicle hours are reduced by 16,233 hours. This results, on average, in having four more vehicles available for service on this line.

Table 2 shows the detailed subsystem evaluations for the modified schedule. Subsystem evaluations are listed in terms of the expected man-hours required for regular inspections (that is, preventive maintenance) and emergency repairs, the estimated number of failures per year and associated annual vehicle hours out of service. Note that subsystems are maintained at different intervals: some at a 4000-mile interval; others once every 8000 miles.

A comparison of Table 2 with a counterpart table for the standard (5000-mile interval) program would show the expected net changes required for preventive maintenance and nonscheduled repairs. For each subsystem which has been shifted to a 4000-mile inspection interval, the number of failures will decrease while the preventive maintenance effort will increase. The opposite occurs for those subsystems which have been shifted to an 8000-mile interval. The total annual cost related to any particular subsystem, however, may either increase or decrease depending upon the net aggregate change between the preventive and

Exhibit 10.11 *continued*
Sample output from MASSTRAM

failure-responding efforts. On balance, considering all of the vehicle subsystems together, this modified schedule represents a less intensive preventive maintenance program than the standard 5000-mile inspection.

MASSTRAM can be used to examine a broad range of trade-offs between increased preventive maintenance and decreased in-service vehicle failures. A set of efficient schedules can easily be determined for which the expected number of failures is reduced with the minimum increase in the associated expected total cost. Table 3 presents such a set of results for schedules when 4000-mile *or* 8000-mile vehicle subsystem inspection intervals were the only ones permitted. For each line of the table, MASSTRAM will have determined a complete maintenance schedule (such as that shown in Table 2). As shown in Figure 1, a plot of this cost-failure frequency trade-off can also be generated by MASSTRAM. The cost increases arise when some of the subsystems are switched from an 8000-mile interval to a 4000-mile interval. The specific sequence of these changes is designed to be the most cost-effective way of achieving a particular reduction in the total number of failures. Management must then select the maintenance schedule which it feels will best serve the opposing cost and service objectives of the transit property during the current planning horizon.

Table 1
Transit Line Evaluation: Red Line

	Estimated labor hours required for maintenance				
	Straight	Overtime	Total	Inspection	Emergency
Standard	17110	6844	23954	5967	17987
Modified	17110	4572	21682	5112	16570

	Maintenance Costs (in Thousands of Dollars)				
	Labor costs				
	Regular	Overtime	Total	Parts	Total Cost
Standard	222	102	324	0	324
Modified	222	68	290	0	290

	Daily Number of Vehicles in Service	Vehicle Hours out of Service	Number of Vehicle Failures
Standard	105	197771	3444
Modified	109	181538	3185

Table 2
Sample MASSTRAM output: subsystem evaluation

System Description	Maintenance Interval (in Miles)	Expected Man-Hrs. Required for Maintenance			Vehicle Hrs. out of Service per Year	Number of Vehicle Failures per Year
		Regular	Emergency	Total		
cineston and d-man ctl	8000	83	73	157	122	5
batteries	8000	75	160	235	1523	23
general condition	4000	442	680	1122	9443	227
window glass	4000	233	678	911	2594	75
destination signs	4000	83	9	93	97	9
door/light/crew sig eqp.	4000	525	2475	3000	27831	619
motor generator	8000	71	53	124	2520	42
compressor	8000	71	206	276	4263	137
compressor motor	4000	0	0	0	0	0
governor switch	8000	63	33	95	1105	33
heat and fan	4000	125	1936	2061	3228	242
d-bar cable and button bks	8000	112	137	250	1246	91
cineston	8000	79	201	280	2361	101
relays and switches	8000	500	1803	2303	20193	451
grids and connections	8000	75	561	636	3930	70
inspect traction motors	4000	508	2202	2710	11512	183
motor brushes	4000	0	0	0	0	0
truck frame	4000	600	1931	2531	14093	161
wheels	8000	292	572	864	2551	36
contact shoes	4000	250	2039	2289	23652	255
emergency trips	8000	150	189	339	1777	47
hand brake and cable	8000	83	81	164	1268	40
drawbar	8000	100	6	106	139	4
brake shoes	8000	125	20	145	1038	20
suspension	8000	192	309	501	5691	206
operating unit	8000	275	215	490	4412	108

Table 3
Sample MASSTRAM output: maintenance-failure trade-offs

Expected Maintenance Cost per Year	Expected Number of Failures per Year	Expected Maintenance Cost per Year	Expected Number of Failures per Year
289768	3185	299799	2985
292271	3069	303416	2969
292637	3062	305236	2962
296130	3016	306024	2960
296995	3005	307835	2956
297999	2997	310929	2951
298736	2991	311841	2950

Figure 1
Plot of expected number of failures per year as a function of expected maintenance cost per year

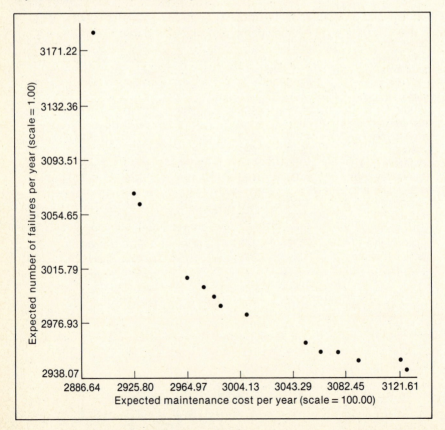

Discussion questions

1. Improving the level of maintenance at the MBTA might involve several different types of initiatives. As a recently hired consultant, you have been asked by the Director of Operations David Gunn to prepare a memo discussing specific changes needed to deal with (a) management capacity, (b) staff skills, (c) union interests, (d) work force attitudes and capabilities, and (e) outside constituencies of the MBTA. This memo should also discuss the feasibility of such changes in the short run (less than one year).

2. In anticipation of the implementation of MASSTRAM, Gunn has requested a memo from Chief Mechanical Officer A. R. Goodlatte explaining the collection of data to support the new program. Gunn has asked you to outline: What data should be collected to determine the optimal level of preventive maintenance? Which of these data are currently available? What would you do to acquire the other needed data?

3. To assess the value of MASSTRAM, Gunn has requested an evaluation from his staff. You have been asked to prepare a response to his request for the following information: Will MASSTRAM be a valuable tool for maintenance planning at the MBTA? Do you foresee any significant problems in successfully implementing this model at the MBTA? What changes could have been made during the MASSTRAM development project that would have improved the likelihood of acceptance and use of the model by the MBTA?

4. In addition to MASSTRAM, the MBTA is planning to introduce the Computerized Maintenance Records System (CMRS). It is designed to tell management day by day, week by week, what has been happening in regard to inspections, repairs, and breakdowns. If you were director of maintenance at the MBTA, what kind of information would you want to be available from this system? Would this be an operations, planning, or evaluation MIS (or some combination)? How do the data needs and information output differ between the CMRS and MASSTRAM?

Notes
*This chapter is a revised version of a case prepared by Stephen R. Rosenthal with the assistance of Robert Kent. Funds for its development were provided by a grant from the Duke University/Rand Graduate Institute's Public Policy Curricular Materials Development Project, which is sponsored by the Ford Foundation. The case is intended to serve as a basis for class discussion, not to illustrate either effective or ineffective handling of a managerial situation.

Part 3
Case management in government

Chapter 11
Case management and policy implementation

A *case*, according to Webster's dictionary, is "a situation requiring investigation or action, or the object of investigation or consideration." In the world of purposive organizations, the nature of an enterprise immediately suggests the type of case it would handle. Manufacturers process orders. Services are offered to customers. Charities solicit donors and distribute to recipients. And government provides service to target groups and individual clients and carries out mandated missions. Loosely speaking, any of these enterprises can be considered to handle "cases."

The field of case management, then, is a special form of operations management. It focuses on relationships between different cases and their processing requirements. It also includes a series of design, control, evaluation, and revision activities that are related to but distinct from the direct processing of cases. As with any other form of operations management, case management in government is essentially concerned with organizational performance in the implementation of public policy. In this chapter we will examine some of the dominant attributes of case processing systems and the range of government activities that are included under the label "case management." We will begin with an exploration of the nature of case processing.

Definition and scope of case-processing activities

When a case is "opened," neither its desired outcome nor its processing requirements are immediately apparent. A case thus retains an element of ambiguity and an associated need for investigation or analysis. By this definition, manufacturing organizations fall outside the realm of case management. Regardless of whether they are geared to mass production, batch processing, or customized orders, manufacturers must know in advance the physical or performance specifications of their products. Production orders must contain full specifications for any attribute of the product about which the customer cares. And the technology and man-power of the manufacturing firm will dictate, for all practical purposes, the production process to be followed and the required processing time.

The same kind of argument leads to the elimination of many services from the domain of case processing. The maintenance of checking and savings accounts by banks, the provision of transportation services by airlines, the delivery of fuel, the activities of restaurants or hotel opera-tors, or the staging of cultural or sporting events are some examples of services which are not case oriented. Customers for these services select the options they desire, and the organization follows a prespecified set of activities to satisfy their demands. Little flexibility or discretion remains in the nature of the service developed once the customer appears and specifies what he or she wants or after a service representative explains the available options and the customer makes a specific selection.

The fact that the scope of a production activity may be defined through the specification of the service itself does not imply that the service is easy to deliver but only that its content is predictable. Many choices may be inherent in the delivery of a service. But as the service delivery system is designed, these choices are often made in advance of delivery. Then, existing operational policies and processing rules are applied consistently to all customers or clients whose requirements are easily established from the start. An organization that delivers service in this way will not be in the case management business.

In contrast with these well-defined service delivery activities, the cases that form the subject of this chapter are handled according to choices made during the course of processing them. Thus each case will be han-dled individually according to its characteristics, as those characteristics become better identified in subsequent stages of processing. In particular, a case-processing activity has the following attributes:

- ☐ Cases are handled on an individual basis and the exact path that a case will take through the processing system cannot be determined from the start.
- ☐ A number of choices will exist in any case-processing program. Each choice embodies an aspect of program policy.
- ☐ The type and level of response to any particular case is usually a matter of discretion.
- ☐ Caseworkers must have some specialized knowledge and be capable

of making judgments. They will usually be considered "professionals."
☐ The outcome of a case is often unclear until its processing is complete. Some cases are not even expected to have an outcome within
a normal planning course.

Each of these attributes contributes to the administrative complexity of
successfully implementing an organization's policies.

Case processing is not necessarily the entire mission of an agency of
government nor the entire business of a firm. One must look within an
organization for those particular activities that have the identifying features of case processing. It makes little sense, for example, to say that an
insurance company is a case-processing enterprise: opening of new accounts, billing of customers, receipt of premium payments, and payment
of covered benefits do not fit the definition of case management as presented above. The claims-handling activity in an insurance company,
however, may well involve case processing since the discretion involved
in the investigation and resolution of each claim is a significant aspect of
that kind of operation. Similarly a credit card company might not normally be thought of as being in the case-processing business. And as long
as accounts are routinely processed and paid, that is likely to be a valid
assessment. But every company of this type has a division which is responsible for the resolution of nonroutine matters such as errors in billings
or overdue accounts, and such operations involve extensive case processing. Some familiar examples of case-processing systems, including grant
proposals as discussed in chapter 6, are presented in Exhibit 11.1.

A functional approach, which attempts to categorize and analyze different case-processing operations, is an important step toward the improvement of managerial practice in this common class of government
activities. The central assumption of this chapter is that successful policy
implementation requires a series of related actions: goals must be translated into designs, designs into operations, operations into evaluations
and controls, which in turn may lead to changes in goals, designs, and
operations. This view of case management provides a language and a
framework for synthesizing the many pieces of this kind of managerial
puzzle. It also encourages the identification of problems in context. This
approach is a positive response to the common criticism that, in its application in government, operations research has usually sidestepped important issues by overemphasizing tractable, low priority problems which
can be solved by standard analytic techniques (Savas, 1975). To over-
simplify the case management function so that it can be represented by an
independent set of planning, scheduling, and quality control models intro-
duces unacceptable misrepresentations of most actual situations.

Exhibit 11.1
Examples of case-processing systems

Organization	Case	Purpose
State Department of Public Welfare	welfare client	provision of social services
Hospital	patient	provision of in-patient medical services
Municipal Office of Housing Code Enforcement	multiple dwelling	enforcement of housing maintenance code
Nuclear Regulatory Commission	nuclear power plant	review and approval of proposed and completed facilities; enforcement of regulations
Public or Private Foundation	grant proposal	review and selective funding and monitoring of proposals
Insurance Company	property damage claim	claim resolution
State Labor Relations Board	labor dispute	mediated resolution

The importance of case management in government

The activities, structures, and legal bases of government all combine to make case processing a common administrative activity in the public sector. A large number of government programs are aimed at either service delivery or regulation, and both of these areas tend to deal with the public on a case-by-case basis. Most public service delivery occurs at the local or state level, although it is subject to federal policy guidelines. As a result of this delegation of authority there is a great organizational distance from policy formulation to implementation. Under such conditions operations managers are likely to have a great deal of discretion, and there is a corresponding need for detailed monitoring and control of case-processing activities.

Legislation that launches government regulatory or service programs is typically vague. Individual programs must then establish guidelines for all aspects of program operations. Ambiguity inevitably creeps in. There is a consistent need to refine general rules and to gather case-related information to support particular case decisions. Increasingly, the reverse problem arises—not enough ambiguity—as legislative bodies and courts begin to impose operational restrictions on existing programs. Several recent examples of such externally imposed processing constraints can be cited. The Federal Speedy Trial Act of 1974 provided that accused persons must be indicted within thirty days of arrest, arraigned within ten days of indictment, and tried within sixty days of arraignment; failure to meet either of the first two time requirements was grounds for a dismissal of the charges. In the late 1970s, a federal court ruling imposed on the Department of HEW's Office of Civil Rights specified processing time limits on various stages in the handling of its cases. In response to threats of periodic judicial review of all foster care cases, the Commonwealth of Massachusetts developed its own supervisory case review procedures and mandated review frequency.

As discussed elsewhere in this book (see especially chapter 7), resource and staffing constraints in the public sector are growing more severe, while the demands on programs using the case approach (in both service delivery and regulation) often appear unbounded. A significant requirement of government programs is, therefore, to select potential cases carefully and to try to adjust the varieties and levels of responses in order to use what limited resources are available in a reasonably effective manner. In such situations, two factors—the desire for equity and the complexity of program response—combine to create an especially difficult management challenge.

The desire for equity has a clear ideology in this instance: similar cases should be treated in similar fashion. Such consistency of response—in other words horizontal equity—ought to be sought, regardless of the type of program or its level of funding. Attainment of this goal requires a carefully designed and well-managed case processing system. Discretion cannot (and should not) be eliminated. And yet those who exercise discretion in case screening and handling should be consistent in the decision criteria they use and in how they apply the criteria in similar situations. Furthermore, different employees with the same case-processing responsibilities should be expected to treat any particular case (or similar cases) in the same manner.

Unfortunately, the ambiguity of cases and the complexity of government services often work against the desire for equity. The amount of information that private individuals or organizations will offer to (or conceal from) the government agency handling a case often varies considerably. Honest differences of opinion about the proper response may exist, the cost of information gathering may become prohibitive, and the range of possible program responses (including those which are allowed under extenuating circumstances) is often quite elaborate. Despite management's best attempts to limit worker discretion to prescribed options under specified conditions, additional discretion naturally creeps in: it is prohibitively expensive to monitor and audit every aspect of every case. Careful training of new caseworkers is especially important in this regard.

Case processing, therefore, becomes an act of elaboration aimed at consistent, responsible decisions. Such elaboration must occur in stages as the government agency learns more about a case and begins to focus on a reasonable response to it. The structure of an organization, the design of jobs, the development of operating procedures, the allocation of resources, and the attention of management must all work together to promote an intelligent system for handling cases in government.

Case-processing programs, such as those described in this chapter, are defined through operational action rather than through preliminary design and planning. This is largely because government agencies do most of their learning on the production line. Private sector organizations usually have staff groups for product design, marketing, process engineering, and testing. Government, in contrast, is characterized by the lack of a tradition of planning, inadequate technical resources, political urgency to get a program started shortly after the formal policy is defined, the frequent lack of prior experience with the business of a new program, the strong likelihood that it will be difficult to predict in advance the range and volume of cases that will arise, and the corresponding operational requirements that are accordingly imposed on the program. One should expect, then, that a series of small program decisions in government will exert a large impact on performance and that policy in practice may differ considerably from policy in rhetoric.

An example of the policy implications of seemingly administrative choices in the housing code enforcement program (chapter 9) is summarized below.:

States and municipalities often issue statutes relating to the maintenance and operation of rental housing. Such statutes are enforced by municipal Code Enforcement Offices. The statutes specify that every building must meet certain physical standards which are deemed necessary for the public welfare, and that the landlord keep his property in good repair.

An Office of Code Enforcement typically will be organized to ensure compliance with these statutes. Such an Office will engage in the following activities: receiving complaints and processing them for subsequent inspection; issuing violations and removing them; and preparing cases for court action. Many administrative choices can shape the ways in which these activities are conducted. These choices may concern various issues such as: how, where and by whom complaints will be received; the priorities for allocating inspectors to complaints (e.g., by type of complaint, history of building, or neighborhood); the nature of the inspection visits and the kind of information that is collected as a result of such visits and the "trigger points" (e.g., certain numbers or types of violations) which indicate when buildings are in such difficulty that court referrals must be made. Choices may also determine the reliance on periodic review inspections, rather than on complaints alone, and the relationship between the Office of Code Enforcement and the courts in specifying the level of fines that are to be imposed on landlords under various conditions.

Although none of these issues is addressed in a typical Housing Maintenance Code (which is the primary policy document of a Code Enforcement program), each implementation decision will clearly affect what the program policy will be, in fact. The special response to an "emergency" complaint, and the operational definition of emergency, for example, are not normally specified in the Code. Neither is the coding scheme used by inspectors, which may be more or less precise in indicating the severity of an observed code violation. (Such "procedure development" activities typically get delegated to the agency's operational staff.) The degree of uniformity of skills and training of inspectors can affect the consistency of violation placement and subsequent sanctions. Administrative decisions to focus code enforcement attention on "marginal" neighborhoods can be viewed as a policy of paying less attention to those neighborhoods which are either in above-standard or highly-deteriorated conditions. (Teitz & Rosenthal, 1971)

The structure of case-processing programs

In order to accomplish their case-handling goals, public sector agencies must begin to make large-scale commitments to case management activities. Evidence of movement in this direction can be found in many organizations at all levels of government. State and local welfare agencies around the country are instituting eligibility tracking systems and social service management information systems. Hospitals have been at the forefront of deliberate attention to case management, since careful monitoring of cases is frequently a matter of life and death. Many federal regulatory agencies are devoting significant resources to developing methods to monitor their investigatory and administrative resolution processes. Numerous systems have been developed to support case management efforts in prosecutors' offices and police departments. The exchange of ideas about case management among similar organizations in different jurisdictions is beginning to occur through limited federal coordination (for example, the Title XX program of the Department of Health and Human Services) and through specialized "trade" organizations (for example, the National Association of Attorneys General and the International City Management Association). Typically, such exchanges have focused exclusively on the particular kinds of activities in one type of organization. But many of the same types of issues concerning effective case management arise in all organizations that undertake this activity.

While no two case-handling programs are exactly the same, strong similarities exist among different levels and missions of government. These similarities are both functional and structural. To describe them is to classify the field of case management. This classification can promote the generic study of case management, thereby encouraging the transfer of models and findings from one area of application to another. Such efforts will also lead to the improved diagnosis of problems in implementing policy through case management. The dual goal of such work is: (1) to encourage more reasonable public policy (in the sense of promising more of what can be delivered and less of what can't be); and (2) to promote administrative and operational decisions which either retain the spirit of the original policy or use operational experience to force the reworking of overall policy.

An informal review of the various government activities that process cases suggests these common functions: delivering a service, enforcing a regulation, or providing a formal authorization. Exhibit 11.2 outlines these different functions in terms of the major characteristic of a case, the kinds of choices and actions which need to be taken, and the meaning of

Exhibit 11.2
Different functions of government case-processing programs

Function	Input	Process	Intended Output

Service Delivery
  social services
  medical services
  legal services
	Client with
	  needs
		Assessment of
		  needs
		Delivery of
		  service
			Satisfied or
			  "cured" client

Statutory
  Enforcement
  housing
  trade
  civil rights
  prosecution
	Potential
	  violation
		Investigation of
		  complaint
		Issuance of
		  finding
		Determination of
		  penalty
			Compliance or
			  punishment

Authorization
  licensing
  grant awards
	Applicant
	  with request
		Review of
		  request
		  (comparison
		  with standard)
		Decision
			Approval or
			  rejection

having "resolved" a case. It should be noted that some cases may proceed through cycles of authorization and monitoring, followed by relicensing or the possible imposition of sanctions.

In addition to classifying government case-processing activities according to their functional categories, we must also look at the structural requirements of organizations which try to perform these functions. What are the needed tasks, skills, and activities for processing cases? When the particular jargon of the individual programs is stripped away, how similar is the central processing structure? Simply put, all case-processing systems have four stages: identification, analysis, response, and resolution. A schematic diagram of this structure is shown in Exhibit 11.3. Note that identification is a distinct initial stage, and resolution must be the last.

Exhibit 11.3
The case-processing pipeline

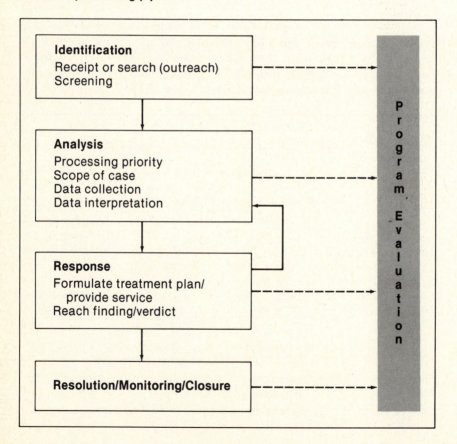

Analysis and response, however, are likely to be iterative activities since new information can lead to case-processing actions that, in turn, require additional analysis before eventual resolution and closure are possible. Finally, program evaluation, if it exists at all, is an independent staff activity in which all stages of the case-processing operation are observed. Highlights of each of these structural stages are discussed below.

Identification

The *case identification* process through which potential cases are initially received is vital to any case-processing program, since it sets the stage for all subsequent operational activities. Identification activities must be designed to take both case characteristics and available resources into account. This process consists of two sequential activities: acquiring new potential cases and screening them. Acquisition may be centralized or decentralized. It may involve only staff of the case-processing program, or it may depend on the assistance of staff from other related programs (for example, the referral to a job training program of a new recipient of unemployment insurance).

One way to acquire cases is through *search* or "outreach" activities, as staff go out to seek new cases to bring to the attention of the program (for example, on periodic site visits, inspectors from the Occupational Safety and Health Administration discover apparent instances of statutory noncompliance). A more passive method of case acquisition is to accept complaints or requests from groups or individuals "outside" the program. In responding to a complaint-originated case, a staff member may uncover additional cases requiring separate attention.

Screening involves determining the eligibility of potential cases. Eligibility may be a matter of statutory specification (as in the regulations of a particular federal agency), seriousness of the condition under consideration (as in a hospital emergency room), or membership in a certain subset of the population (as in a youth services program), to give a few common examples. The more precise the formal definition of case eligibility and program obligation, the more mechanical and consistent the screening process will be. Once eligibility and associated obligations have been established, cases are logged in and referred for subsequent analysis and response. Those deemed ineligible never become cases (unless there is an appeal mechanism, which is itself a case-processing system). The legitimacy and priority granted to different sources of case identification are usually matters of administrative policy, as are exceptions to the general rules. A well-designed screening activity is a critical part of any case-processing system. An appreciation of inherent weaknesses in the screening process (outlined below) is essential for case management and policy implementation.

Analysis

Various activities in which different specialists determine how and when a case is to be processed constitute case analysis. Once a case is accepted, it becomes part of the active case load. It is then assigned to a processing unit where one or more caseworkers are designated to handle some or all of the stages of case analysis and response. In some organizations (for example, workmen's compensation units), these workers are treated as a "pool"; no individual has full responsibility for a case and assignments are interchangeable within the unit. In other situations, a case is assigned to a specific worker who remains responsible for it until the particular problem is resolved successfully. Depending on the type of program, a caseworker may have any of a number of job titles, such as investigator, inspector, hearing officer, social worker, or adjustor. The work actually done in the analysis and response stages will naturally depend on the type of case being handled.

Establishing a case's priority is an initial step which involves categorizing the case with respect to the rest of the case load and deciding its relative urgency; some cases will warrant special treatment—that is, faster processing than cases which arrived earlier—because they are deemed to be "emergencies," politically visible, or particularly significant in terms of overall program goals. The scope of a case will then have to be defined. Although occasionally the agency will have no choice concerning scope, often it will have considerable latitude. For example, in a social service case, a familiar question is whether to include an entire family or just the family member with the "presenting problem." In an enforcement case, the range of charges to pursue is often a matter of discretion. The data collection activity begins with determining the information required to yield a proper response (that is, how to prove the case). Data collection takes many forms (for example, issuing subpoenas, administering psychological tests, or conducting interviews) and has a variety of labels: "investigation" in law, "performing lab tests" in medicine, "taking client profiles" in social services. Data interpretation is the review and analysis of collected information to formulate an appropriate response. Interpretation may be called diagnosis in medical areas, assessment in the social services, and determination of probable cause in an enforcement case. In practice, these four analysis activities are highly interactive. A new piece of information can result in a redefinition of either the scope or priority of a case. Conversely, a change in case priorities, as a result of (say) outside pressures, may require the collection of additional information or the development of a more sophisticated analysis.

Response

The response stage of case processing varies by type of organization. In organizations which deliver services, the response will usually be a service (or treatment plan) designed to achieve some particular impact on the client and the method chosen to deliver services according to that plan. Such plans are likely to be modified continuously as new data (lab tests, reports about a client's behavior) are collected and interpreted. The scope or priority of a service case may also shift as a result of information collected while delivering services to a client. In an enforcement (or authorization) organization, a typical response is to hold a hearing or trial and then to reach a finding or verdict. The hearing or trial is in itself a data collection and analysis activity which occurs in response to earlier analytic stages performed before formal charges were issued. Sometimes, however, especially in licensing situations, the response stage requires continual monitoring or inspection rather than arrival at a decision.

Resolution

Case resolution can take many forms. A fine, a sentence, a plea bargain, a "not guilty" finding, a release from treatment, or an agreement of some type are some familiar examples. Resolution may be the equivalent of case closure (for example, labor mediation), or it may mean passing the case from the jurisdiction of one organization to another—as when a defendant is sent to jail or an inpatient becomes an outpatient—thereby generating a new case elsewhere for each one that is closed. In situations where an agency must monitor its decisions to see if they have been properly implemented, a case may not be closed formally until long after a resolution has been reached. Instances which require such monitoring include lengthy appeals processes and compliance efforts that may take many years of reviewing progress reports until it is clear that the defendant has met the provisions of an agreement (for example, equal opportunity hiring practices). Some agencies may choose to include outcome evaluations of cases as the last stage of their process (for example, ultimate successful employment following vocational rehabilitation services). Sometimes closure may occur without any resolution of a case. This will happen, for example, if resources are scarce and the case is deemed to be either relatively unimportant or unresolvable with a minimum of additional effort. In any event, closure is usually the final step of case processing and indicates that a case is no longer considered active.

Program evaluation

As indicated in Exhibit 11.3, program evaluation depends on selective monitoring of all stages of the case-processing pipeline. A comprehensive evaluation would involve collecting and aggregating data on the types of cases being handled, case-processing trends and patterns, and the distribution of case outcomes. A complete evaluation would also include the identification of changes in the client population that may be attributed to the existing case-processing program.

Issues for operations managers

How does case processing determine the effective policy of a program? To answer this question, we must examine the range of issues that are implicit in the activity of case management. The following discussion of policy-related management issues draws on the conceptual framework presented above. The range of topics considered is meant to be illustrative, rather than comprehensive.

Screening at the intake stage

Specifying and implementing the screening criteria to be used at the intake stage is a necessary case management function. To begin, the relative balance between active outreach for cases and passive receipt of complaints or requests strongly influences how much program targeting is possible. Subsequent screening activities at intake further define operational program policy. The policy implications of case screening should not be underestimated, since these intake procedures serve to distinguish those potential cases which will receive attention from those which will not.

With program planning such a prevalent concern in budget preparation today, organizations are being forced to state their overall priorities. Government agencies must then choose which cases to accept in accordance with these priorities. But when case-screening criteria are not sufficiently refined, when staff training is inadequate, or when management is not effective at monitoring the intake activity, inconsistencies will result. In 1979, the U.S. Department of Justice, for example, conducted a nationwide survey of the types of cases that its attorneys declined to handle and the frequency with which such refusals occurred. The purpose of the study was to see if formal priorities were actually being implemented.

It is not difficult to find examples of the ways in which operational inconsistencies can arise in intake screening. Consider a situation related to the example presented in chapter 8: an intake clerk in a housing code enforcement program may refuse to accept one case because the tenant's tone of voice makes the condition seem not "very important." A short time later, another intake clerk, hearing a more emphatic plea for the same type of assistance from another tenant, may decide that the city ought to respond with an inspection. Similar inconsistencies may be found in the actions of intake clerks in local welfare offices (Pesso, 1978). Such inconsistencies can occur frequently and may be particularly costly when emergencies are not adequately identified. Until intake activities are adequately controlled through staff training, explicit procedures, and supervisor monitoring, an agency can never be sure that its established policies are being followed. Yet rigid adherence to rules in the blind pursuit of consistency can have disastrous effects on program equity.

Since improper case screening seems to be unavoidable, the sources and implications of screening errors must be understood. Whenever yes or no decisions must be made on the basis of incomplete information, two different types of errors are possible: (1) the incorrect rejection of a potential case, or (2) the acceptance of an inappropriate case. Both of these types of errors may result from incorrect data on certain prespecified surface attributes of the case; for example, formal conditions of eligibility (for example, age, residence, income) may be specified in advance by legislative mandate or administrative rulings. Some case-processing programs lack such simple indicators of eligibility. Then one must search for evidence of the case's legitimacy; the question is always how far to carry that search. Limitations of time, resources, and authority will prevail in such situations; there is a trade-off between the accuracy gained through additional screening and the incremental cost of such diligence. The fewer the number of screens, conversely, the greater is the risk of both "Type I" and "Type II" errors. (For a further explanation of the technical meaning of these two kinds of errors, consult any statistics text on the subject of hypothesis testing.) In a well-designed screening process, the likely social and economic cost of each type of error must somehow be factored into the specification of processing routines and decision rules. The nature of this trade-off, however, is inescapable; the screening process will inevitably contain some degree of uncertainty.

Setting case-processing priorities

It is frequently impossible for a public sector case-processing program to satisfy the potential demand for its services. Also, some cases will be difficult or impossible to resolve and will remain active for a long time. A successful program may thus develop a sizable backlog of cases through the years. The history of the federal Equal Employment Opportunity Commission (EEOC) is a good example of this ever present management problem. Empowered by Title VII (Section 706) of the Civil Rights Act of 1964 to receive and investigate complaints of employment discrimination, the EEOC had amassed a backlog of 127,800 unresolved charges by the end of the 1976 fiscal year. A sizable backlog of any sort is likely to provide an excuse to seek budget expansions for additional staff. Court systems, for example, perennially demand more funds to remedy long delays in reaching trial. Program management may also try to specify processing priorities or insist that existing priorities be implemented. Managers often wonder whether to emphasize newly opened cases that have just begun to be processed or to stress older cases that are currently still unresolved. Sometimes the question is what mix of these two extreme strategies is appropriate.

Unfortunately, there is no one correct set of priorities for reducing backlogs, since program goals are often multidimensional and, to some extent, conflicting. More specifically, equity often has multiple attributes, each of which would lead a manager to emphasize a different priority rule. The priority issues differ between enforcement/approval organizations and those delivering services. Exhibit 11.4 outlines a variety of potential priorities for processing enforcement cases and identifies the methods of implementing these schemes and the probable side effects (which may be unintentional).

Although these may seem to be oversimplified priority rules, they have a strong appeal to public managers who wish to issue clear signals to caseworkers and to assure the public that a definite action is being taken. The visibility and impact (and deterrent effect) of a given program will be highlighted by adopting methods 3, 5, and 7. The appearance of program responsiveness will be supported by use of methods 1, 4, and 7. The evenhandedness of program administration is demonstrated by methods 2 and 6. Clearly the adoption of any one, or a combination, of these methods is ultimately a statement of the organization's policies.

In organizations that deliver services, backlogs are often the result of the kinds of services that are deemed appropriate. The goal is not so much to reduce backlogs by closing cases as it is to serve as many people as effectively as possible. In social service agencies, for example, choices between treating a group or an individual, or between treating specific conditions or taking action to prevent the emergence of problems, have broad managerial and clinical implications. Overall response patterns

Exhibit 11.4
Examples of possible priorities for handling enforcement cases

Goal	Method	Side Effects
1. Quickly close as many cases as possible.	Locate potentially simple cases regardless of age and process only these.	Will create backlog of complex cases and will have less latitude to juggle slack time.
2. Close all cases opened prior to X date.	Use a great percentage of investigator time on old cases.	May waste time on irrelevant cases and lose momentum on important ones.
3. Affect the lives of as many citizens as possible.	Select cases based on size of jurisdiction or organization and/or number of employees, constituents, or members affected.	Fewer cases will be closed because larger, more complex cases take much longer to investigate.
4. Make some significant response to every new case within X number of days.	Assign *all* cases to investigators regardless of work load and require that they collect applicable data immediately even if they can't begin analysis for months.	Expectations may be raised then reduced because it will take longer to complete analysis.
5. Process the most important cases quickly.	Screen incoming cases to identify those that are most important and give them top processing priority.	Some cases will take longer to process than otherwise but targeted processing may make greater impact.
6. Process cases equitably (if slowly).	Assign priority based on date case was opened. Always handle oldest case first (first-in-first-out).	May waste time on irrelevant cases and lose momentum on important ones, but cases will receive equal treatment under law.
7. Process *all* cases as quickly as possible.	Close trivial or simple cases as soon as possible. Avoid expanding scope of other cases; interpret scope as narrowly as possible. Do minimal analysis necessary to substantiate some finding.	Quality of case analyses will be harmed; cases may be prepared so simplistically that compliance will be minimal.

generally should be consistent with publicized program goals. In particular, when program managers seek to reduce backlogs, they may choose to emphasize one type of treatment over another and may thereby redefine program policy. Operational responses implicitly define the market for a public program.

A case-processing program may be described as a complex queuing system of responding to policy decisions. A case arrives at the agency and takes its place at the end of the line or queue; a service is delivered that permits the case to move into place in the next queue; when that step is completed the case moves to the next queue; the process continues until the case is discharged. The nature of the arrivals will naturally vary widely from one type of case to another; they may be voluntary (as in a welfare office) or involuntary (as in a regulatory proceeding). They may occur at a fairly regular and predictable rate, or they may bunch up, as with disaster relief applications. Similarly, the services performed may vary all the way from certifying that a necessary document has been filed to providing ongoing counseling for an entire family.

The critical management choice is the design of the whole queuing system: (1) determining the most efficient sequence for the separate steps or services performed, and (2) deciding on the queue discipline—the order in which cases will be serviced—in each of the queues. Moreover, the nature of the arrivals and the services will significantly influence the choices made, while arrivals and services will, in turn, be both directly and indirectly affected by the choice of queuing system and priority scheme. First, arrival rates are directly affected by policies concerning the extent of outreach and mechanisms for screening cases. Arrivals also depend indirectly on service time, capacity, and case outcome since complaints on noncompliance (or requests for service) are likely to increase as enforcement ''muscle'' is strengthened (or service quality improves). Conversely, slow case processing, large backlogs, and ineffectual outcomes are likely to discourage potential complaints or requests for service, thereby reducing future arrival rates. Second, service times depend in part on operational procedures that can be changed at the discretion of policymakers. Different kinds of cases, for example, will be expected to receive different levels of analysis and investigation. But even such differentiated norms are easily violated when program case loads begin to vary. In the face of (implicit or explicit) monthly quotas, or the appearance of especially ''interesting'' cases, service time patterns may also shift drastically.

Policymakers may decide to intervene more directly by affecting the queue discipline in a case-processing system. This would be the result of imposing one or more of the priorities listed in Exhibit 11.4. If such changes were implemented in a program in which each caseworker simultaneously handles a variety of cases, then service times (and, perhaps, new case arrivals) would probably change as well. Changes in the quality of a case-processing system may arise, therefore, from the interaction of a number of factors: changes in service times and waiting times for different kinds of cases; ultimate case outcomes; impacts on the future flow (arrival) of new cases; and, ultimately, the deterrent impact of the overall compliance program.

Determining the scope of a case

For each problem/complaint/referral brought to the attention of a case-processing program, a decision must be made about how narrowly or broadly the case is to be interpreted and the extent of an appropriate response. In enforcement programs, the amount of work needed to resolve a case is determined to a great extent by the breadth of the case—the set of issues that the case is defined to include—and its depth—the degree of sophistication and intensity of its analysis. For example, an individual complaint about discrimination in a local government's handling of a job promotion might be investigated as:

- ☐ An individual complaint only: Did the government agency discriminate against *this person*?
- ☐ A class complaint: Does the government agency discriminate against *all persons* in certain categories?
- ☐ A broadly construed class complaint: Does the *entire government* discriminate against *all persons* in certain categories?

The ultimate determination of the breadth of this case will clearly affect the work to be done as well as its potential impact.

Several factors tend to affect the scope of a job discrimination case:

- ☐ If a complainant brings other complainants to meet the investigator, the case may change from an individual to a class issue.
- ☐ If the investigator is pressed for time, the case may be construed as narrowly as possible to limit the length of field visits and analyses.
- ☐ If the data supplied by the government is orderly, printed by computer, and highly detailed (making analysis easier), the investigator may be more likely to expand the case scope than if the data is very difficult to read and requires much manipulation.
- ☐ If the investigator is more experienced, the scope of the case may more readily be broadened.

The scope of a case may, thus, be the result of numerous idiosyncratic factors totally unrelated to the merits of the case.

In any one of these situations the extent of data collection and analysis (that is, the depth of the case) may vary a great deal. In response to an individual complaint a caseworker will often have to decide how intensively to investigate a range of different factual issues. For class complaints of racial discrimination against one government agency, several levels of analysis are possible:

☐ The percentage of minorities in the labor pool of the area can be compared to the percentage of minorities employed by that agency. If the percentage in the labor pool is significantly greater than that in the agency, discrimination (although not necessarily intentional) is assumed to exist.

☐ The above analysis can be augmented by an analysis by job classification. Thus, the percentage of minority employees could be roughly equal to the percentage in the labor pool, but minorities might be in custodial or clerical, rather than supervisory or managerial positions.

☐ More sophisticated analyses might look at practices of hiring and promoting over time or at the actual hiring process, uses of testing, and special requirements.

Similar issues concerning the scope and complexity of cases arise in service delivery systems. Consider the case of a child who has been exhibiting antisocial behavior. Depth of treatment for the child may be punishment, extensive counseling, or placement in a special living situation. The breadth of the case might be expanded if the entire immediate family of that child is considered to be involved and intensive family and individual counseling services are recommended. As the scope of a case broadens, options on depth and breadth of treatment begin to blur, as when baby-sitting assistance is provided to help the child's parents care for other children in the family. The scope of investigation is also an issue in such a case, since in order to analyze the client's needs, the caseworker might rely on direct observation, interview the child's teachers or doctors, or administer numerous psychological tests.

A given case may be handled very differently in different situations or by different caseworkers. Actual policy will be determined on a case-by-case basis by those who have direct processing responsibilities. Here again, there is a need for carefully specified guidelines, although sometimes the feasibility of such specification is questionable. In the absence of guildelines, standardized case processing may exist only to the extent that supervisors communicate with one another and with their staff through training sessions, informal discussions, and formal meetings. Developing workable guidelines for defining the scope of a case is a much more difficult task than that of developing intake criteria. The guidelines must be specific enough to reflect the organization's priorities, yet sufficiently broad to enable caseworkers to use their professional discretion.

Measuring the performance of processing activities

Performance measurement—with respect to either individual workers or to the system as a whole—is very difficult for case-processing systems. Several factors contribute to this complexity: case mix, quality standards, processing time, demand management, and case closure criteria. We will discuss each of these factors separately, although in practice they are highly interactive.

Case mix   A single caseworker is responsible for a case load that includes a variety of cases; time must be allocated among all cases that are active. It will generally be impossible to handle the case load in a purely sequential fashion, that is, to complete one case before moving on to the next. Instead, the caseworker will engage in parallel processing and will constantly have to decide when to switch from one case to another. It is difficult to measure a worker's performance over a short period under these conditions, since overall progress is necessarily a function of the current case mix. It is also difficult to forecast the progress of any particular case without an explicit appreciation for the other cases that are being handled by the same caseworker. The case mix, similarly, is a critical factor in the assessment of the performance of the entire case-processing system.

Quality standards   For many case management programs, the final output is not well defined and it is often unclear to determine when to close a case. Findings in compliance-related investigations are made when the caseworker believes that the existing evidence is adequate; definitions of adequacy, however, may vary from one caseworker to another, or even from one case to another. Treatment plans for those in need of medical services are often highly subjective, and the extent of analysis preceding this response may vary considerably within any particular program.

The desired scope of a case will largely determine the appropriate standard of quality. Note that setting quality standards too high may turn out to be a problem. For example, in regulatory organizations, investigators will often gather and analyze more information than is actually needed to obtain voluntary compliance from a cooperative subject. If this becomes common practice, considerable staff resources may be wasted.

The more that management emphasizes the quality of analyses or response, the longer processing times are likely to be. On the other hand, if employees are encouraged to handle cases quickly rather than well, quality standards may be hard to achieve.

Defining case-handling times   As discussed in chapter 4, two different measures of case-handling time are of concern to management.

Throughput time is the period from the initial acceptance of a case to its
ultimate resolution. It is a measure of how long the case stays in the
system. Regardless of the specific function of the program, it is always
better (in some sense) to maintain a low throughput time. Delays can harm
clients, be unjust, or make reaching a resolution more difficult.
Throughput time will normally relate to the effectiveness of a case-
processing program. Unlike throughput time, *processing time* is a measure of the direct labor required to handle a case and is an important
indicator of program efficiency. It is a measure ot the total time that
various employees actually spent on the activities associated with processing a particular case. For some service systems, processing times and
throughput times are not very different from each other. Waiting times in
such systems are relatively short. But in case-processing systems where
demand usually outstrips supply, the opposite will be true: cases will
bunch in processing pipelines and waiting times are likely to become
lengthy.

Processing times will vary with the complexity of a case. In fact, when
we say a case is *complex*, we typically mean satisfactory resolution of a
case is likely to require greater than average processing time. As the
number of complex cases in the active case load increases, the demand on
program staff also rises. Large backlogs may occur either through growth
in the number of active cases or as a result of the increased complexity of
those cases (or some combination of the two).

Direct processing time eventually affects throughput time, since it is the
existence and growth of backlogs that lengthen throughput times.
Throughput time will also be affected by the caseworker's skill in parallel
processing of the existing case load. The rates at which outsiders contribute information requested by caseworkers is yet another important factor.

Opportunities for demand management   In chapter 7 we presented the
general issues and opportunities inherent in the management of the demand for public service delivery systems. Some case management systems are confronted with demand that is essentially uncontrollable.
Emergency situations that require disaster relief (for example, storms or
earthquakes) have this characteristic: government programs offering low
interest loans are likely to be deluged with a large demand which must
receive prompt and careful attention. Other case management systems, in
contrast, face demands that are partially controllable, thereby offering
public managers a chance to take strategic advantage of this quality.

In private sector services, some of the most effective demand management strategies are peak-hour pricing or altered business hours. But these
strategies don't solve case management problems for which the total case
volume and mix, rather than the timing of demand arrrivals,
are the essential factors. In the public sector, the level and timing
of demand may be altered directly by various policy or administrative

procedures: eligibility requirements for social services or medical assistance programs usually emerge from formal legislative policy, while screening procedures are often used to eliminate inappropriate or unimportant cases. These actions are relatively immediate ways of managing demand. More gradual and indirect impacts on demand will arise from the performance of the case-processing system; for example, an enforcement program will have a deterrent effect. The use of a variety of demand management approaches can help match the requirements placed on a case-processing system to the available capacity of that system, thereby promoting the improved handling of the pending case load. Conversely, if demand is not explicitly managed, the case-processing program is probably not performing as well as it might. In the extreme, government may "manage" the effective demand by ignoring it, as when a program is terminated.

Case closure criteria   The criteria for closing a case, as described earlier, are often a matter of discretion. Typically, such criteria are not even identified as part of program policy. Accounting systems that contain the single catchall category "cases closed" often mix several different kinds of resolutions and/or closures (for example, compliance has been promised, is ongoing, or has been verified as being completed). Such measurement problems make assessment of program outputs difficult.

Staffing the case-processing program   Staffing decisions made in the program design stage will strongly influence the capabilities of a case-processing program. Staff may turn out to be either overqualified or underqualified for their jobs; either type of mismatch can be costly. Such questions need resolution at two stages: job design and staff recruitment. Job design issues begin with the definition of required experience: When should an investigator be an attorney? When should a "social worker" have formal training in the field? Job design also calls for specifying work activities and associated responsibilities. A typical challenge at this point (discussed elsewhere in this chapter) is to anticipate the levels and variety of discretion that are likely to be required in handling cases. The next set of challenges is to find or train people to meet the requirements of these positions.

Ideally, job tasks will be consistent with the skills and training of the caseworker. But if they are not, when should the nature of the job be altered? And when should management ignore this mismatch, in the hope that problems will be spotted and corrected on an individual basis? Questions concerning the organization of work also arise. When should a case be routed from one staff specialist to another, rather than assigned, from start to finish, to a single caseworker? These kinds of issues are common in government case-processing programs and are exacerbated by the rigidities of civil service systems. When staff-related decisions are made, the most expedient, rather than the most cost-effective, option is often selected.

Mistakes in the general job definition of caseworkers or in their recruitment and training will generate operational problems at the supervisory level. Supervisors must decide how much discretion to leave to individual caseworkers, even when this general issue has been covered in the caseworker's job specification. If caseworkers are highly competent and careful and the choices they make are highly technical, the program is likely to benefit from giving them considerable discretion: doctors in clinical settings exemplify this situation. When the opposite conditions are true, such a decentralized strategy may backfire and lead to inefficient processing and (even worse) inconsistent, inequitable program response. There can be no uniform rule about the proper level of supervision and standardization in case management, but serious attention to this matter in the context of job design is essential. In summary, staffing a case-processing program is likely to be a continuing challenge to case management.

Summary

Case management is a common administrative form for implementing organizational policy. It characterizes many public sector programs in which services are delivered or regulations are enforced. Although there are many different varieties of case management systems, they all share certain structural attributes and a limited number of generic functions. Thus, they present similar kinds of challenges to those who design or manage them.

Formal statements of public policy are often intentionally general and global. A few major program options may be debated politically and eventually resolved through negotiation and compromise. In general, however, most implementation issues are considered "operational details" and receive little or no advance policy analysis or discussion; they are simply left to be worked out by program managers and their staff. For case-processing systems, the resolution of many of these details will largely determine the overall performance of the program. Since these systems are rather complex and are typically poorly understood, many counterproductive choices are made. Often policy-in-practice turns out to be very different from policy-in-theory.

At present, case management is more an art than a science and public managers must continue to grapple, largely intuitively, with the dilemmas of case-processing programs. Regardless of whether government is providing services or imposing sanctions, program staff must determine the eligibility of potential cases, gather additional information to further categorize the new cases, and then develop appropriate responses. Performing these tasks in an equitable manner, through a program that is relatively efficient and coherent, is not likely to be easy. The central managerial challenge is to appreciate the variety and extent of operational discretion that must be left to agency personnel. Management must decide which staff positions should have what kinds of discretion. They must develop staff trained to use this discretion wisely for the range of cases that are likely to arise. And they must design their organization and procedures to encourage professional use of such discretion. Sometimes managers must even be prepared to modify existing policies when program experience proves those policies to be unreasonable. Most importantly, these managerial actions must work together to create a case-processing system which operates consistently with overall program policy.

Discussion questions

1. Many organizations have some production activities which are suitable for case management and some which are not. Consider the example of a university. Make a list of activities usually performed at a university and decide for which activities case management is appropriate. Explain why. What similarities are apparent among the case management activities? Among the other activities?
2. Courts and legislatures occasionally intervene in the operations of public agencies which require improved case management. Possible reasons for such interventions include concerns for timeliness of response, equity of decisions, low staff productivity, or budget overruns. Identify some actions that you, as an operating manager, could take to avoid such intervention. Could you eliminate all such problems by improving your case management? If not, what types of problems could be most readily handled?
3. As discussed in chapter 3, government programs develop through the stages of an operations life cycle. How do the needs for case management differ in each stage of the life cycle? Which of these requirements are unique to one of the five stages? Which requirements continue to exist through all of the stages?

Notes
* This chapter is adapted from "Case Management and Policy Implementation" by Stephen R. Rosenthal and Edith S. Levin, *Public Policy*, Vol. XXVIII, Fall 1980, No. 4, pp. 381–413. Copyright © 1980 by the President and Fellows of Harvard College. Published by John Wiley & Sons, Inc. Reprinted by permission.

Chapter 12
Designing case management support systems

In chapter 11 we introduced the concepts and issues of case-processing programs in government. In this chapter we will explore options for designing systems to aid operating managers who are responsible for case-processing programs. The major questions to be addressed are: How should a manager determine what information is needed? How should one plan to collect, present, and use that information? These questions, discussed generally in chapter 9, lead us to define options for what is termed a case management support system (CMSS).

To begin, consider the general notion of a case management support system. A CMSS is an organized set of methods, procedures, and technical capabilities for providing information to those who need to know about the status or performance of a case-oriented program. Although a CMSS may be limited to manual methods of data collection, processing, and reporting, it will be likely to benefit from some form of computerization. A CMSS may support decisions at several different levels of a single organization, or it may serve more than one organization. The challenge in designing such a system is to consider the many aspects of the case-processing activity including organizational structure, policy concerns, and managerial decisions, as well as the more technical issues of data collection, manipulation, and distribution.

Chapter 9 introduced the concept that all information systems design decisions can be reduced to a single basic trade-off: the value of additional information versus the cost of acquiring it. In other words, up to a point, it pays to invest in a system with more information processing and reporting capabilities because the related decision process, and thus program performance, will be improved considerably. Beyond that point, however, information systems become too expensive if the additional capabilities do not improve the quality of decisions sufficiently to justify the cost of the system. From this trade-off, we can proceed to an examination of more detailed issues about informational support for case management activities: How much information is needed to describe a case? How frequently must changes be recorded? How precise must the records on file be? What are the reporting requirements for successful case management? In this chapter we will outline the implications of these questions, first in terms of the overall scope of the system and then in terms of particular design options. As in other portions of this book, we will consider both operational and policy issues.

Deciding on the scope of the system

Questions of the value of a case management support system usually precede those of cost. An organization must decide who are to be the primary beneficiaries of the system. Several users are possible: case-workers, supervisors, program managers, agency managers, budget analysts and planners in the agency, or external officials who affect program appropriations. Correspondingly, the system can be designed to produce a variety of benefits for the different users: improved client interaction (for service delivery or regulatory enforcement), strengthened management control of operations, enhanced policy implementation, better resource allocation, more rigorous program analysis and planning, or more direct program oversight. The point here is that as one adds new functions to such a list, one simultaneously increases the complexity of the required information system. Increased complexity, in turn, leads to increased costs.

The most important strategic decision regarding a CMSS is, therefore, determining its scope. Practitioners must avoid the temptation to be overly ambitious in deciding how comprehensive a CMSS is to be. At the same time they should try to seek the advantages of a system which can serve several purposes simultaneously. In the following review of the basic choices available to those who would design a CMSS we shall begin with a presentation of the functions which might be served by a CMSS. Next we shall examine how one might satisfy these functions using several associated "ideal types" of systems. Some common variations on these simple models are then identified. The section concludes with a description of ways in which an organization's environment might affect the choice of CMSS scope.

Potential functions served by a CMSS

A case management support system, like most information systems, may serve one or more of the following functions.

Function	Type of Information
External Reporting	Statistics on current status of case load
Program Evaluation	Measures of efficiency, effectiveness, equity
Planning/Budgeting	Projections of reserve requirements
Learning	Insights to aid in future evaluation or planning

External reporting requirements, or the threat of their imposition, often provide the impetus for the development of a CMSS. They may even define the shape of a new information system. One state welfare department, for example, had to report the status of all cases every six months in order to avoid a threatened judicial case review process. A federal regulatory agency, in a different situation, began to acquire better data about its consent negotiations (out-of-court settlements) with respondents after a congressional study called attention to intolerable delays in reaching final agreements. In each of these two situations, a CMSS was developed simply to provide the case-oriented information required by externally imposed mandates. In contexts like these, program managers must try to understand the differences between the information they need to collect to satisfy outside demands and information to support their own case management activities. Information requested by outsiders will probably be more general, or in different categories, than that needed for internal program management.

A CMSS may serve operating management by collecting data and providing reports that enable evaluation of the case-processing program. Reports might show, for example, historical trends in case processing (for example, how many children, by age, have been placed in how many foster homes?). For programs in which case-processing standards already exist, reports might be designed to help managers identify the processing stages at which cases tend to receive insufficient attention. Such reports may address a variety of questions relating to the efficiency, effectiveness, or equity of a program. Evaluations may be directed at correcting known operational problems, or they may attempt to raise new questions of program impacts. More generally, a CMSS might lead to the development of alternative processing strategies or to the reevaluation of a particular policy.

Much of the information resulting from meeting case management needs can be used in long-range planning and budgeting. Effective planning, however, often requires the collection of extra information so that case attributes and processing activities can be analyzed in greater detail. In particular, long-range planning and budgeting often require the categorization of cases complete with specifications of quality standards, response priorities, and resource utilization. Developing such categories and standards requires a considerable familiarity with the characteristics of different cases, the difficulties of processing such cases, and the potential impact of case processing on overall program policies. In many organizations, when cases are fairly routine and a limited number of processing alternatives exist, the categorization necessary for long-range planning and budgeting may be quite straightforward.

Sometimes, however, classification of the many highly complex and unique cases in a particular organization will seem unreasonable. In such situations the search for patterns and the development of categories will remain elusive until the program starts to collect adequate descriptive data. Thus one possible function of a CMSS is to research itself; that is, to develop a data base which will aid in future analysis and planning. Once rudimentary case categories are created, case-processing standards can be specified. Only then can one talk in earnest about accountability and evaluation and avoid the generalities that prevail in most organizations today. In this way a case management support system can help agency officials to learn more about the production side of their business and how to improve it.

Models of case management systems

As the scope of a potential CMSS needs to be explored, so does its technical configuration. Each of the CMSS types described in this section has its own strengths and weaknesses. Public managers and their systems designers should begin with a review of these three basic models to help identify their own needs.

CMSS Type	Purpose
Oversight	To provide a periodic descriptive summary of current case load characteristics and volumes, presented by case category.
Case Tracking	To encourage the monitoring of case loads through time, the periodic evaluation of the progress of individual cases, and improved planning for the future handling of cases. This kind of system seeks to enable the identification of problems incurred by cases

	as they move through the processing pipe-line.
Resource Allocation	To help managers make resource allocation decisions by reporting on staff utilization.

In practice, the most appropriate CMSS may turn out to be a blend of these ideal types that suits particular managerial needs.

One might easily argue that the oversight system is too basic to be useful for case management, but since it is often viewed as a substitute for a CMSS, it has been included in this discussion. The oversight system collects descriptive case data and provides summary counts. Statistical distributions are collected periodically, but ongoing historical information is not maintained for any case. There are no records for individual cases. This type of CMSS provides answers to questions such as: How many fraud cases are we handling at a given time? What percentage of children for whom we are responsible are now in foster homes, group care facilities, or in adoptive homes? More complex cross-tabulations might also be possible if large amounts of detailed data were collected: How many children between seven and ten years of age have been in the same foster home for more than five years? (Here, not only would it be neces-sary to know that a child is in a foster home, but "age" and "length of time in current placement" would have to be available as well.)

Typically an oversight system is seen as a simple, quick response to high-level external requests for information: budget reviews, federal re-porting requirements, professional standards committee reviews, con-gressional inquiries, and background investigations for community boards are some examples of clients for such a system. While they may eventu-ally effect improved case management, such systems do not assist operat-ing managers in making specific program decisions. Whether manual or computerized, an oversight system requires that descriptive information about a case be entered each period, rather than letting the computer maintain such information on an ongoing basis. This creates a burden on support staff. Such systems, on the other hand, are easily designed, im-plemented, and operated. Furthermore, they raise no confidentiality prob-lems, since all reporting is statistical and client identifiers aren't needed.

The case-tracking system contains both descriptive data and status data for all cases. Simple descriptive items might include a client's name, number, age, and service category. Examples of status data are the last service rendered on a particular case and the date of such an action. The requirements for descriptive data will vary with the scope of the system and with the ability of its users to interpret data. Status data is best captured by entry of a set of predefined "milestones" or "events" in the case process. As each event occurs, a status change is reported to the CMSS. In criminal litigation, for instance, the events to record case prog-ress might be: indictment issued, pretrial motions heard, jury selected, trial begun, testimony completed, verdict issued, sentence announced, case closed. Additional events might be included to follow the appeals process or to keep track of various phases of the trial. With a case-tracking system, planning of deadlines for future events becomes possible. For example, when an investigation begins, management can require that a target date for a final report be entered into the system. If the final report has not been issued by that date, the system can notify the manager or caseworker so that case processing can be reevaluated. The number and types of events required for a given CMSS and the degree of attention paid to meeting deadlines will depend on the type of case-processing activities and on the organization's needs. Staff members will be required to report the status of all cases assigned to them. Since this can be a bothersome task, managers must be committed to ensuring that data is provided in a timely and efficient manner.

In a case-tracking system, as in the overview system, reports that answer questions about the aggregate case load can be produced. Case tracking also addresses questions concerning the histories of specific cases and case loads. Some examples: When cases required social workers to make home visits, what was the average length of time between such visits? How many cases were not reviewed by a social worker within six months of foster care placement? Which ones? Which cases have been delayed for more than three months awaiting a court date assignment? More indirect analyses are also possible: Is a high-level special approval process creating a major bottleneck? Are caseworkers paying uniform attention to their entire case loads or are they concentrating on emergencies? These and similar analyses may result in important, timesaving operational or policy changes. Such systems can provide all levels of management with useful information about program capacity and the processing activities performed within a reporting period.

Although the case-tracking system may provide a great deal of information concerning elapsed time in case-processing activities, it does not provide information about the utilization of workers' time. This capability makes the resource allocation system potentially the most useful type of CMSS. It is also the most ambitious. In many organizations, resource allocation is viewed as the essence of the case management process. Managers not only want information about "movement" of cases, they also want to know how much staff time is being spent on various case processes in order to budget such time. The collection and analysis of staff time reports is time-consuming and costly to a busy operating program. The resource allocation CMSS is not always warranted. The payoff from such a system is the use of historical data to improve future decisions on the allocation of scarce staff time across the case load. A resource allocation system tends to be most useful in organizations that have some discretion over which cases to take or how quickly to handle each case. In contrast, for those settings where "everything is an emergency" or where "total equity" prevails, managerial discretion on resource allocation is more limited and thus this type of CMSS is more difficult to justify. Furthermore, in some organizations, informal staff resistance to the collection of work performance data—a subject discussed in chapter 6—may limit the practical utility of the resource allocation CMSS.

The additional dimension of staff resource accounting significantly increases the power of the CMSS. Progress of cases can be matched with staff time utilization, overall productivity begins to be measurable, and budget development choices become more explicit. A manager can get straightforward answers to direct questions such as how much staff time, on average, is required to place a child in a suitable foster home? Analysis of these data may lead to new operations insights on more indirect queries: Why has one particular case required an unusual amount of staff time? Why has some other case not received staff attention this month? Should a new service approach be tried for the activity which now takes an excessive length of time? Complex policy choices may be identified. For example, reports produced by a resource allocation system might show that considerable staff resources are needed to provide counseling, baby sitting, and child care services to a family in order to keep a child with an emotionally disturbed single parent. If one case of this type engages over 20 percent of a caseworker's time for several months (although the case represents less than 5 percent of the worker's case load), other cases will clearly suffer from lack of attention. If such a resource problem occurs frequently, management might begin to question the basic program goal of "keeping nuclear families intact at all costs." A review of this social service policy may lead to new initiatives in foster care placement. Moreover, even if the original policy is not changed, such a review process can demonstrate that more funding should go toward foster care payments. A CMSS, therefore, can be a critical catalyst in the broad resource allocation decisions of an agency, in its policy formulations, or in both.

Variations of the ideal types

Typically, as the members of a case-processing program become involved in designing a case management support system, they will adapt these three basic models to their unique needs. The result, while hard to predict, is likely to include one or more of the following kinds of variations.

☐ Add case "snapshots" to the oversight system.
☐ Report staff effort only upon case completion in the resource allocation system.
☐ Provide an index capability in the case-tracking system.

☐ Collect sample data rather than complete records.
☐ Add the case selection activity as a preliminary processing phase.

Each of these variations is outlined below.

Perhaps the most common tendency is to start with a simple system whose demands on personnel are minimal, then to expand the system as increased power is needed and justified. The oversight system, for example, presents aggregate descriptions of the pending case load. Such a system might be extended by retaining individual case snapshots that contribute to the aggregate statistics for each period so that dynamic profiles of individual cases can be constructed over time. To expand the system requires development of unique case identifiers, usually code numbers, for each new client, customer, or patient. By retaining information from a series of consecutive reporting periods, the system can match information about any given case and thereby achieve a limited kind of case-tracking capability. This type of extension to the CMSS requires a substantial development effort. In addition, operating staff will be entering much more data each period than would have been necessary had a case-tracking system been developed in the first place. The original virtue of the oversight system—simplicity—has been sacrificed.

In another variation—a simplification of the resource allocation model—the power of this CMSS concept is sacrificed in order to reduce the demands on caseworkers. Some data processing effort can be saved by reporting the level of staff effort as an aggregate figure when a case is closed, rather than periodically entering bits of such information during the life of the case. This variation is not likely to make much of a difference to planners and top management; one can still compare and contrast resource requirements for different kinds of cases with an eye toward future staff utilization or analysis of the efficiency of various operational policies. To supervisors, however, the loss can be severe. Since information about actual resource inputs to date will not be available, the CMSS will not help the supervisor to allocate future time among active cases. Another "hidden cost" of this apparent CMSS improvement is the loss in accuracy which will occur because staff members will submit time reports long after the time was actually spent on the case (and with the distraction of other cases in the interim).

A third variation of the basic case-tracking model is the addition of an indexing capability for all important case attributes. By referring to this index, caseworkers or managers could check the historical file when specific questions about the case load arise. For instance, the organization could easily identify all cases involving a particular client, violation, or medical diagnosis. A system with this variation is particularly useful for comparing a current case with processing strategies adopted in the past for similar cases. This capability can improve case management practice as well as promote consistency and equity over time (for example, with respect to fines, settlements, or placements). This variation requires the investment of some extra computer programming (or manual card filing) effort to provide managers and planners with more powerful and flexible access to the historical case-processing data base.

A fourth type of variation represents the most direct attempt to save data processing costs: the collection of sample data rather than comprehensive records. This method can capture staff input time when managers want a sense of how staff time is allocated but don't need detailed case-by-case staff utilization data. Unfortunately, considerable distortions may occur when some of the caseworkers are observed more closely than others (for example, the Hawthorne effect). Problems may also arise in drawing reliable samples where case volumes and types are varied. This issue is explored more fully in the discussion of system design issues.

A reasonable balance of validity, comprehensiveness, and cost may often be achieved by periodically collecting the few most crucial items of data from the entire organization. Supplementary sample studies can collect detailed data which are less important but nevertheless useful. This strategy can apply to the characteristics of particular cases, to different milestones in the case process, or to the use of staff time.

In a fifth variation, the evaluation of case-processing activities can be greatly improved by understanding how cases are selected. Case status tracking begins at the intake point, prior to acceptance or rejection of a potential case. The system records the potential cases which were referred elsewhere, those which were rejected for failure to meet formal eligibility requirements, and those otherwise declined. The system might also record the reasons for the action which was taken. Then, as mentioned in chapter 11, insight into this process can lead to the specification of appropriate intake procedures and standards which can improve the equity of service delivery.

Other variations on the ideal types of CMSS are certainly possible, but those outlined above are the most commonly observed. For each variation, the same trade-off issue must be resolved: What is the optimal scope of the CMSS, given the cost of additional features and the likely benefits from having them?

Systems design issues

After the scope of the planned CMSS has been identified, the more detailed system design activity begins. The development of the desired design specifications may appear to be a straightforward technical matter, but it is not. Major design issues to be considered are: How much information should be collected and reported? Who should provide the input data and receive the output reports? How often should these activities take place? The resolution of such issues requires a sophisticated cost-benefit analysis, especially since they are highly interrelated. Agency management must be actively involved at this preliminary design stage. Delegating these matters to the computer professionals could be disastrous. Later, as the dimensions of cost and benefit become better understood for a given CMSS, the designers will probably want to modify the overall scope of the system to improve the chances for successful implementation and institutionalization. Some of the most common major design problems are presented below. Related operational issues are discussed in the final section of this chapter.

Collecting information

The extent of substantive detail in a CMSS is largely determined by the way in which a case is described, what type of coding scheme is established, how the status of a case is recorded, and how staff utilization is reported.

Describing the case   How should a case be identified in the CMSS? In the simplest situation, a unique "case identifier" will suffice—perhaps the name of a client or an account number. Depending on the type of case, some possible embellishments might include address, names of relatives, aspects of client or family history, references to specific violations or rules or statutes, statements of charges, or medical diagnoses. For the sake of simplicity and economy, case descriptors should be brief. Nevertheless, designing elaborate case description capabilities into the system may be seen as an investment. When an unanticipated question arises in the future, such a CMSS will probably be able to provide data to answer it. Comprehensive descriptive information greatly extends the possibilities for managing cases and for conducting sophisticated operations analyses. Aside from the obvious risk that an undue burden may be placed on staff who supply these data, two key considerations—maintaining confidentiality and service quality—argue for moderation in the amount of detail collected.

The right of clients to privacy is a dominant theme in organizations that provide services in many fields including mental health, social welfare, and law enforcement. Current laws protect the public from computer systems that may infringe on this right. In the system design stage, choices may be made which inadvertently permit potential exposure of confidential information. Clearly, the more detailed the descriptive information collected about a client, the more sensitive the client's file becomes. It is usual, in such situations, to omit specific client identifiers such as name and address from records and to use identification numbers instead. However, the larger the number of other client characteristics maintained, the greater the chance that a client can be identified by the unique conjunction of such descriptors.

Coding the descriptive information Consistency and precision in the representation of data are hallmarks of a successful case management system. *Data codes* are the language through which caseworkers communicate with management and program analysts. If each doctor were to use an idiosyncratic language to diagnose a given condition, for instance, the confusion of terms could make it difficult, if not impossible, to discern patterns of demand for services and to evaluate program impacts. In any organization, an appropriate set of codes must be developed for all caseworkers to use in providing input to the CMSS.

A data category, such as the "diagnosis" of medical cases, may be described by a small set of general codes or by a larger set of more specific ones. The degree of specificity will be determined by balancing the need for detailed information against the problems resulting from attempts to collect it. Insufficient precision means that operations managers may not have the information to make key choices. For example, suppose "broken bone" is given a single code; all kinds of broken bones would be grouped into a single statistical category. If, however, it is important for management, when evaluating the progress of a case, to be able to distinguish between a broken wrist and a broken leg, or between a simple and a compound fracture, then the coding system should be more elaborate to reflect such variations. Such coding choices naturally exist in all kinds of case-processing settings. In making such choices, operations managers and analysts must be sensitive to the range of hidden indirect costs which, as discussed in chapter 9, can result from attempting to implement elaborate coding schemes.

Recording the status of a case As a case moves through a sequence of stages from initial intake to final resolution and closure, a CMSS can keep track of its current status. What information will best describe the status of a case? Two types of CMSS design are possible, one of the number of case events which are recorded and the other of the kinds of status descriptors which are used. Each of these types is outlined below.

A case usually passes through many discrete steps from the time of its opening to its closure. It is tempting to try to incorporate many of these steps in the data base in order to provide a detailed case-tracking capability. Typically, however, managers are not concerned with following each step of the case's progress. Only certain key events are vital to effective monitoring. Capturing unnecessary information is costly in several ways. First, there are the direct costs of entering and processing additional data. Furthermore, continuous requirements for status reporting may place excessive impositions on staff, thus causing incomplete and inconsistent data entry. Under this burden, the tracking system may tend to deteriorate. Perhaps only a subset of the case-processing milestones will continue to be recorded. There is no guarantee that the most important milestones will consistently receive greatest attention.

How much information about case status is useful to management? Many processing choices exist in most reasonably complex situations. It may be important to know why one case action was taken rather than another. One would certainly want to know if a particular criminal investigation had been closed; but it may also be important to know whether the case was closed because there was a lack of evidence, because there were no resources to pursue it further, or because the violation in question was no longer considered important. It may even be important to know who decided to close the case. The general issue, however, remains: is such detailed information worth collecting?

Recording utilization of staff resources   If a case management system is to be a tool for improved staff allocation and program productivity, data about the utilization of staff time must be collected. Traditionally, workers periodically record their levels of effort for their various cases on time sheets. Such time sheet reports may capture overall time spent on each case or time spent on various kinds of case-processing and administrative activities. Agency personnel, however, may be reluctant to report their time in a system which can be assessed by all levels of management. Questions of time reporting methods and levels of detail and accountability require careful attention during the initial design stages for a new CMSS.

Information about time utilization may be gathered by consistent periodic reporting or by occasional sampling. As discussed earlier, sampling reduces the total cost of reporting but raises many questions of validity and timeliness. A sample data base may not enable program planning and budgeting staff to analyze staff needs adequately, and certainly it will not provide managers with the ability to monitor expenditures of staff time. Periodic reporting, on the other hand, attempts to capture all reportable time. This method tends to give a more valid profile of how time is spent, although it is more costly and staff may be rather careless about what they enter.

The simplest time recording categories are the cases themselves, plus several broad types of non-case-related activities (for example, administration, personnel, vacation). But often supervisors, managers, and program planners want more detailed reports about what staff is doing rather than mere counts of the number of hours spent on each case. It may be important, for example to know how much time was spent on specific case-processing activities such as preparing reports, reviewing submitted documents, administering aptitude tests, or appearing in court. Categories for recording activities, as for encoding other items of information, can be general or specific. The costs and benefits associated with the choice of activity codes closely parallel the trade-offs discussed above in reference to descriptive data.

Regardless of whether the time sheets are completed on a regular or a sampled basis, there remains the question of how much time needs to be accounted for. Caseworkers presumably spend most of their time processing cases, but they are likely to perform other activities as well. Asking employees to account for only their productive case-processing time has theoretical appeal but creates problems in interpreting data. If not all staff submit reports as required (a likely occurrence), it is impossible to determine the percentages of error in the time data that the system produces.

Types of output reports

As discussed in chapter 9, a common initial step in designing any management information system is defining the types and contents of output reports required by various system users. Such requirements definitions are particularly important in any CMSS design, although they are not likely to be accomplished in a single discrete initial activity. Some of the specifications of information, formats, and frequencies will be easily identifiable early in the design process; other output requirements will become obvious only after several preliminary design choices have been made; still other output information needs may not emerge until the CMSS has been operational for some time. In general, reports should be designed to be as simple as possible and to contain only information which will be useful to those who receive the reports. Some of the most useful kinds of reports to support case management are outlined in Exhibit 12.1.

Integration with other information systems

Since the capturing of case status information is one of the key interactions between the caseworker and management, a CMSS is frequently seen as the center of a broader and more comprehensive information system. The potential integration of the CMSS with other information systems within an organization adds another level of complexity to the already overwhelming task of synthesizing the many choices involved in CMSS design. Integrating the CMSS with other information systems is a decision that must be carefully considered. Two types of synthesis are commonly sought—vertical integration and horizontal integration.

A vertically integrated CMSS will include some of the information requirements which are associated with, but distinct from, the operational management of cases. Information concerning financial activities is a common addition, and the need for data-related planning and coordination capacities may also exist. Some examples of functions which may be added are:

Type of Capability	Description
Financial	Issuance of third-party payments (that is, checks to organizations which provide direct service under contract with the government agency, such as foster homes or physicians who handle Medicaid patients); Financial management (that is, development of total case resource accounting including staff, travel, materials costs, as well as the costs for support personnel such as mother's helpers, hospital attendance, court stenographers, etc.); Client billing (as in a clinic with sliding fee scale).
Planning	Budget development and analysis; Facilities utilization analysis (as in physical therapy class registration).
Coordination	Intraagency referral tracking (of particular importance in a decentralized service delivery system in which different service centers provide different services, as in the medical service model).

Exhibit 12.1
Case management reports

Type	Description
Current Case Profiles	Each caseworker gets a list of current case descriptions and a summary of the status of each case assigned to him or her.
Case Status and Resource Utilization Summaries	Supervisors and middle managers get an overview of the cases in their charge; the overview presents brief descriptions of each case, its status, and the time spent on it by individual staff members.

Exhibit 12.1
Case management reports (con't)

Type	Description
Exception Reports	Caseworkers, supervisors, or middle managers get lists of cases which are potentially "in trouble" according to guidelines specified in advance (for example, whenever over 1000 hours of accumulated staff time have been spent on any single case; whenever a case has had no change in status for the past 6 months).
Action-Due Reports	In some case management systems, particular actions can be planned to occur on certain dates. Caseworkers, supervisors, or managers receive periodic reports which list those cases which did not meet their planned schedules or those cases for which actions should take place in the near future. This type of report is equally useful whether the action deadline was scheduled automatically according to an agency-wide rule or was established by a caseworker for a single active case.
Volume Summaries	Middle and top managers, as well as external overseers, receive periodic summaries of such statistics as the number of cases which have been opened, closed, or processed through a given milestone, or the amount of staff time spent handling particular types of cases. Summaries of cases handled, or resources used, by each operating division, program, or office may also be useful.
Cross Tabulations	Program planners or middle managers get reports that indicate the distribution of the case load according to some policy-relevant variables (for example, the number of children between six and twelve years old who have been in foster care for more than five years, with no adoption review during that period). The capability to produce such reports is important and is often overlooked in design efforts. Since the need for such reports will increase as the organization becomes more familiar with handling and analyzing data, this is one area where easy-to-use report production software systems become essential.
Statistical Analysis	Program planners and evaluators receive reports that summarize particular statistical analyses of items of data which are available in the CMSS data base.

There are several advantages to developing vertically integrated information systems along these lines. Information about the status and progress of any single case, which is the heart of the CMSS, can be used directly as input for related agency activities. Financial management, budgeting, planning, or client-tracking can be as up-to-date as the direct management of the cases themselves. Consistency of data across the agency is promoted. The information seems to offer government agencies a cost-effective approach to acquiring several related information-based capabilities. Public managers, however, must heed the potential risks in this type of collaborative information system ventures (see the general discussion in chapter 9).

In contrast to the vertical variety, horizontal integration is restricted to the core activity of case management. This type of synthesis adds to central case management the activities of those in other parts of the agency or even the case management activities of other organizations. Some examples are:

☐ Tracking cases across multiple subdivisions within one operating directorate (for example, across two sections in the criminal division of the Department of Justice);

☐ Tracking cases across more than one directorate (for example, across the criminal and civil divisions of the Department of Justice);

☐ Tracking cases across different agencies (for example, the mental health, welfare, and rehabilitation departments in a state government; the state, county and private welfare agencies in one geographic area; federal and state civil rights enforcement agencies).

Requests to integrate a CMSS system horizontally are likely to come from the top management in an agency, since these officials often seek a broader understanding of how case management activities interrelate. Sometimes an overview requirement imposed by the legislature, the Office of Management and Budget, or the courts forces managers to answer questions concerning relations between similar, although organizationally distinct, case management programs. These external sources argue that the need for a CMSS in one program or office typically demonstrates a similar need in other programs or offices. The argument continues that horizontal integration will result in compatibility among reports and, in some situations, will produce the added benefits of improved coordination, evaluation, and planning capabilities for higher levels of management.

As with vertical integration, horizontal integration also incurs hidden costs. Horizontal integration clearly requires a much more complex effort than development of a freestanding or unintegrated CMSS. Combining organizational entities with very different operating styles into a single design process creates difficulties in specifying case description and case status characteristics which are meaningful to all organizations.

Horizontal integration of a CMSS also generates operational problems deriving from the method of identifying a case. When the case identifier is the name of a person, misspellings and other kinds of inconsistencies may arise, (for example, nicknames or middle names may be used). The use of numbers in order to avoid names raises other difficulties. Numbering schemes do not necessarily ensure consistency when services are delivered in a decentralized fashion (unless not-so-confidential social security numbers are used). For example, it can be difficult to arrive at an unduplicated count of clients served at walk-in mental health clinics, because the clients may not identify other offices where they have received similar treatment. In a centralized operation, inconsistency may develop if cases are identified differently according to stage of processing. For example, a regulatory agency may identify an initial investigation with a sequential intake number and the subsequent litigation stage by a totally unrelated court-assigned docket number. Clearly, this identification problem is compounded when more than one agency is involved, or when seemingly similar operations are approached differently within the same organization. Inconsistencies in case numbering and the operational difficulties in implementing consistent case numbering schemes have prevented many horizontal integration attempts from getting off the drawing board.

Problems with case identifiers become even more complex when entirely separate agencies are involved or when the services provided are private. In one northern California county, county-funded counseling organizations in the communities refused to submit the names of their clients to the county's mental health department or to use client identifiers assigned by the county. In another state, a group of social service agencies paid by the state for services rendered to the clients referred by the state refused to report to the state welfare agency about individual cases either by client name or by the state-assigned client identifier. In some urban areas, community groups fought to have information such as psychological diagnoses removed from case records lest the information, even by remote chance, be shared with other agencies. Resistance to the sharing of client service information between two state agencies may not be quelled by the consideration that such sharing might prevent the delivery of duplicate or conflicting services to a given client. At the state and local levels, these confidentiality issues generate impassioned controversy, which has already stifled many attempts at horizontal integration.

Attempts to integrate a basic CMSS either vertically or horizontally are common but tricky. When to integrate and to what extent are questions that do not have simple answers. Clearly, possibilities of integration should be explored even if the responsible official (or some important outsider) does not push for such an initiative. If some degree of integration does seem feasible, designing an integrated system from the start may be advantageous. Nevertheless, experience has shown that a healthy degree of skepticism about such synthesis is warranted.

Operational issues

The general problems encountered by operating managers in the implementation of information systems in government were discussed in chapter 9. In this section we will examine the specific versions of those problems which are most prevalent for case management support systems.

Haphazard entry of data

Elaborate case coding schemes require a caseworker to make many distinctions in entering data on new cases. As the coding choices grow, the manuals describing them become unwieldy and are used less frequently. Haphazard data entry may then result. Attempts to categorize all of a caseworker's productive time through the use of periodic reporting schemes—unless such plans are strictly enforced—are likely to have a similarly disappointing result.

Intentional distortions of data

Managers must also expect some intentional distortions in reports of "time worked" as employees try to look good. No one really works a full eight-hour day, but who is likely to record that fact? Attempts to record overtime will generate other distortions. A common tendency is for employees to charge all extra time to their major case. In some organizations professionals are expected to work extra hours. Pressures will thus exist to report more time than was actually spent working. The main danger in such situations is that managerial and analytic attention will be wasted in the study of such distorted resource utilization data. The indirect costs of basing personnel allocation decisions—such as those discussed in chapter 6—on such distorted data can be considerable.

Interruptions of work

Continuous requirements to provide status reports on existing cases tends to interrupt the operational activities of caseworkers. For any middle-level employee reporting a case's status is often seen as a distracting clerical chore which frequently becomes a task of lowest priority. In some situations an agency may assign a set of well-trained clerks to provide this support service for all caseworkers. In other instances, the status reporting activity might be integrated with a managerial process, such as a systematic review by a supervisor of the work done by subordinates. In this situation it might be better for casework supervisors to be responsible for recording case status changes.

Timing of status reporting

In addition to the question of who should report the status of cases, there remains the matter of when this should be done. The reporting of changes in case status may be either event-triggered or "snapshot." In the first approach, a case status form is completed each time a reportable event occurs in the case. Forms announcing single status change are entered into the CMSS frequently, typically daily or weekly, thus providing a current data base. In the second approach, case status "snapshots" are taken periodically, typically monthly or quarterly. When the snapshot status report is due, the caseworker, clerk, or supervisor must enter all events which have occurred since the last snapshot was taken. With this approach the CMSS will, to some extent, always be out-of-date and will not reflect the true status of some cases. However, many organizations do not need case-tracking information more frequently than monthly or quarterly; in these instances snapshot reporting is appropriate. Snapshot reporting significantly reduces the volume of input forms (but not the number of transactions) and enables better management control of the reporting process. Since caseworkers must systematically review their entire case loads, they are thus more likely to report everything that happened. Supervisory reviews of the status reports can ensure that everything is kept up-to-date. In contrast, with event-triggered reporting there is a greater possibility that a caseworker will neglect to submit information about a status change. Clearly, serious operational implications may result from the choice of when to report the status of a case.

Relationships between clients and caseworkers

In clinical settings, attempts to collect detailed descriptive information about clients' cases may inadvertently strain the often delicate relationships between caseworkers and clients. This problem is particularly acute when the requested information is not clearly related to the clinical problem at hand: hospital admission procedures, for example, are often criticized because a lot of extraneous information about patients is collected. This negative effect on caseworker-client relationships may be significantly greater if, in the attempt to keep files up-to-date, caseworkers are required to enter data directly onto a computer terminal while interviewing the client, rather than to complete forms for subsequent computer entry. Whenever clients are uneasy with caseworkers' procedures, subsequent interactions, and hence the quality of service delivery, may suffer.

Operations costs of integrating information systems

The costs of consolidating information systems may include undesirable delays in implementing the basic CMSS, inadequate attention paid to CMSS design issues, or failure to develop an operational CMSS. For example, since a great deal of additional time may be required to specify and develop a highly integrated CMSS, there is a chance that the system, once operational, may be somewhat obsolete. Organizational priorities and case-processing strategies may change enough to require significant changes to be made to the CMSS, even before it has been implemented.

Summary

The subtlety and significance of choices in the design of information systems is rarely appreciated. The performance of a case-processing program can be affected as much by the operational implications of its information support system as it is by the nature of the case load and the available program resources. Public managers must help technical system designers to anticipate and then resolve the many issues involved in the design of a CMSS. The process may be time-consuming, since the issues often have no obvious solution. In this chapter we have indicated the general issues to be considered, but each situation needs to be worked through by those who are most familiar with the case-processing program and who have the greatest stakes in the success of its decision support system.

Discussion questions

1. A case management support system can be designed to support an agency's internal users as well as its external constituents. Consider these two examples: a system to support social workers would provide information that is of little value to an individual client; a system to process claims should be designed to inform the claimants of the status of their cases. What differences exist between a system de-

signed primarily to assist the service provider and one designed to assist the service recipient? Can one system be designed for both types of users? Is such a system practical?

2. There are two basic approaches to the design and implementation of a CMSS. One may begin with a simple system and then enlarge its capabilities over time, or one may design and implement a comprehensive system from the beginning. What are the advantages and disadvantages of these two alternatives? As a manager faced with a growing backlog of existing cases, which approach would you recommend? What specific capabilities would you want in your design prior to implementation of the system?

3. As with any MIS, a CMSS can suffer from the "garbage-in/garbage-out" syndrome. What steps can a manager of a government agency take to reduce the probability of faulty input?

4. Many case management support systems routinely monitor the utilization of staff time. Such a system could be expanded to aid managers in planning their staffing requirements based on data already collected. Under what conditions would you want to adopt this approach? (Recall the issues of personnel planning discussed in chapter 6.) What problems do you foresee? How might they be overcome?

Notes
* I wish to thank Edith S. Levine for working with me on the unpublished manuscript from which this chapter was developed.

Chapter 13
"Revenue sharing compliance"

On October 20, 1972, the State and Local Fiscal Assistance Act became a federal law. This act was heralded as a major step toward a "New Federalism" which would restore the importance of state and local governments in this country. Under this act the federal government provides state and local governments with considerable levels of funding to be used largely at their own discretion. The major restrictions on the use of revenue sharing funds were that they could not be used as matching funds, that they must be spent in certain (broadly defined) priority areas; and that they could not be used to support discriminatory programs. Congress and President Nixon clearly wished to avoid letting this legislation lead to yet another federal bureaucracy: the Office of Revenue Sharing (ORS), created by the act, originally contained only three professional staff members to ensure compliance (with fiscal and civil rights provisions) by the 39,000 governmental jurisdictions receiving these funds.

In September 1973, Director of ORS Graham Watt testified at House committee hearings that ORS aimed to secure "comprehensive compliance" without creating a new army of federal auditors, investigators, and analysts. He thought it important to keep matters simple so that even a small jurisdiction could "do that which is asked and required of them." He saw no point in "collecting a tremendous amount of data and statistics" on the recipients of General Revenue Sharing (GRS) funds; Graham intended that such information would be collected only if a locality were suspected of practicing discrimination. ORS expected occasionally to sample localities for investigation but to rely primarily on the receipt of complaints of alleged discrimination.

In the autumn of 1975, further hearings were held by the House Civil and Constitutional Rights Subcommittee and the House Intergovernmental Relations and Human Resources Subcommittee of the Committee on Government Operations. These broad-ranging hearings raised a number of issues about General Revenue Sharing practices and policies. One of the criticisms raised was the fact that ORS had not yet instituted any termination hearings for GRS recipients found to be in noncompliance. Another was the "astounding" delays in processing cases.

The amended revenue sharing bill was approved on October 15, 1976. It contained, among other items, a trigger mechanism built into the enforcement process. This mechanism stipulated that if an ORS investigation determined that a governmental recipient was not in compliance with the provisions of the Act, a notice was to be sent that GRS funds will automatically be cut off. The sequence of specified time periods for written response and hearings was intended to guarantee due process to the jurisdiction while speeding up ORS enforcement procedures.

The Office of Revenue Sharing has grown steadily since 1976. Trends in budget and staffing are shown in Exhibit 13.1. In 1977 the Office of Revenue Sharing was organized into ten operational areas (see Exhibit 13.2).

Exhibit 13.1
Trends in budget and staffing: Office of Revenue Sharing

	Fiscal Year			
	1976[a]	1977	1978	1979[b]
Budget Category	(Millions of Dollars)			
Legal and Support Services	.42	.50	.76	.88
Operations and Technical Assistance	1.34	1.70	2.60	2.70
Monitoring and Enforcement	.69	1.20	2.13	2.90
Antirecession Financial Assistance	—	.65	1.24	.72
Total program costs, funded	2.45	4.11	6.73	7.20
Personnel Summary				
Total Number of Permanent Positions	108	184	209	185
Average Salary (Thousands of Dollars)	18.5	18.5	19.5	21.2
General Revenue Sharing Payments[c] (Billions of Dollars)	6.35	6.69	6.85	6.85

Source: Appendix to Annual *Budget of the United States Government*, 1976–79.

[a] Does not include transition quarter (July 1, 1975, to Sept. 30, 1976).
[b] Estimated.
[c] Does not include Antirecession Financial Assistance Fund.

Exhibit 13.2
Office of revenue sharing

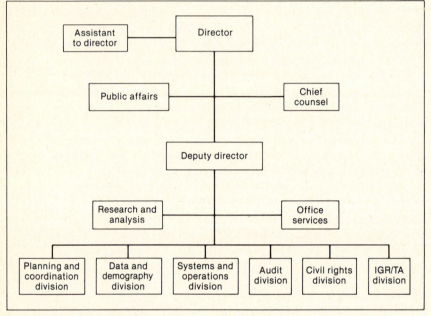

Source: ORS Director's Office, September 21, 1977.

Compliance activities

Three of the operational areas of ORS—the Audit Division, the Civil Rights Compliance Division, and the Public Participation Unit of the Intergovernmental Relations/Technical Assistance (IGR/TA) Division—are responsible for the actual performance of compliance-related activities. The activities involved in handling complaints and referrals of non-compliance are similar for all three operational areas. Each division follows these general steps to resolve a case:

☐ receipt of complaint/referral
☐ initial determination of likely ORS jurisdiction
☐ screening and acknowledgment of receipt
☐ request for information/field investigation
☐ analysis of information
☐ reaching a conclusion (finding)
☐ preliminary, informal notification of jurisdiction
☐ second, formal notification of jurisdiction
☐ administrative hearing
☐ withholding of funds

At any point in this process, however, resolution may be reached through a finding of "no jurisdiction," "compliance," or "violation" with a subsequent agreement for resolution.

Public participation compliance

The State and Local Fiscal Assistance Act requires a recipient jurisdiction to engage in several sequential public participation activities. Initial regulations requiring publication of reports of planned and actual use of revenue sharing funds were expanded in 1976 to include GRS funds in the public participation requirements (if any) of state and local budget laws. Hearings on both the proposed use of revenue sharing funds and on the budget itself were required during each budget cycle in those jurisdictions not subject to other more stringent state or local requirements.

To ensure compliance with these statutes, a Public Participation (PP) Compliance Unit was set up in the Office of Revenue Sharing's IGR/TA Division. At the beginning of 1979 this unit included five persons. The unit responded to complaints from the public, requests for waivers, and referrals of potential problems from within ORS and from other government bodies. In addition, the unit initiated reviews of public participation compliance activities of a limited number of the state and local governments receiving general revenue sharing funds. To a small degree, the unit also engaged in outreach activities to inform citizen groups of legal opportunities for public participation.

Public participation complaints arise when notification of hearings is inadequate, when citizens' groups discover that required hearings have not been held, or when the substance or procedures of the hearings themselves seem inadequate. The PP unit has jurisdiction only when procedures impinge on the ability of persons to participate. Other procedural and substantive problems are generally considered to be beyond its jurisdiction and are referred to appropriate agencies either inside or outside ORS. Three typical cases are outlined in Exhibit 13.3.

Civil rights compliance

In addition to complying with the public participation requirements of the act, each recipient jurisdiction must abide by certain civil rights provisions. The act prohibits discrimination on the basis of race, color, national origin, sex, age, religion, or physical disability.

Discrimination can be found in two general areas of local and state government activity: (1) employment and (2) the location of public

---

Exhibit 13.3
Three illustrative public participation cases

Town A   Case opened 5/77 and closed 10/77. A citizen of Town A complained of not having seen a public notice of a revenue sharing budget hearing. An investigation by the PP Unit disclosed that a budget hearing was held in accordance with the regulations. However, the revenue sharing budget hearing announcement was published less than ten days in advance of the hearing, did not contain a budget summary, and did not mention that the proposed budget was available for public inspection. The PP Unit determined that these were technical violations, notified the jurisdiction how to go about rectifying them, and closed the case.

Town B   Case opened 1/78 and closed 7/78. This case was opened by the PP Unit in a compliance-monitoring effort, rather than in response to a complaint. When asked to document its compliance, the local government of Town B discovered that it had neglected to hold a revenue sharing budget hearing. A Determination Letter was mailed to the jurisdiction informing it that it was in noncompliance with the law. The jurisdiction took corrective action (conducted the budget hearing with public notice), and a Close Letter was sent informing the jurisdiction that, with exception of a technical violation (the hearing notice did not include a summary of the budget), it had succeeded in coming into compliance and that the case was closed.

County C   Case opened 1/78 and closed 9/78. This case began as a compliance-monitoring case but was expanded when a citizen's complaint alleging that the proposed use and budget hearings had not been held was sent to the PP Unit. Information submitted in response to the PP Unit's investigation revealed that neither the proposed use hearing nor the budget hearing had been conducted and that no notice had been published indicating that a copy of the enacted budget was available for public inspection. The county explained that it had ignored the provisions because it had requested a waiver for the proposed use hearing during the previous year and had assumed that the waiver had been granted. However, the case file contained evidence that the jurisdiction had been notified that a waiver could not be granted under the regulations prevailing at that time. The PP Unit issued a noncompliance determination and recommended steps for the jurisdiction to take. Three months later the jurisdiction submitted evidence of its actions. Since only one technical violation remained—the hearing notice did not mention that the public could make oral and written comments about the proposed use of revenue sharing funds—the jurisdiction was notified that the case was closed.

---

facilities or delivery of public services. The most common types of discrimination cases handled by ORS are individual and class complaints of racial discrimination in employment. Such complaints may be about hiring practices, employee selection procedures, or recruitment practices. The act prohibits discriminatory selection criteria, perpetuation of past discriminatory practices, and impairment of efforts to overcome past discrimination. Complaints of discrimination in the delivery of services on the basis of race are also common and include denial of services, inequitable services, segregated provision of services, restriction of services, unequal treatment, denial of opportunity to participate in a program, and denial of opportunity to be a member of an advisory board. The regulations also prohibit discrimination in the location of facilities which has the effect of excluding individuals, denying benefits, and denying use.

Almost all civil rights compliance cases develop as a result of citizen complaints or referrals from other government sources (inside or outside ORS). A case may reflect an individual problem—as when a person is denied a promotion based on race—or it may incorporate a class action issue—based on patterns of discrimination in employment or services. Employment discrimination may occur in hiring, promotion, assignment of duties, firing, employee harassment, or the underutilization of a certain class of employees. Discrimination in the delivery of services or in the quality or location of facilities covers a broad area of municipal activities including provision of paved streets, street lighting, water and sewerage systems, police and fire protection, libraries, hospitals, or particular parks or recreational buildings. All such complaints and referrals are handled by the Civil Rights Compliance Division of ORS, which is legally mandated to reach findings within ninety days of the initiation of a case.

In addition to responding to complaints and referrals, the Civil Rights Division also selects jurisdictions for compliance review. These active attempts to see whether a jurisdiction's employment and service patterns comply with civil rights provisions are generally seen as deterrents to deliberate governmental violation of such provisions. However, by 1978, the consistent backlog of cases initiated by complaints or referrals left little time for compliance reviews.

In 1978 both the Public Participation Unit and the Civil Rights Compliance Division were experiencing continued problems in case closure, accumulation of a case backlog, and delays in processing cases. The nature of the compliance process and associated problems seemed more complex in the Civil Rights Division. The division manager was under growing pressure to improve overall performance but knew many questions needed to be answered before a resolution could be achieved.

Organization and staffing

The Civil Rights Division is organized into four regional units, each staffed by seven to nine equal opportunity specialists (or investigators) including a supervisor. The units are supported by six clerical workers. A fifth supervisor (the control supervisor) operates the control section, which is staffed by one control clerk and a clerk typist. The manager has an administrative staff of two secretaries. Staff levels from January 1977 through October 1978 are shown in Exhibit 13.4. By November 1978, the division had a staff of fifty consisting of twenty-eight full-time investigators, four supervisors, a division manager, and support staff.

Exhibit 13.4
Civil rights division staffing levels

Date	Number of Supervisors[a]	Number of Investigators			
		Senior	Junior	Trainee	Total
January 1977	1		1		1
April 1977	1	4	1		5
July 1977	3	11	2	7	20
October 1977	3	12	2	6	20
January 1978	3	13	3	4	20
April 1978	4	15	6	12	33
July 1978	4	14	6	11	31
October 1978	4	14	5	9	28

[a] One additional supervisor heads the control section.

The division manager supervises the day-to-day functioning of the division, a task which includes managing personnel, authorizing substantive changes in procedure when necessary, and assuring the smooth functioning of the office. Other responsibilities include making division policy through the preparation of technical memoranda and procedural outlines and seeking consistency in case handling through frequent meetings with supervisors. Exceptional cases are discussed with the chief counsel, and often the manager also participates in negotiations with jurisdictions. All compliance cases which reach the prefinding stage (described below) are reviewed and signed by the division manager.

Supervisors are responsible for the quality and amount of work performed by the investigators in their regional subdivisions. Much of their time is spent advising investigators in the handling of particular cases. Supervisors also become involved in negotiations with recipient jurisdictions after a prefinding or finding has been reached. Supervisors also share with each other, with the manager, and with their investigators their combined experiences of case handling to help ensure consistency among regional units.

The control supervisor develops and implements case-tracking systems for the entire division, supervises the maintenance of files of closed cases, and is responsible for the updating of the Compliance Tracking System. In addition, initial outgoing letters are typed in the control unit.

The equal opportunity specialists (investigators) are responsible for investigating all complaints and referrals and performing compliance reviews. In addition to investigating cases, senior level investigators may also be called upon to train new investigators. In each regional unit at least one senior level investigator (and possibly a trainee) is assigned, as a "follow-up monitor" to review all cases awaiting progress reports from jurisdictions which have made plans to comply.

In the course of their work, investigators interact a great deal with the control supervisor and their own regional supervisor. The supervisors in turn have frequent meetings with the manager. Investigators and supervisors are also available for consultation with the chief counsel's office.

The civil rights compliance case

Individual cases of discrimination (in hiring, for example) are usually brought to the attention of ORS by persons who feel discriminated against. Complaints lodged by civic organizations, such as the NAACP, or local organizations, such as a neighborhood coalition, usually involve patterns of discrimination rather than an individual act of discrimination. The Civil Rights Division also receives occasional referrals from other federal agencies (the Departments of Justice or Health and Human Services, the Equal Employment Opportunity Commission, etc.) or from other divisions within ORS.

All allegations first cross the desk of the control supervisor, who judges whether they are within ORS jurisdiction. In cases of dubious jurisdiction, the division manager may be consulted. If a case is judged to be outside ORS jurisdiction, the complainant is notified of that decision. Where appropriate, the control supervisor will refer a complaint to a more appropriate agency and will notify the complainant of this action.

Problems may arise in determining, on the basis of the complaint alone, which level of government is responsible for hiring and promoting a given individual or group, or for funding or delivering a given service. As a result, many cases are opened against one recipient government when the next highest level of government is actually responsible. For example, the commonwealth of Massachusetts administers the civil service process by which some employees of some cities and towns in that state are hired. A complaint about discrimination in hiring in a given town might eventually be treated as a case against the commonwealth. Often such issues of institutional responsibility are not determined by ORS for several months after a complaint is received.

Once jurisdiction over an allegation is established, the ORS supervisor sends an "Acknowledgment Letter" to the government, notifying it that a complaint or referral has been received and that an investigator will be in contact "soon" in order to request information and to arrange interviews with government officials. The complainant also receives a letter advising that the case has been opened. Division policy is to issue these letters within thirty-six hours after receipt of the complaint or referral. Delays may arise occasionally but generally last no more than a week.

Types of findings/resolutions

When a Civil Rights Compliance case has been opened and information pertaining to the alleged instance of discrimination has been collected, an investigator analyzes the information and makes a tentative finding of either compliance or noncompliance. Office policy dictates that an investigator must make a convincing argument not only for a "cause" finding (noncompliance) but also for a "no cause" finding (for example, compliance, no ORS jurisdiction over the case, or state rather than local responsibility for the action).

If the actions of a jurisdiction are inconsistent with the civil rights requirements of the State and Local Fiscal Assistance Act, the investigator will issue a noncompliance determination and will develop an appropriate remedy. In cases of individual discrimination typical remedies for noncompliance are reinstatement with back pay of the person who was discriminated against and reassessment of the complainant's personnel record. In contrast, findings of discrimination against a class of employees call for changes in the system, such as the validation of entrance requirements (for instance, written tests), the elimination of discriminatory benefit policies having to do with pregnancy leaves, or the broadening of recruitment efforts. A common recommendation in such cases is the establishment of an affirmative action plan to be drawn up according to guidelines developed by (and perhaps with the assistance of) the federal Equal Employment Opportunity Commission (EEOC). If a jurisdiction already has an affirmative action plan, the ORS may require a redefinition of goals or a more rigorous timetable. In many instances, ORS will require the jurisdiction to submit periodic reports to be reviewed by ORS. These reports must demonstrate that the new (or original) affirmative action plan is in fact being carried out.

Service discrimination cases are idiosyncratic and often require creative resolutions. When, for example, street paving and maintenance practices vary by neighborhood, depending on the ethnic composition of the neighborhood, the remedy might include the development of plans for paving or maintaining a specified list of streets; ORS may even call for the postponement of existing paving plans until the specified streets are paved. Or if a library in a section of town inhabited mainly by minorities is open for fewer hours than libraries in other parts of town, ORS is likely to recommend that such disparities be eliminated. In cases of planned or existing inequitable location of facilities (such as parks or recreational buildings), ORS may recommend that plans be changed to locate new facilities in more suitable locations or may require that any future planned facilities be built in the neighborhood which has been discriminated against.

Cases are closed as soon as remedies are determined and action is taken. Sometimes the full response can take considerable time: if extensive street repaving is recommended, the jurisdiction may take several months to develop a plan and several years to pave all of the itemized streets. ORS may then close the case and demand that progress reports be submitted until the work has been satisfactorily completed. Once an agreement has been reached on a case of noncompliance, the supervisor will assign it to a follow-up monitor whose activities follow no formal procedures.

Although the civil rights specifications in the act are simply stated, the Civil Rights Division of ORS handles a wide variety of cases. Illustrations of three different types of Civil Rights Compliance cases—individual employment, class employment, and services—are given in Exhibit 13.5. Division employees often say, however, that no single case is "typical."

Case-processing procedures

The case-processing procedures for civil rights cases are quite complex. Highlights are presented below.

Case opening

Once ORS jurisdiction has been determined, the case is opened. Relevant information (such as name and number of jurisdiction, nature and source of complaint, and date letters were sent out) is entered onto the Compliance Tracking System, a case file is started, and the case is passed directly to the appropriate regional supervisor. (All Civil Rights compliance activities operate out of the same office, but they are grouped by geographic region.) The supervisor examines the case and assigns it to one of the investigators. Bases for assignment are estimated difficulty of the case, the skills and available time of the investigators, and sometimes the location of jurisdiction. Supervisors also try to abide by the first-in, first-out provisions of the law. However, in some cases, the nature of the complaint in an individual discrimination case may cause the supervisor to give precedence to that case. For example, if a complainant failed an exam believed to be invalid, and a second exam for a limited number of persons is to be held in sixty days, the supervisor may give that case priority and assign it first. Supervisors tend to limit investigator responsi-

Exhibit 13.5
Three illustrative civil rights cases

County A   Case opened 4/11/78 and closed 9/7/78. The Civil Rights Division received a complaint alleging racial discrimination in firing. The complainant, an employee of a youth community center, claimed that he had been discriminated against by harassment on the job and by being fired without recourse to grievance procedures. The Civil Rights Division investigator requested all necessary information by telephone. Materials requested included a termination memo signed by the local Equal Employment Opportunity officer; an earnings statement by the complainant; written records of phone interviews with the complainant, the complainant's representative, and the Community Center Director; a roster of current employees; relevant written personnel policies; notes from current employees; and notes from follow-up interviews. The investigator assessed the information and recommended a finding of "no cause." To substantiate the finding, the investigator found that three other employees (two white, one black) in identical positions had been fired over the previous two years for similar reasons and that similar disciplinary actions had been taken against other employees. Although ORS acknowledged that grievance procedures were not followed, the division found no evidence of racial discrimination. (The procedures were newly established and few people knew of them.) The jurisdiction and the complainant were notified and the case was closed. The complainant's representative protested the finding. In a letter, the division manager offered to review any additional information received in light of the finding.

City B   Case opened 3/7/77 and closed 11/21/77. This case was opened by a referral from the Department of Justice which found, in the course of a routine investigation, that the city had never had women employed in uniformed police and fire positions. The investigator conducted a two-day field investigation which included interviews with several city officials. While in the field, the investigator examined employment policies of the police and fire departments and of a local hospital partially supported by revenue sharing funds donated by the city. Based on all information collected (job descriptions, application forms, employment rosters, labor market statistics, rules and regulations of the police and fire departments, physical agility exams, and other relevant information), the city was found in noncompliance. Specifically, it was found that women were underrepresented, that a firefighter's exam had potentially discriminatory impact on women, that a job title ("patrolman") was sex-restrictive, that minorities were underutilized in the hospital, and that the employment application form requested potentially discriminatory information such as height, weight, and marital status. The city demonstrated sincere efforts to respond to the charges and take corrective actions: adoption of recruitment plans for women, elimination of the physical agility exam, elimination of sex-restrictive job titles and discriminatory preemployment inquiries, adoption of an affirmative action plan, advancement of minority hospital staff, and submission of annual progress reports. The case was closed in response to the city's first reply to the ORS finding.

Town C   Case opened 3/23/76 and closed 3/16/77. A complaint was lodged by the local branch of the NAACP alleging discrimination in the provision of services to the black community. Specifically cited were street and roadway construction and repair, health and social services, education, social development, housing and community development, and economic development. The investigation was expanded to include a class employment investigation as well. A two-day field investigation was conducted, and several violations in both employment and services were found. Discrimination in employment was found in both underrepresentation and underutilization of women and minorities in the city's work force. Discrimination in service delivery was found in the provision of unequal fire protection (four-inch water mains in black community, six-inch water mains in white community), provision of unequal water service, and provision of unequal recreation equipment and fewer improvements of facilities located in the black area. Suggested remedies set forth in the Finding Letter included the submission of an affirmative action plan, putting in writing the employment practices and procedures for the police department, the submission of a plan to provide streets of the same quality in the black community as in the white community, submission of plans to provide equivalent water service (both water mains and fire hydrants) to the black community, submission of a plan for equal provision of recreational facilities, elimination of height and weight requirements for police and fire departments (or proving that such requirements are valid), elimination of certain preemployment inquiries, and submission of annual progress reports.

When the city failed to respond to the Finding Letter, a Ten-Day Hearing Letter was sent. This time the city responded but did not indicate its willingness to enter into a compliance agreement. Furthermore, its plans were inadequate to fulfill the remedies outlined in the Finding Letter. The director then ordered the suspension of funds on the grounds that the jurisdiction was not acting in good faith. The jurisdiction finally submitted a more detailed compliance plan, and the director restored funds and closed the case pending the receipt of acceptable progress reports.

bility to five to eight cases at any one time, a practice which can cause delays in the assignment of new cases.

The investigator is responsible for all aspects of a case until it is eventually turned over to a follow-up monitor in the same compliance unit. After receiving the case from the supervisor, the investigator examines the complaint or referral as well as any substantiating evidence the complainant might have sent. He or she then draws up a list of documents that will be required for the investigation, telephones the recipient jurisdiction to request the documents, and follows up with a form letter. This "Fifteen-Day Letter" is sent to the jurisdiction with the request that it submit the itemized data within fifteen days.

Analysis of response to the Fifteen-Day Letter

Responses to the Fifteen-Day Letter usually provide investigators with information upon which to base their analyses. In some cases, however, the response may indicate that the problem is the responsibility of another jurisdiction, that the case has been resolved in another manner (for example, an out-of-court settlement or a subsequent promotion for the complainant), or that a time extension is required.

Should the jurisdiction fail to respond to the Fifteen-Day Letter, the investigator may call to ask for an explanation and then follow with a new and strongly worded request for information, indicating that the ORS has the legal authority to request such data. Investigators make every effort to obtain as much information as possible before a field investigation since this will increase their subsequent effectiveness.

Field investigation

Field investigations are performed only when the information gathered by mail is insufficient for reaching a conclusion. Most major cases require field investigations, but for many smaller cases sufficient data can be collected by mail. Investigators are responsible for making their own travel plans, although these are submitted to the supervisor for approval. In order to conserve travel funds, an investigator attempts to schedule several field investigations on each trip. For areas like the West Coast to which travel is expensive and time consuming, supervisors often assign several cases in the same geographic area to one investigator. The agenda of visits is always subject to modification by the investigator in response to changing conditions in the field. An investigator may travel alone, with a trainee, or occasionally with a team. The investigation will last from one to five days, depending on the complexity of the case. Most field investigations take two or three days. Exhibit 13.6 lists the variety of data which may be collected for different kinds of cases. Other information may also be collected, depending on the type of case and the experience and imagination of the investigator.

In the field, investigators will almost always rely on their own judgment in determining the scope of an investigation. For example, if an investigator, in responding to a complaint of individual employment discrimination on the basis of race, discovers (through interviews with the complainant, the complainant's supervisor, or co-workers) any possibility of discrimination on the basis of sex, the scope of the investigation might be broadened to include sex discrimination as well. Similarly, an investigator examining one department against which a complaint has been lodged may choose to examine all departments of the jurisdictions simply because the data are easily obtainable. In still other cases, an investigator may broaden the scope of the complaint based on the altered allegations of the complainant resulting from an interview. Civil Rights Division policy places the burden on the jurisdiction to prove that any particular department or agency has never received revenue sharing funds and is therefore exempt from the provisions of the State and Local Fiscal Assistance Act.

In an exit interview with the chief executive officer or a designated representative, the investigator will summarize the evidence found for corroboration but will otherwise make no comment regarding a finding.

At this point a request for additional information to be collected and forwarded to the investigator's office as soon as possible may also be issued.

Exhibit 13.6
Field investigation data: civil rights compliance

The following items of data may be collected by Civil Rights Compliance investigators during field investigations (if such data were not supplied by mail prior to the investigation). The nature of the complaint or referral, the scope of the case, and the availability of records will determine what data are actually collected. Other types of data may also be sought.

Employment discrimination cases
number of employees by sex, race, date hired, last date promoted, salary, job title, starting salary, starting position, current position
attendance records by name, race, sex
written personnel policy statements, memoranda, and notices regarding hiring, firing, reprimands, recruitment, promotion
application forms
job descriptions
health benefit policies
informal notes from interviews of job applicants
all entrance and promotion tests
evidence of recruitment practices such as classified ad clippings, locations of notice boards, itineraries, or recruitment drives
local labor force statistics
evidence of test validation (reports by consultants)
interviews with personnel directors, immediate bosses, and/or other supervisors, department directors, co-workers
interviews with specialists
position statements regarding specific employee dismissal
individual employee records

Service discrimination cases
maps of: sewer lines, water mains and hydrants, street lighting systems, current and future street and sidewalk paving plans
for streets and roads: width, type, age, durability of surfaces, number of "Children Playing" signs; degree of lumination by streetlights
for fire protection: number of hydrants per block/mile, gallons per minute per hydrant, width of fire mains
for water, sewer system: width, material, age of sewer pipes and water mains; location of pipes; source of water; type of sewage disposal system
for libraries: hours open per week, percent of books in foreign languages, pay discrepancies in various neighborhoods, number and types of books and periodicals available
for jails: employment rosters, housing assignments by race
interviews with specialists such as fire chiefs, civil engineers
photographs of conditions

Case analysis

Upon return to ORS, the investigator will meet with the supervisor and briefly review the trip and data. If the investigator decided, while in the field, to extend the scope of an investigation, the reasons for doing so are explained to the supervisor, who will either approve such a decision or, occasionally, will instruct the investigator to limit the case to the original charges.

It usually takes between one and two weeks to analyze a case. Preparation time is determined to a large extent by the type of investigation (individual employment, class employment, or services), the scope of the investigation (one department, all departments), and the size of the jurisdiction.

Upon completion of case analysis, the investigator sends a memo containing written recommendations for a finding to the manager of the Civil Rights Division. If the review reveals no evidence of discrimination, the investigator prepares and attaches a draft "Close Letter," to be signed by the manager of the Civil Rights Division, notifying the jurisdiction that no violation was found. A letter to the complainant and other interested parties is also attached.

If the investigator finds instances of discrimination, the memo must briefly describe the violations and outline possible actions the jurisdiction should take to come into compliance. Also drawn up for the manager's signature is a "Prefinding Letter," notifying the recipient jurisdiction that it may be in violation and outlining required actions for compliance.

The Prefinding Letter states, in a somewhat standardized format, the issue, the finding, and the remedy. Appended to this letter is the Case Report, which outlines the issues investigated, the data reviewed, the analysis performed, and the investigator's conclusions. The Case Report Appendix tends to be somewhat idiosyncratic in format; its style and content reflect the style of the supervisor, the scope and complexity of the case, and the level of experience of the investigator. The Case Report is the most detailed item of correspondence produced by the Civil Rights Division. Investigators are supplied with a format outline for this report, but it is quite general and does not specify particular required coverage for each type of case. If other explanatory letters to interested parties were drafted, these are also attached to the case file. The file, memo, and appropriate letters are then submitted to the supervisor for review in draft form.

The supervisor reviews the case, asking two basic questions: "Does the evidence support the findings?" and "Do the remedies suit the violations?" If the supervisor is not satisfied, the memo and letters are returned to the investigator for changes. If the case is judged satisfactory, the material is typed and proofread by the region's clerk/typist and the memo, letters, and case file are submitted to the manager of the Civil

Rights Division. If in agreement with the analysis, findings, proposed resolution, and style of presentation in the letters, the manager signs the Prefinding Letter (which may be a Close Letter if there were no violations found) and sends it to the control staff where it is logged and sent out. Clarification from either the investigator or the supervisor may be requested if the manager does not agree with any part of the case. The manager may also discuss aspects of the case with the chief counsel. Once mailed to the jurisdiction, the Prefinding Letter must be answered within fifteen days.

Analysis of reponse to the Prefinding Letter

In most cases (more than 75 percent of the time), recipient jurisdictions respond to the Prefinding Letter by agreeing to comply, negotiating with the supervisor and the manager on the terms and deadlines of a compliance agreement or, in the simplest cases (for example, a single act of employment discrimination), redressing the problem on the spot. Although the remedies set forth in the Prefinding Letter generally are non-negotiable, recipient jurisdictions often ask for (and are granted) extensions of time in which to come into compliance; it may, for example, take a jurisdiction longer than the allotted time to draw up an affirmative action plan comprehensive enough to suit the standards of ORS. Once the jurisdiction and ORS agree on the process to be followed to bring about compliance, responsibility for the case is transferred to the follow-up monitor. Jurisdictions are obliged to submit a letter agreeing to take the required steps to reach compliance and are then required to submit periodic progress reports. Review and acceptance of these reports are responsibilities of the follow-up monitor.

In those instances where jurisdictions respond either inadequately or not at all to the Prefinding Letter, the investigator will prepare a "Determination Letter" for the director's approval and signature. This letter iterates the violations stated in the Prefinding Letter and asks the jurisdiction to indicate within thirty days efforts being made to take corrective action. The procedure for issuing the Determination Letter and the subsequent (but rarely needed) follow-up activities are outlined in Exhibit 13.7.

Defining case remedies

Once a finding has been reached in a case, an appropriate remedy is required. The type of remedy is determined by the specifics of the situation. In most cases, however, the prescribed remedy falls into one of several categories: (1) Define and implement a new affirmative action plan

Exhibit 13.7
Civil rights compliance procedures related to determination letters

Preparation of the Determination Letter   Accompanied by the case file and draft letters to interested parties (including the governor of the state in which the jurisdiction is located) the draft Determination Letter is forwarded to the director's office. There the file is reviewed by the assistant to the director, the deputy director, and the director. The deputy director will frequently ask the chief counsel's opinion before submitting the Determination Letter to the director. If there are any questions, the director may consult the chief counsel before allowing the Civil Rights Division control staff to mail the letter. Modifications to the draft letter are common, often requiring its return to the Civil Rights Division for changes once or even twice before final signing. The process of securing approval from the director's office for a Determination Letter usually takes a minimum of a week to ten days and, occasionally, the delay can be as long as a month.

Response to Determination Letter   The follow-up monitor must take one of a number of actions within ten days after the jurisdiction responds to the Determination Letter. If the jurisdiction has submitted proof that it has come into compliance with all of the findings made in the Determination Letter, the follow-up monitor writes a memo summarizing the case and recommending closure and also prepares a Close Letter for the director's signature. A letter to the complainant is attached for the manager's signature and a letter to the governor is prepared for the director's signature.

There is much opportunity for negotiation concerning the jurisdiction's response to the Determination Letter. Even in instances where a jurisdiction has complied with many of the recommendations in the letter and is quite willing to agree to follow other recommendations, further negotiations, revolving around time limits for compliance (rather than around the substance of the remedies) may still be required. If the jurisdiction is less cooperative, more extensive negotiations will be needed.

If the jurisdiction does not reply to the Determination Letter, or if the response signals inadequate plans to comply, the follow-up monitor prepares a memo identifying areas of noncompliance and illustrates the lack of satisfactory response to the charges. Also prepared is an "Administrative Hearing Letter," to be signed by the director, advising the jurisdiction that it has ten days either to agree to come into compliance or to request an administrative hearing. Letters to other interested parties notifying them of the status of the case are included with the case file, Ten-Day Hearing Letter, and memo.

Once again, this material is routed from the supervisor to the manager of the Civil Rights Division who reviews the wording of the letter and sends it to the director's office. There it is reviewed by the assistant director, the deputy director, the chief counsel, and the director. By this time, the chief counsel will be familiar with the case and will advise the director if the need arises. According to one supervisor, in only about 5 percent of the cases handled by the Civil Rights Division is the mailing of the Administrative Hearing Letter necessary.

Response to the Administrative Hearing Letter   Of those few jurisdictions that receive Hearing Letters, most request an administrative hearing. A few respondents to the Hearing Letter agree to comply with ORS.

If the jurisdiction is uncooperative, the follow-up monitor prepares a memorandum from the director to the manager of the Systems and Operations Division authorizing the suspension of revenue sharing funds to that jurisdiction. This action has been taken only once. Funds were suspended until the jurisdiction agreed to come into compliance, at which point funding was restored.

It is likely that if a jurisdiction still refuses to comply after an Administrative Hearing Letter has been sent, it is because the ORS charge is felt to be unfair. In this situation the jurisdiction will request an administrative hearing. At this point the responsibility for the case is passed to the chief counsel.

or implement an existing one; (2) Alter hiring practices to eliminate invalid or unnecessary tests or irrelevant physical requirements; (3) Build equivalent facilities in minority neighborhoods or stop building new facilities in nonminority areas; or (4) Provide special facilities for handicapped or elderly people. Sometimes the selection of a remedy may not be obvious. For example, if a new baseball diamond is to be erected for the white community, how far along must the approval/construction process be for the remedy to be "build another in the black community" rather than "stop building this one and put it someplace else?" In order to help standardize such determinations, supervisors review the investigators' work and regularly have informal discussions with one another.

Case follow-up

When a compliance agreement of any sort has been reached, the jurisdiction typically agrees to supply the Civil Rights Division with periodic progress reports. The case is then closed (a Close Letter is sent) and placed in "follow-up" status. The follow-up reports will typically consist of documentation that required long-term actions are taking place as scheduled. The follow-up monitor is responsible for ensuring that these reports are submitted in a timely fashion and for reviewing the reports when they are received. These reports are required until the monitor is satisfied that all violations have been corrected.

Administrative closings

Occasionally a case may be closed administratively. This procedure occurs either in cases in which an individual complainant withdraws the complaint or in cases in which the case has been found, upon investigation, to be outside of the jurisdiction of the ORS. In both cases a letter is sent to the complainant, and another letter is sent to the jurisdiction under investigation. A memo explaining the reason for case closure should be enclosed in the file. Although administrative closings can occur at any point in the case-handling process, they tend to happen before a Prefinding Letter is mailed.

Processing times, case loads, and staffing levels

From its inception in early 1973 until September 30, 1978, the Civil Rights Division closed a total of 458 cases. The open case load, commonly called the backlog, in September 1978 was 626. Exhibits 13.8, 13.9, and 13.10 show, respectively, the age distribution of this backlog, distribution of the time required to close the 458 cases, and trends in monthly case processing from October 1977 through September 1978. Examining these statistics, the manager of the Civil Rights Division commented:

We're doing the best we can, given our limited staff resources. In the last two months we opened and closed a total of more cases than in any comparable prior time in our Division's history. We are aware of the reasons for major delays and usually it is due to circumstances beyond our control. Our Division's case control methods [see Exhibit 13.11] provide an effective source of overall management support. Supervisors and investigators are responsible for keeping track of the processing of cases assigned to them.

An analyst from the ORS Research and Analysis Division expressed a different opinion:

The Civil Rights Division has never been able to close a significant number of cases within the mandated period. Our recent study has pointed to serious bottlenecks in their processing system [see Exhibit 13.12], and increases in the Division's output is not very impressive considering the additional staff they have received in the past year and a half. What we need are standards for judging the productivity of this Division. Right now, it's hard to know what's really happening. We've discovered that different investigators have varying case loads [see Exhibit 13.13], but we're not sure what this means, or what to do about it. Things aren't good, though, when only 26 cases (out of the 1000 or so which we've opened since the Civil Rights Division started) were closed within ninety days or less. And this is especially bad, since only one of these cases reached a finding. The rest were closed early for reasons such as incorrect jurisdiction, referral to other agencies, or withdrawal of the original complaint. This Division has been seriously mismanaged.

Exhibit 13.8
Age of open civil rights cases
(as of September 30, 1978)

Age in months	Cases		Percent of cases in process this long or less
	Number	Percentage	
0–2	27	4	4
2–4	59	10	14
4–6	63	10	24
6–12	128	20	44
12–24	156	25	69
24–36	101	16	85
over 36	92	15	100
Total	626	100	

Exhibit 13.9
Processing time of closed civil rights cases

Total Processing Time (Months)	Cases		Percent of cases closed by this time or earlier
	Number	Percentage	
0–2	15	3	3
2–4	31	7	10
4–6	31	7	17
6–12	105	23	40
12–24	125	27	67
24–36	115	25	92
over 36	26	8	100
Total	458	100	

Exhibit 13.10
Recent monthly case load statistics: Civil Rights Division

Last day of month	1977			1978								
	Oct.	Nov.	Dec.	Jan.	Feb.	Mar.	Apr.	May	Jun.	Jul.	Aug.	Sep.
Cases open at beginning of month	507	513	526	541	543	563	578	581	592	604	621	637
Cases closed this month	12	13	7	14	3	18	23	15	25	16	24	28
Cases opened this month	18	26	22	16	23	33	26	26	37	33	40	17
Total unresolved (backlog) end of month	513	526	541	543	563	578	581	592	604	621	637	626
Received prior to 1/77	318	311	307	295	294	285	268	260	243	236	220	209
Received after 1/77	195	215	234	248	269	293	313	332	361	385	417	400

Source: ORS case load statistics prepared by Planning and Coordination Division.

Exhibit 13.11
Case control mechanisms for civil rights compliance

The methods by which ORS attempts to maintain accurate, up-to-date, and accessible information about each civil rights compliance case are described below.

Case filing system   Each complaint or referral which becomes a case is assigned a number and is filed in a case folder. As events occur during case processing, records are entered into the file. These records include copies of letters sent and received, notes on telephone contacts, data submitted or gathered, and memos to the file. A table of contents and file tabs facilitate the location of items in the file. Collections of data relevant to cases are often attached to the case folders by rubber bands. Stapled to the file folders of many cases are case summary sheets on which investigators can record various events as they occur.

The case folders (with attached data) are filed in cabinets located throughout the division's office area. Closed cases are filed alphabetically by state, and within state, alphabetically by name of jurisdiction. Sign-out sheets posted on the file cabinets are used to record the location of each case file removed from the cabinet.

Control card files   Three files of control cards are maintained. The primary "Open Case Control File" contains one card for each open case in the Civil Rights Division. On this card are recorded the date the complaint was received, the date the case was opened, limited data about the origin and type of complaint, and the dates of various occurrences in the case. When a case is closed, its control card is transferred to the "Closed Case Control File," which should contain an entry for every case closed since civil rights compliance processing began. When the control supervisor becomes aware that a case is awaiting a specific action on a certain date, a "Suspense File" card is created and placed in the proper time sequence location in the Suspense File. This file is reviewed periodically, and all cases awaiting action at a given time are located. The control supervisor also maintains a log of follow-up responses to come from governments after a case resolution has occurred. When information comes in, it is checked against the log and recorded. If a requested progress report has not come in, however, no action is taken.

Computer system (CTS)   The Compliance Tracking System was installed in the Civil Rights Division in 1978. It is intended to replace eventually the Control Card Files with a similar computer file. Both the CTS and the Control Card Files are being used at present. The control supervisor is now responsible for entering data onto the CTS, but regional supervisors will probably be given some or all of this responsibility in the future.

Supervisor case controls   Each supervisor has a particular method to keep track of cases. The information maintained by the supervisors typically includes the name and type of case, the open date, and the name of the investigator to whom the case is assigned. Supervisors do not maintain profiles of activities on each case. Much of the case control supervision occurs during frequent informal interactions between supervisors and investigators.

Management reporting   The reports compiled by the Civil Rights Division consist of the number of cases opened and closed by month by each supervisor. These reports were compiled from the Open and Closed Control Card Files until the CTS was implemented. Now, computer printouts of these counts are produced.

Keeping track of complaints and referrals   When a complaint or referral (internal to ORS) is received and found to be outside ORS jurisdiction, it is filed in a general "no jurisdiction" file folder. Referrals sent to ORS from other agencies but which are found to have no merit are filed here as well.

Correspondence logs   Each piece of information received in Civil Rights is logged in a General Correspondence Log. Information is then logged in a separate Correspondence Log for the manager. When an item is forwarded to another person, a notation is made on the Correspondence Log. Similarly, an item originating in the Civil Rights Division and sent to the ORS chief counsel or director, for example, would be logged as outgoing correspondence. (Items returned to the Civil Rights Division are also noted.)

Exhibit 13.12
Processing bottlenecks for eight of the longest new[a] cases which are still open

Case Number	Length of Time Open (Months)[b]	Last Event	Date of Last Event	Site Visit[c] V/N	Major Processing Bottlenecks	Duration of Bottleneck (Months)
1	15.5	Prefinding Letter awaiting signature	N.A. (after 7/7/77)	N	Data collection	8
2	15	Request for information before Site Visit	1/6/78	N	Acknowledgement out to request for data Investigator left, case awaits reassignment	3.5 10.5
3	15	Prefinding Letter mailed	11/13/78	V	Request for data after site visit to data received Analysis of case to Prefinding Letter mailed	11 3
4	14.5	Acknowledgement Letter mailed	10/5/77	N	Assignment of case to investigator	13.5
5	14.5	Threat to cut off funds if data not sent	10/30/78	N	Jurisdiction not responding to requests for data	12
6	14.5	Prefinding Letter mailed	10/30/78	V	Case assignment to Site Visit Analysis to Prefinding Letter out (no additional data requested)	2.5 9
7	14	Extension granted for data submission	10/24/78	V	Acknowledgement out to request for data Analysis of case	6 6
8	14	Site Visit	11/15/78	V	Assignment of case to request for data	12

[a] New means that the case was opened since September 1977.
[b] To 11/30/78.
[c] V = occurred; N = no visit occurred.

Exhibit 13.13
Case loads of five civil rights investigators

Investigator	Total Active Cases	Post Resolution Monitoring	Post Pre-finding Letter	Being Analyzed (Visit Made if Needed)	Being Investigated	Opened But Not Yet Investigated	Type of Work Performed in a Recent Five-Day Period
		Current Status of the Various Case Loads					
A	18	—	13	1	4	—	Worked on one major case analysis—four days; Wrote letters, made calls for other cases—one day
B	10	—	3	2	3	2	Worked on one major case analysis—five dass
C	14	—	6	5	3	—	Worked on high priority case analysis—five days
D	17	5	6	5	1	—	Rewrite of one case analysis—four days; wrote information request—one-half day; began analysis of a case—one-half day
E	39	10	14	8	—	5	Sent letters, made phone calls for many cases—five days

Source: Interviews with five investigators.

Discussion questions

1. Although the manager of the Civil Rights Division (CRD) feels that the "division's case control methods (see Exhibit 13.11) provide an effective source of overall management," an ORS analyst believes there are serious bottlenecks and low productivity. The deputy director of ORS has asked you, another member of the research and analysis staff, to prepare a memo identifying problems with the existing case management support system and recommending improvements in the system. Specifically, what bottlenecks could be eliminated by improved case status information? How might the CRD manager's ability to assess the current status of the compliance program and to assess staff productivity be improved?

2. The Deputy Director has also asked you, the CRD manager, to prepare a memo responding to these specific questions: How efficient is the current policy of assigning several cases to each investigator and then allowing the investigators to determine their own case-processing priorities? Can you suggest another approach to case assignment? How would you expect it to perform compared to the current policy?

3. Expanding the Compliance Tracking System in the CRD is one solution to the case management problem. If you were the division manager, what information from this system would you want to be provided directly to you? Do you foresee particular difficulties in making the expanded system fully operational?

4. A recent management audit identified other problems in the CRD in addition to its case management practices. The need for more staff, standardization of investigatory procedures, and streamlined flow of paperwork were all mentioned. The audit asked for responses from the division manager. Can you, the manager, estimate (using specific numbers) the staff size needed to process incoming complaints and totally eliminate the backlog within three years? How would you develop standards to promote consistency and efficiency in the investigation and analysis of cases and in reporting the extent to which these standards are met? How would you know if performance had improved? Finally, do you agree that the current flow of paperwork causes delays? If so, suggest a method for improving the distribution of information to appropriate parties.

Notes

* This case was prepared by Stephen R. Rosenthal. It draws heavily on an unpublished study by Edith S. Levine, Stephen R. Rosenthal, Morris A. Shepard, and Susannah Sherman. Funds for its development were provided by a grant from the Duke University/Rand Graduate Institute's Public Policy Curricular Materials Development Project, which is sponsored by the Ford Foundation. The case is intended to serve as a basis for class discussion, not to illustrate either effective or ineffective handling of a managerial situation.

Part 4
Conclusion

Chapter 14
"Managing" in government

Although many of the chapters in this book are conceptual, the text remains grounded in the world of the practicing public manager, who needs to identify and implement appropriate operational techniques. Any analysis of options for the improvement of government operations should consider potential implementation problems. The purpose of this concluding chapter is to identify common institutional barriers to improved operations management in government and to suggest some approaches to dealing with them. Many of the topics are covered in depth in the literature of public administration, public policy, or organization theory; we make no attempt here to summarize any of these fields. Rather, what follows is a synthesis of ideas which are particularly important for those who manage government operations.

The life cycle notion introduced in chapter 2 provides a useful schema for categorizing various institutional barriers into three groups: policy formation, management structure and processes, and operational activities. In the pure life cycle, policy issues come first, followed by questions of management structure, and finally the day-to-day operating activities. At any stage in the life cycle, certain elements will receive more attention than others. A competent public manager should be familiar with the typical barriers in all three categories. He or she should be able both to distinguish between barriers that can be bypassed and those that must be endured and to develop a plan of action responsive to those distinctions. By adopting the systems approach presented in this book, a public manager ought to be able to identify specific operational problems and particular opportunities for improving program performance.

The formation of public policy

Policy formation includes the setting of goals and the broad allocation of resources, tasks that are usually beyond the direct control of the public sector operations manager. Such activities create expectations, deadlines, and resource constraints that inevitably reduce the range of options available at the operational level. When deliberate public debate leads to the informed identification and selection of appropriate constraints, the policy formation process guides the operations manager toward the establishment of a high performance service delivery system. Unfortunately, however, policy formation rarely proceeds in this manner; in policymaking circles at all levels of government the operational perspective is sorely lacking. Policy debates usually are too imprecise to aid an operations manager in setting service delivery standards. Even worse, policymakers often avoid issues of day-to-day operations, with the assumption that these mundane matters should be considered only after broader policy decisions have been made. By then, of course, the operations manager may have been asked to deliver on unreasonable promises, in which case he or she is doomed to fail.

As the interests and expectations of the electorate change, so do the operational ground rules for government programs. Furthermore, since many government mandates evolve from external political processes, programs often have multiple objectives, some of which are intentionally ambiguous, while others (such as improving services while cutting costs) are in conflict. Politics becomes everyone's excuse for ignoring management. The existence of multiple constituencies becomes an excuse for serving no one well. Often, poor performance occurs not because a public manager makes mistakes in the use of existing program capacity, but rather because he or she fails to think in terms of managing capacity at all.

Changing economic and political situations and related policymaking activity create a turbulent environment. Within this environment, operations managers are responsible for developing and managing government programs and processes. Often, such managers cannot predict future requirements based on past performance; those who would like to make informed operational decisions run the risk of overreliance on obsolete or irrelevant data. As they grow accustomed to periodic sharp changes in their organizational environment, managers may come to believe that efforts to monitor the current performance of their programs are useless. As they find that they cannot control the extent or direction of change, they may lose interest in learning about new technological options for improved efficiency or effectiveness. It is no wonder that many public managers, discouraged by numerous checks and balances and reams of red tape, become skeptical about the notion of operational improvement. Instead of continually working to improve program performance, public sector operations managers, particularly those who are experienced, frequently wait for the initial period of a new administration before seeking changes. All too often, changes at such times ultimately are limited to the activity of "the new broom sweeping clean." This may not be the best time for incremental improvements of ongoing operations.

Many program changes require policy endorsement through new or modified legislative or budgetary actions. If policymakers routinely require program information in support of their oversight responsibilities, operations managers may then help their own cause by providing backup data to support such program changes. Recent activity to promote "sunset legislation" also is a healthy trend. Under such legislation, programs in steady-state are required to justify their continued existence on both a political and an operational basis. In addition, such activity promotes the termination stage of the operations life cycle, which must become more frequent if, in a period of overall retrenchment, new program initiatives are to be fiscally feasible. Admittedly, however, sunset legislation may turn out to be an impractical fad. Issues concerning the associated politics and work load lead to basic questions of the operational feasibility of such legislation (Behn, 1977). In general, several overriding factors work in favor of program prolongation; every program benefits some external group; evidence of the failure of any government program is always debatable (no direct measure of "net contribution to profit"); and in any bureaucracy, hesitancy to stress the failure of one's own (or even another's) program is natural (Wildavsky, 1972).

Despite the preferences of program planners and operations managers, the formation of public policy in this country is not likely to become more "rational." Our political traditions simply do not place managerial efficiency or effectiveness high on the list of goals to be achieved by our public officials. A systems design combining policy formation with program implementation, therefore, is not realistic in most situations. Instead, the "successful" operations managers in government will be those who are opportunistic, analytic, and energetic enough to gain a measurable degree of control over program directions, despite frequent buffeting by the shifting winds of public policy. Such control also requires considerable ingenuity, since an operations manager usually works within traditional government structures and processes.

Management structure and processes

While management structures and processes in government may have different labels from their private sector counterparts, their operational implications often are remarkably similar. The frequent claim that "government is too big to manage," for example, is an overused excuse for inadequate performance. The organizational size, structure, and processes of most agencies usually can be modified to improve their manageability. The most common barrier in this area is that managers are not careful to differentiate between external constraints associated with politics or economics and those which are internal and bureaucratic. The substitution of political gamesmanship for conscientious management is an unfortunate but common phenomenon; it is a great temptation in government to become an amateur politician worried about hidden traps, shifting moods, and the next wave of priorities. All too few managers in public sector settings are able to concentrate on solving existing structural problems. When such matters are ignored for long periods, day-to-day operations seem to have their own momentum, independent of desired managerial directions. Capable, hardworking managers frequently are fired for performance failures that are systemic rather than personal. Those who are not fired often burn out and quit in frustration after they have fought the system as long as they could. Only through gradual improvement of underlying structures and processes can situations be created more conducive to professional operations management.

A major impediment to managerial innovation in government operations is the lack of personal incentive. Operations managers frequently do not receive the support they need from public officials, who lack an appreciation for operational accomplishments. At all levels, public managers rarely are rewarded if they succeed in improving a program's operations, yet they are likely to be criticized, if not fired, for failing to accomplish everything they attempted. Bad publicity is common for those who are in charge of government operations; favorable publicity is rare, even when warranted. To date, the ability of the public sector to reward its employees with increased pay for exemplary work is limited. Merit pay systems tend to be used for giving small pay increases to everyone rather than for providing significant increases to the truly outstanding few; this practice is such a deeply rooted part of the culture of public sector bureaucracy that the possibility of a merit increase has ceased to be a serious incentive system for management. Experiments with special bonus systems, notably that of the Federal Senior Executive Service, are too recent to evaluate. A public manager who wishes to reward outstanding employees often is limited to traditional modes of selective promotion based on merit, which are constrained by civil service criteria (or union rules) on eligibility and rating (Savas & Ginsburg, 1973). The granting of special awards is likely to have more symbolic than financial significance and, therefore, may not motivate behavior.

The popular media frequently launch broadside attacks on the multilayered structure of government organization, attributing the day-to-day problems of program performance to "the bureaucracy." Although this layman's view masks more issues than it illuminates, there are some direct implications for the operations manager. For example, reducing unnecessary levels of approvals through the improved design of operating systems (along lines suggested in this book) increases the likelihood that lower level staff will be able to make more of the operating decisions. Trends toward the diffusion of decision making and job enrichment are emerging in the private sector in response to the need for increased productivity. Most government operations managers can find opportunities to take similar actions in their own agencies.

Any review of the major structural barriers facing the government operations manager must acknowledge the impact of the civil service system. Much has been written on this subject in the public administration literature. To propose revolutionary changes in the civil service system is beyond the scope (or intention) of this book. For our purposes, an emphasis on personnel planning, standard setting, and training (as outlined below) is most important. The continued growth of public employee unions also has placed increasing constraints on human resource management. For example, operations managers who use overtime to meet peak demands often are subject to a union work rule that such opportunities must be offered first to those with the most seniority, rather than to those with the most appropriate skills. Also, it is generally difficult for a public manager to change significantly the job responsibilities of existing staff, in response to new service delivery requirements. Finally, to hire a person with a skill not normally required by the agency often necessitates that a new position be created. Public service unions that made significant gains in periods of growth are likely to give ground only grudgingly, when, in times of cutback, such action becomes necessary to increase productivity.

Taken together, these broad structural constraints may seem to create an environment that prevents significant initiative by operating management. However, experience has shown that managerial ingenuity and commitment can lead to innovation in government productivity (Hayes, 1977). General lessons for federal government executives are beginning to be articulated (Lynn, 1981), but public sector operations managers (most of whom work in agencies of state or local government) are not likely to find these lessons to be of direct value. In practice, an operations manager must learn to identify his or her own specific opportunities for program improvement. While radically different management approaches to developing more productive organizations are beginning to be formulated (see, for example, Ouchi, 1981), a more incremental view is probably more appropriate for the operations manager. In particular, in any government office, the manager may be able to take certain small steps to make the work of employees more meaningful, thereby beginning to enfranchise those in the civil service. A noticeable increase in the number of concerned workers will serve as a catalyst to others, thereby encouraging the restoration of a work ethic in corners of government where inattention to employees has bred indifference or laziness.

Operational activities

Many policy and structural constraints are beyond the immediate control of operations managers. Nevertheless, these managers may use a variety of tools and approaches to achieve creative, productive action. One basic strategy for managers is to identify and take actions to improve the quality and relevance of existing resources. Another is to design, control, and, when necessary, revise the operating system to suit its primary task. Taken together, these strategies encourage the successful management of capacity that is the essential operational responsibility in government (as well as elsewhere).

A key ongoing task of operations management is to determine what is "best practice" in the field—those operating activities, achieved by some, that should be adopted as widely as possible. Many public managers are so far removed from day-to-day operations that they do not know which of their various operating groups have developed the best practice. Lacking this information, such managers cannot hope to achieve consistent and productive program operations. Regardless of the particular management structure and organizational context, managers must develop mechanisms for learning more about the best practice in their field. Admittedly, there are many social psychological resistances of individuals and groups in planning to learn and in learning to plan (Michael, 1973). Nevertheless, a public manager who is sensitive to the opportunities inherent in different stages of the operations life cycle can take steps to design and implement appropriate monitoring and evaluation activities for identifying critical aspects of best practice. Armed with this knowledge, a manager can then proceed to the equally challenging task of guiding the necessary innovations.

Management of information

The management of information will provide both opportunities and constraints for the operations manager in government. Think of the common complaints: "I keep getting buried in reports but when I need a piece of information I never know where to look" or "I'm too busy writing reports and memos to deal with the problems that really need my attention." These two symptoms become increasingly common throughout government, as mandated reporting requirements combine with managerial initiatives to generate burdensome flows of information. In chapter 9 we described the different kinds of information systems that can be of value to a public sector operations manager and suggested that it is important to avoid both information overloads and information shortages since the two situations often have the same conclusion: uninformed decisions and wasted time. However, attempts to clarify the basic measures of agency performance and to streamline the flow of information may be hindered by political and bureaucratic forces. The manager's desire for explicit objectives and quantitative performance measures is often in direct conflict with the politician's frequent need for ambiguity. In the extreme, this conflict presents a classic information dilemma. A competent operations manager will build a useful base of information to support his or her internal decisions, without forcing policymakers to embrace a simplistic view of program success that might be politically disastrous.

The potential value of an adequate information management system is its use as an impetus to the operations manager who is faced with implementation barriers. A public manager should strive to develop a system that provides information pertinent to daily operations, as well as information needed to convince policymakers of needed program changes. An operations manager must expect information capacity, like service delivery capacity, to be developed over time. Even if employee resistance to such a system can be overcome, its implementation will disrupt the normal production process. Further, the existing capacity will disintegrate if it is not used. Managers must decide what information they would like to keep, develop a workable document storage and retrieval system, and then remember to use the system to identify operational issues and to diagnose appropriate responses.

Selection of appropriate resources

Using the systems approach to production processes outlined in chapter 3, operations managers request funds and associated personnel positions, equipment, and facilities sufficient to deliver required services. Overall budget levels and the amount and type of possible resources are likely to be constrained by current policies and economic conditions, existing manpower and technology, civil service regulations, and purchasing procedures. Nevertheless, a manager always has some flexibility to reallocate existing resources, perhaps by redefining operational tasks of personnel. Admittedly, existing personnel may resist such changes, but a competent manager can overcome some of these tendencies. Finally, the selection of appropriate resources requires timely and accurate information on resource requirements and their availability. It may be difficult for a manager to acquire all the information that would be helpful (for example, resources required to implement alternative production designs), but judicious identification of priorities and constraints should facilitate reasonably well-informed judgments.

Management of capacity

The management of productive capacity is a major job of the operations manager. This job is made more difficult by the general lack of work standards in government, by the difficulty in determining the value of public sector outputs, and by the often conflicting goals of efficiency, effectiveness, and equity. Furthermore, the difficulty of forecasting in the public sector makes capacity planning less scientific than operations managers might like. The long lead time needed to acquire most government capacity additions further complicates the situation, especially in light of the traditionally short-term perspective of most public officials. In fact, the highly politicized nature of many government enterprises creates an environment which seems to resist capacity management in every way.

Even the traditional reluctance to terminate programs constrains the public manager who wishes to free resources by eliminating unnecessary operating systems. However, the government operations manager is not completely helpless in the face of these many constraints. One capacity management strategy, discussed at length in chapter 7, is to manage the demand that is imposed on the capacity. A public manager can begin to develop criteria that narrow the effective demand for service. If the definition and imposition of such guidelines are within the authority of the operations manager, problems of capacity management may be solved directly. If the approval of higher level policymakers is required, an astute operations manager will anticipate the need for such action and will recommend and justify criteria for approval. To implement this kind of strategy, the operations manager will have to develop an information system which can signal upcoming capacity shortages. He or she must be prepared to test the practicability of different demand management options.

Finally, a manger in the public sector, following the approaches outlined in chapter 4, can adjust the production process within certain limits, thereby changing the productive capacity (as well as other characteristics of the operating system). For example, if the existing production process has been appropriately selected, the primary task is to manage it more carefully. An inappropriate production process may be changed. A line operation may be converted to a job shop to enable the handling of diverse situations; conversely, when diversity is not needed, a job shop can be converted to a line operation to encourage efficiency and consistency in the production process.

Development and implementation of standards

Standards are the essence of effective service delivery. Without standards, an operations manager has no way to judge program performance. Specific operations questions can be resolved as they arise, but standards provide an aggregate sense of the quality of program operations. Input standards, discussed in chapter 6 in the section on work measurement, allow a manager to check a program's efficiency. The problems of setting such standards, given a program's core technology and the likely resistance of employees to the introduction of work measurement practices, already have been discussed. Nevertheless, a persistent operations manager must proceed with the implementation of such input standards, particularly in times of fiscal austerity. In addition, quality and quantity standards for the output of government programs must be expressed as aggregate production targets. The manager who sets any of these standards must be familiar with the productive capacity of the organization and with the service needs of its clients. The measurement of equity in service delivery is particularly difficult; it requires not only that a meaningful index be developed but also that the agency compare the levels of this index across different segments of the client population. The identification of serious anomalies requires strong assumptions of both the values of clients and the outcomes of services. A change in existing output standards is, in essence, a change in public policy (as described in chapter 11 for case-processing programs) and must be done with care. Improved standard setting, both for work measurement and for service output, requires careful historical record keeping. The successful implementation of standards, in turn, requires an ongoing monitoring system.

Training of employees

One of the major differences between private sector and public sector employment is the relative lack of on-the-job training in the latter. In the labor-intensive world of government, the successful operations manager will make sure that the first line production workers understand the requirements of their jobs and will encourage them to develop the skills necessary to do those jobs well. No matter what the stage of the operations life cycle, the training of personnel, from clerical to professional, is appropriate. At the start-up stage, employees are being placed in jobs which often are new to them and sometimes are also new to the agency. Managers need to develop operational job specifications, to screen candidates carefully, and to develop operating procedures that will mold the newly formed team into a productive system. In steady-state, managers must arrange training for new employees and provide written instructions for longer term employees when minor changes arise in operating procedures. As part of their routine responsibilities, supervisors should seek to identify those employees who seem to be having difficulties with ongoing operational activities and provide them with informal, periodic training. During revision, training requirements increase and, if the revision is extensive, the need for training may be similar to that needed during start-up. At any stage of the operations life cycle, changes in the nature of external demand, program objectives, or service delivery technology are likely to require associated training components. Regardless of the type of internal training activities being offered, a public manager must be careful to monitor the competence of the trainers and the quality of their services. Training must be managed carefully if it is to achieve its objective of supporting the primary operating capacity of an organization.

A successful public sector operations manager periodically will explore the need for different training activities designed to improve performance. Depending on the needs of an agency and on the availability of financial support for training activities, different kinds of external training programs may be considered. These include technical schooling, such as training for maintenance personnel, and executive development programs for supervisors who have been promoted to the ranks of management. Organizational development programs may include group exercises designed to promote cooperation and creative collaboration among co-workers. Two of the major constraints on training are money and time. Financial support for training must be provided in annual program budgets. Managers in state and municipal agencies should investigate the possibility of federal support for training programs in their field. Unfortunately, the greatest barrier to adequate training often is the apparent time constraint on those who ought to be trained. Those at supervisory levels in government, in particular, often feel that day-to-day job pressures make breaks for training an unaffordable luxury. Ironically, with better training many supervisors would be less overwhelmed by their jobs.

Conclusion

Public officials concerned about the performance of government operations should try to introduce operational perspectives early in the process of policy formation, thereby anticipating potential problems. Typically, however, operations managers in government have little direct impact on the formation of public policy. Furthermore, a newly appointed operations manager steps into an existing organizational structure and culture that combine to limit further his or her potential actions. These constraints include the layers of bureaucracy through which operational decisions traditionally are made and implemented, systems of incentives and rewards (or their opposite equivalents), and related personnel practices for hiring, assigning, and promoting staff.

Admittedly, the barriers to improving the performance of government programs are formidable. Indeed, the better a public manager understands these barriers, the more likely it is that he or she will become generally discouraged. Discouragement in the face of complexity leads naturally to indecision, whereupon effective management ceases. The challenge is to avoid such debilitating discouragement by identifying opportunities for converting knowledge into action. The effective public manager constantly looks for ways to make an incremental difference. Despite external constraints, most managers can improve the quality of operational decisions by strengthening the existing information base. Managers who understand the nature of program resources and constraints can become more skilled in planning and implementing changes as needed. In particular, these managers can always try to define more appropriate and realistic production standards and to see that employees are trained to meet those standards. Operations managers also can seek ways to match the capacity of the existing operating system to prevailing work loads.

In summary, those who are responsible for the performance of government operations must begin by making a personal commitment to manage, in the context of political and organizational constraints. An effective public manager learns which constraints to respect and which to modify to improve program operations. Many apparent *general* barriers to successful program performance can be overcome if appropriate *specific* actions are identified early enough. "Managing" government operations requires care and compromise, as well as the basic approaches to resource allocation and evaluation presented in this book.

Discussion questions

1. The barriers identified in this chapter can be found in all programs at any level of government. Taking sound operational actions to respond to the barriers will help produce effectively managed public programs. Recall the discussion in chapter 13 of the Civil Rights Division of the Office of Revenue Sharing. If you were the manager of this division, what barriers would you identify as being the result of (a) policy formation, (b) management structure and processes, and (c) operational factors? How would you deal with each of these barriers as you respond to the problems identified in the Revenue Sharing Compliance case?
2. Answer the above questions from the perspective of the deputy commissioner, Office of Housing Code Enforcement, Housing and De-

velopment Administration, the City of New York, as discussed in chapter 8.

Bibliography

Behn, Robert D. "The False Dawn of the Sunset Laws." *The Public Interest*, no. 49 (Fall 1977), pp. 103–18.

Biller, Robert P. "On Tolerating Policy and Organizational Termination: Some Design Considerations." *Policy Science* 7 (July 1976):133–49.

Churchman, C. W., and A. H. Schainblatt. "The Researcher and the Manager: A Dialectic of Implementation." *Management Science* 11, 4 (February 1965): B69–B87.

Drucker, Peter F. "Managing the Public Service Institution." *The Public Interest*, no. 33 (Fall 1973), pp. 43–60.

Feller, Erwin. "Public-Sector Innovation as 'Conspicuous Production.' " *Policy Analysis* 7, 1 (Winter 1981): 1–20.

Hayes, Frederick O'R. *Productivity in Local Government*. Lexington, Mass.: D. C. Heath and Co., 1977.

Lynn, Laurence E., Jr. *Managing the Public's Business*. New York: Basic Books, 1981.

Michael, Donald N. *On Learning to Plan—And Planning to Learn*. San Francisco: Jossey-Bass, 1973.

Nelson, Richard R., and Douglas Yates. *Innovation and Implementation in Public Organizations*. Lexington, Mass.: D. C. Heath and Co., 1978.

Ouchi, William. *Theory Z*. Reading, Mass.: Addison-Wesley Publishing Co., 1981.

Roessner, David J. "Federal Technology Policy: Innovation and Problem Solving in State and Local Governments." *Policy Analysis* 5, 2 (Spring 1979): 181–200.

Savas, E. S., and Sigmund G. Ginsburg. "The Civil Service: A Meritless System?" *The Public Interest*, no. 32 (Summer 1973), pp. 70–85.

Shafritz, Jay M. *Personnel Management in Government: Politics and Process*. New York: Marcel Dekker, Inc., 1978.

Stahl, O. Glenn. *Public Personnel Administration*. New York: Harper and Row, 1962.

Walton, Richard E. "Work Innovations in the United States." *Harvard Business Review*, July–August 1979, pp. 88–98.

Weiss, Janet A. "Substance vs. Symbol in Administration Reform: The Case of Human Services Coordination." *Policy Analysis* 7, 1 (Winter 1981): 21–45.

Wildavsky, Aaron. "The Self-Evaluating Organization." *Public Administration Review* 32 (September/October 1972): 509–20.

Index